Architectural Guide
Australia

Architectural Guide Australia

Edited by Sarah Zahradnik

With contributions from Harry Seidler, John Gollings, and David Bridgman

DOM publishers

Contents

Appendix

Territorial cities

Australia consists of eight states: New South Wales (NSW), Australian Capital Territory (ACT), Tasmania (TAS), Victoria (VIC), South Australia (SA), Western Australia (WA), Northern Territory (NT), and Queensland (QLD). Each of these states contains its own capital city: Sydney (NSW), Canberra (ACT), Hobart (TAS), Melbourne (VIC), Adelaide (SA), Perth (WA), Darwin (NT), and Brisbane (QLD). I have dedicated an entire chapter to each of the capital cities in order to capture the variety of projects within them. The chapters on Hobart, Darwin, and Brisbane include projects in the surrounding areas. Although modern architecture makes up the leading architectural trend in Australia, historical and tropical architecture has played a large role in forming the country's culture. Research carried out for this book has shown that many architects have drawn inspiration from the country's rich history, culture, and natural landscapes. I hope readers will be inspired and get a taste of what this vast land has to offer. *SZ*

iStock (Totajla)

Surabaya
Malang
Bali
Denpasar
Lombok
Flores
Sawu Sea
Dili
EAST TIMOR
Kupang
INDONESIA
Timor Sea
G
Darwin
Indian Ocean
NORTHERN TERRITORY
Broome
Port Hedland
Karratha
Great Sandy Desert
Lake Mackay
MacDonnell Ranges
Gibson Desert
WESTERN AUSTRALIA
Carnarvon
191
Uluru / Ayers Rock
Meekatharra
SOUTH AUSTRALIA
Geraldton
Great Victoria Desert
Kalgoorlie
F
Perth
Mandurah
Bunbury
Great Australian Bight
Albany
Indian Ocean
Australia
0
500 km

Kerema
PAPUA NEW GUINEA
Port Moresby
SOLOMON ISLANDS
Arafura Sea
Torres Strait
Coral Sea
Gulf of Carpentaria
Cape York Peninsula
Great Barrier Reef
Pacific Ocean
Cairns
228
Townsville
Bowen
204
Mount Isa
Mackay
Great Dividing Range
Rockhampton
Gladstone
217
218
QUEENSLAND
Bundaberg
Maryborough
Gladstone
Sunshine Coast
Brisbane
H
Toowoomba
219
Gold Coast
Lismore
Lake Eyre
Sturt Stony Desert
Lake Torrens
Coffs Harbour
Tamworth
Port Macquarie
Dubbo
Broken Hill
NEW SOUTH WALES
Whyalla
Port Pirie
Orange
Newcastle
D
Sydney
A
Mildura
Gawler
Port Lincoln
Goulburn
Wollongong
Adelaide
E
Wagga Wagga
Canberra
B
A. C. T.
Albury
Kangaroo Island
Horsham
Shepparton
Mount Kosciuszko
2.228 m
Bendigo
VICTORIA
Ballarat
Melbourne
D
Mount Gambier
Sale
Geelong
Warnambool
Tasman Sea
Bass Strait
TASMANIA
080
Devonport
Launceston
088
089
081
C
Hobart
061
079

Coastal Shores, Swimming Pools, and More: Introducing Australia's Architecture

Growing up on Australia's southern coast, I have always had an appreciation for Australia's bold culture, remarkable landscapes, and varied works of architecture. I studied architecture at the University of South Australia. After graduating, I spent some time in Central and South America as well as Europe.

By the end of 2015, I was in Berlin, working as an architect for Natascha Meuser and Philipp Meuser, who run the international studio Meuser Architekten as well as the firm DOM publishers. Before I returned to Australia, the Meusers asked me to produce an architectural guide on Australia – an opportunity I could not miss. Once I was back in Australia, I based myself in the city of Melbourne, which has a thriving architectural scene. It was from here that I began working on the *Architectural Guide Australia*. My appreciation for the sheer scale of the project developed over the course of my research, and the biggest challenge proved to be reducing the never-ending list of buildings that merited inclusion in the guide. I decided to divide the book into eight chapters, based on Australia's eight capital

Villa Marittima, St Andrews Beach, Victoria. Architect: Robin Williams, 2014.

Australia between tourist cliché and celebrated icon: a kangaroo on a sandy beach.

cities, and to present a balanced range of historic and contemporary buildings. I chose the buildings based on their architectural merit, materiality, and uniqueness of design. I managed to visit most of the country's eight capital cities by car. For the buildings I couldn't reach personally, the architectural office that had designed the respective building provided the material for this book. Texts provided by architects are attributed to those architects with the initials *PA* (Project Architects). I would like to particularly thank Polly Seidler for her permission to use her father Harry Seidler's essay, 'Sunlight and Architecture' (see pages 28–31); architectural photographer John Gollings – whom I personally met at his exhibition 'John Gollings: the History of the Built World' in Melbourne – for his essay 'A Lucky Country' (see pages 36–41) and also for contributing many of his spectacular images; architect David Bridgman for his knowledgeable essay 'Design for the Hot-Humid Tropics' (see pages 368–371); and last but not least the many architectural offices for their generous contributions. *SZ*

Caroline Voelker

Bondi Icebergs, Bondi Beach in Sydney. Restored by Marchese Partners in 2002.

Terra Australis

Australia is the only country in the world which occupies an entire continent. It is the sixth largest country in the world, with an area of 7.692 million km^2 and at the same time has one of the world's lowest population densities with a population of approximately 24.6 million (2017). Of those Australian inhabitants, more than 80 per cent live within 100 kilometres of the coast, which makes Australia a remarkably urbanised coastal settlement. It has the highest proportion of migrant settlers among the world's developed nations. Although the primary language spoken by Australians is Australian English, there are over 200 different languages and dialects spoken in the country. Australia is the driest of all continents aside from Antarctica. The driest state is South Australia (SA) whilst the wettest is the Northern Territory (NT) with its tropical climate. This vast land boasts seventeen heritage-listed sites of natural wonders including the world's largest living organism, the Great Barrier Reef, in Queensland, which has been listed as one of the Seven Wonders of the Natural World. Another spectacle is Uluru, also known as Ayers Rock, which is located in the Northern Territory and is known as the largest monolith in the world. This large sandstone rock formation is over 8 km wide at its widest point and is sacred to the Aboriginal people of the area. Australia's man-made wonders include works of architecture, of which the Sydney Opera House (by Danish architect Jørn Utzon, 1973) and the new Parliament House in Canberra (by Italian architect Romaldo Giurgola, 1988) are among the most remarkable buildings in the country, both groundbreaking and polarizing.

Uluru (Northern Territory) is considered a sacred site by Aboriginal Australians and is estimated to be around 600 million years old.

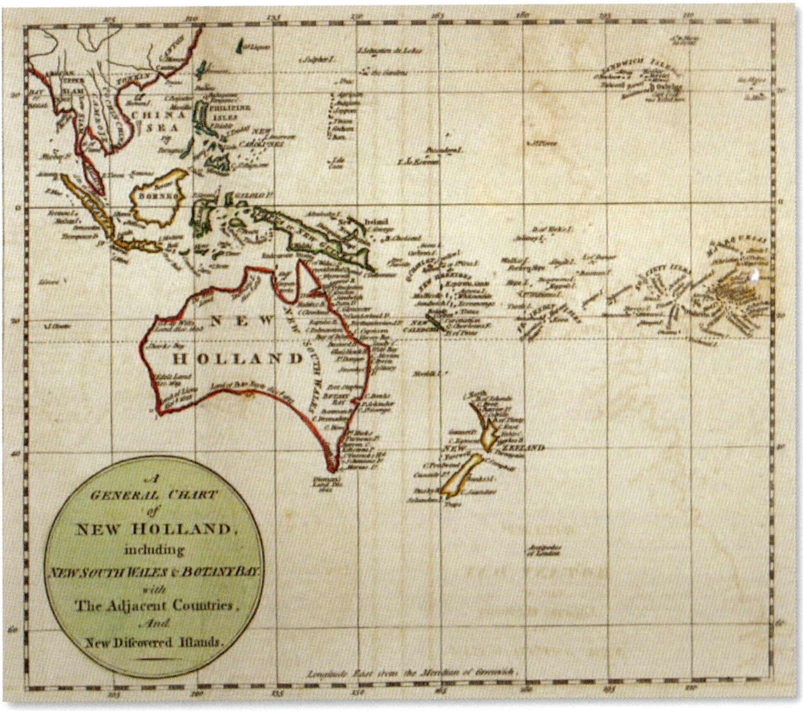

A general chart of New Holland (today Australia), including neighbouring countries and newly discovered lands, circa 1786

Map of Terra Australis Incognita, from Petrus Bertius's *P. Bertii Tabularum geographicarum contractarum*, Amsterdam, 1616

Unknown South Land

For centuries, Europeans believed a great land existed in the southern hemisphere and often referred to it as 'Terra Australis Incognita' or 'Unknown South Land'. Legends of this unknown southern land date back to Roman times and earlier and were common in medieval geography, although no actual knowledge of the continent had been documented. The first records of European mariners sailing into Australian waters date back to circa 1606. The Duyfken, captained by Dutch explorer Willem Janszoon, was the first ship to chart the Australian coast and greet the original inhabitants of the land, the indigenous Aboriginal people. Between 1606 and 1770, an estimated 54 European ships, many of which were merchant ships from the Dutch East India Company, made contact with the land. The 17th century discoveries of the western and northern coastlines made by the Dutch resulted in the western section of the continent being referred to as 'New Holland'. The Dutchman Abel Tasman, charted the south coast of the land in 1642 and named it Van Diemen's Land, today known as the state of Tasmania. In 1768, the British explorer Captain James Cook set out on a voyage to further investigate this unknown land. His ship reached the east coast of Australia in 1770, landing at Point Hicks and then proceeding to Botany Bay. Cook claimed the east coast on behalf of King George III of England and named it New South Wales. The remaining extents of the continent remained unknown until explorer and mariner Matthew Flinders made his voyage in the late 18th century. This charter made him the first to circumnavigate the entire continent. By 1803, a complete outline of the Great Southern Land had been mapped out.

Portrait of Captain James Cook, circa 1780, by artist John Webber

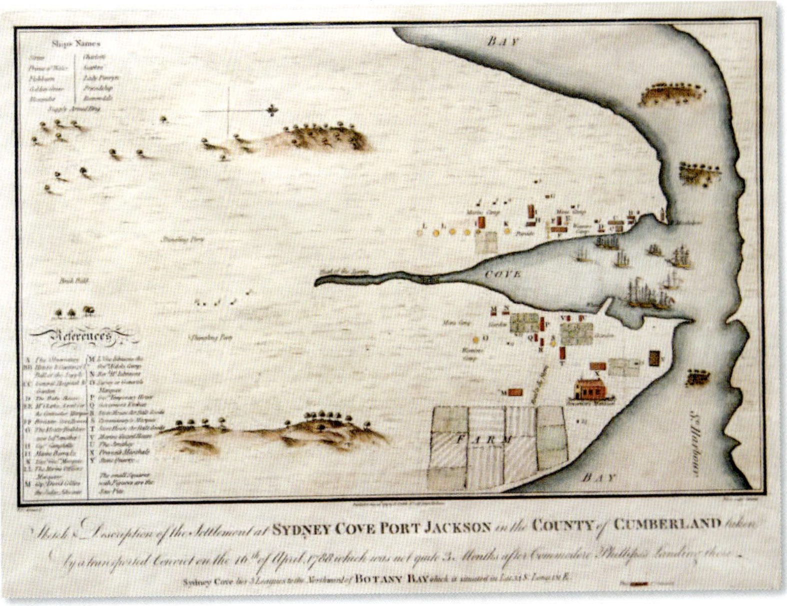

Sydney Cove, Port Jackson, by F.F. Delineavit, 1789

British Settlement

On 13 May 1787, Commodore Arthur Phillip set sail from England, commanding the First Fleet, 11 ships that were intended to establish the first British Colony in Australia. The fleet carried approximately 1,350 people, who arrived at Botany Bay in January of 1788. This area was later deemed to be unsuitable for settlement, so the settlers moved northwards to Port Jackson, arriving at Camp Cove (Sydney Cove). Sydney was the first Australian colony to be built from the ground up. The colonisers mainly consisted of convicts, marines, and their wives. It wasn't until 1793 that free settlers began to arrive. The British settlement extended to Van Diemen's Land (Tasmania), and the city of Hobart was established in 1804. In 1824, the penal colony at Redcliffe, in the state of Queensland, was established and later moved to the site now called Brisbane. Western Australia's Swan River Colony (today Perth) was officially established in 1829, and the first convicts arrived in 1850. South Australia was established thereafter, and the Adelaide colony was founded in 1836. The city of Melbourne in Victoria was established in 1837 with the first immigrant ships arriving at Port Phillip in 1839. The Northern Territory's city of Darwin was established in 1869 and was originally known as Palmerston.

A 19th century engraving of an Indigenous Australian encampment, showing the lifestyle in the cooler parts of Australia at the time of European settlement

The colonial town of Hobart, with its modern-day array of colourful suburban rooftops

iStock (David Lade)

First Nation

Although Europeans were the first to officially found this unknown continent, the land itself had been occupied by Aboriginal Australians 40,000 to 60,000 years prior to British settlement. These first inhabitants, Aboriginal and Torres Strait Islander people, numbered up to 750,000 at the time of colonisation and had their own boundaries of the land which were often based on intimate cultural relationships with the land and sea. At first, the relationship between British settlers and the Aboriginal Australians was hospitable and revolved around trading food, water, axes, cloth, and artefacts. It wasn't until the Aboriginal people realised that their land and resources were threatened by the continuous presence of the colonisers that the Eora clan in the Sydney area began a campaign of resistance. This resulted in several coordinated attacks against the English colonisers between 1790 and 1810, a period later known as the 'Black Wars'. This land-ownership dispute eventually led to the Proclamation of Governor Burke, in 1835, which nullified all land-ownership claims in Australia prior to the settlement by the British crown. This law would not change until 1992, when the Australian High Court revisited the matter and issued a public apology. The first National Sorry Day was held in May, 1998.

Colonial Architecture

Many of Australia's first permanent buildings were built by convicts in order to meet the immediate needs of the colonies. These were typically of the modest Georgian style and rendered in brick or stone, with multi-paned windows and gabled roofs. Convict architect Francis Greenway, known for his designs of the Hyde Park Barracks (Sydney) and the Macquarie Lighthouse (Sydney), was one of the primary architects of this era where architectural services were limited. Early 19th century architecture in Tasmania was greatly influenced by the works of architects such as John Lee Archer (Parliament House, Hobart) and James Blackburn (Holy Trinity Church, Hobart), who were influenced by the styles of the Greek Revival and Romanesque Revival.

The Gold Rush

In 1851, the first discovery of gold was made in Bathurst, NSW. This led to the Australian gold rushes and a population influx which ultimately had a huge impact on the Australian economy and the development of the nation. Australia's economy boomed dramatically with around 370,000 immigrants arriving in Australia in 1852 alone. By 1871, the country's population had risen from roughly 430,000 (in 1851) to 1.7 million. The number of eager new arrivals in Australia during the

State Library of New South Wales

Gold diggings in Ararat, Victoria, circa 1854. Oil on canvas, by Edward Roper

Preliminary plan of Canberra by Walter Burley Griffin, signed 1913

gold rush was greater than the number of convicts, which in turn precipitated the end of convict transportation to the entire country. Immigrants from the US, France, Germany, Hungary, Italy, Poland, and China made up the largest groups of incomers entering Australia.

Victorian-era Architecture

The broad mix of nationalities that entered the country brought with them their own cultures, ideas, and skills, and also introduced Victorian architecture to Australia. Victorian architecture entailed a range of different revival styles that were used during the reign of Queen Victoria (1837–1901). This blend of architectural styles developed in Australia between the 1850s and 1890s and was possible thanks to the increased wealth of the land. Architects who distinctly incorporated these styles into their designs included Joseph Reed (Royal Exhibition Building, Melbourne; State Library of Victoria, Melbourne; Melbourne Town Hall, Melbourne), John George Knight and Peter Kerr (Parliament House, Melbourne), James Barnet (General Post Office, Sydney), and William Pitt (Princess Theatre, Melbourne). These works set a standard for Renaissance Revival, Gothic Revival, and Italianate architecture in Australia. Following the economic boom, Australian cities grew rapidly. The construction of elaborately adorned multi-storey buildings and suburban houses reached a peak in the 1880s. This era was referred to as the 'Boom-Style' era, of which late-Victorian architecture became the most decorative, with designs embellished with excessive columns, balustrades, entrances, decorations, and highly detailed ornamentation on façades. The Gothic and Italianate styles were also popular during this time as they provided the opportunity to display prosperity through rich and ornate decorative features such as carved stone sculptures, dentil detailing, cast iron lacework, and slate roofs.

Economic Depression

During the 1890s, Australia spiralled into economic depression as the demand for wool, which made up the country's biggest industry, decreased significantly. Public works projects were put on hold, and banks were closed. Within three years the recession spread worldwide and accelerated the collapse of Australia's economy, causing widespread unemployment. Fortunately, the wheat industry grew along with gold and silver mining in Western Australia, and the nation's economy was back on its feet by the 1900.

The coat of arms of Australia, the formal symbol of the Commonwealth of Australia

Federation Architecture

The Federation of Australia took place in 1901, uniting the six British colonies – New South Wales, Victoria, Queensland, South Australia, Western Australia, and Tasmania – to form the Commonwealth of Australia. This process lent its name to Federation architecture, an architectural style that prevailed between 1890 and 1915. The style was an amalgamation of the Arts and Crafts style, the Edwardian style, and the Queen Anne Revival style. Prominent features of this style include red or brown brickwork, terracotta tile roofs with decorative gables, and white-painted window frames. American architects Walter Burley Griffin and his wife Marion Mahony Griffin were advocates of the Arts and Crafts movement, bringing into the country their winning 1911 design for Australia's new capital city, Canberra. Their design was inspired by the Art Deco and Art Moderne movements and was based on circles and rectangles joined by long avenues structured to fit within the natural landscape of the site.

Modernism

Modernism emerged in Australia in the mid 1910s. The style was introduced to the country by migrants and further propagated by exhibitions and publications. This movement drew inspiration from early European avant-gardes and was enabled through technological advances. With the rise of new technologies and materials, Australian architecture began to take on a new form, with an emphasis on function and a responsiveness to social conditions. Australia's modern residential architecture began to reflect this change with the use of new environmental materials and designs that responded to the Australian landscape and climate. Early buildings, in particular Queenslander houses and wool sheds, provided

State Library of Queensland

Federation house in Cairns, Queensland, circa 1914. State Library of Queensland

shading from the strong Australian sun, and new designs encouraged ventilation to cool down houses. These distinctive designs typically included broad verandas, corrugated iron roofs, roof ventilators, lattice structures, and slatted flooring, and were often raised from the ground with stumps. Roof pitches varied, depending on the latitude and climate conditions of the region, and often favoured the Northern sun. These innovative design techniques spread to tropical regions such as the Northern Territory, Queensland, and northern New South Wales, and inspired Australian modernist architecture, including the designs of one of Australia's most renowned architects, Glen Murcutt. The First World War led to a shortage of tradesmen and materials, which made it necessary to reduce housing costs. One of the solutions to save on building costs was to lower ceilings, which led to the emergence of low-rise houses known as 'bungalows' between 1915 and 1940. Post-war housing redevelopments of the 1950s and 1960s ranged from three-storey buildings to flats and town houses through to villas and multi-dwellings. These were built from weatherboard, cement, or brick veneer. Harry Seidler's Australia Square Tower (1961–67) design is widely regarded as a symbol of Sydney's high-rise modernism. At the time of its completion, it was the world's tallest lightweight concrete building, and it is praised to this day for its sculptural qualities. The Space Age further inspired modernist designs, leading to dome, shell, and spiral structures. Australia's most outstanding architectural achievements of this movement include the Australian Academy of Science (Roy Grounds, 1959) in Canberra and the Sydney Opera House (1973).

Australian Architecture

Australia's history is reflected in its wide range of architecture, from the grand colonial style and elaborate Federation architecture, to the practical minimalism of Australian modernism, through to modern-day architecture which continues to tread new ground with new technologies and methods. Characteristic Australian architecture expresses a local identity. The 'Queenslander house', the 'wool shed', and the 'beach house' respond to their regional climate conditions and are made of local materials. But local identity was often disregarded in suburban developments, where 85 per cent of Australians have lived since the start of the twentieth century. Australian architects such as Roy Grounds, Robin Boyd, Glenn Murcutt, and Harry Seidler are leaders in Australia's modern architecture movement, favoured for their influential residential and contemporary contributions.

State Library of Queensland

A 'Queenslander House' in Queensland built in the early twentieth century, with a short-ridged roof and a generous wrap-around veranda. The roof and veranda feature architectural ornamentation at the edges and posts.

Harry Seidler's Australia Square Tower, centre, with the Sydney Harbour in the background. Sydney Opera House in the back right

Harry Seidler & Associates

The Henty House/Round House (1953), Mornington Peninsula, Victoria

wikimedia commons/Crystalsong92

Grounds House and flats (1954), Melbourne, Victoria. The Grounds House went on to influence the overall form of the National Gallery of Victoria.

Rory Hyde

Baker Library (1979), Bacchus Marsh, Victoria

Roy Grounds

Roy Grounds (1905–1981) was one of Victoria's most renowned architects and a leader in Australia's modern architecture movement. He was awarded the RAIA Gold Medal in 1968 before being knighted as Sir Roy Grounds in the same year. Grounds was born in Melbourne, Victoria. He studied at the University of Melbourne Architectural Atelier and in the evenings took classes at Brighton Technical School, which was where he developed an interest in the Bauhaus and modernist styles of design. After graduation, he began working with Blackett, Forster & Craig, a firm that focused on merging living and dining areas and minimising passageways. In 1928 he won the RVIA's annual war memorial scholarship, which allowed him to travel to the UK. Once on that side of the world, he also worked for several employers in Europe. In 1929, he set off for California, US, to work alongside Cram & Ferguson, designing sets for acclaimed Hollywood studios Metro-Goldwyn-Mayer and Radio-Keith-Orpheum Pictures. Grounds returned to Australia in 1933 and entered into a partnership with Geoffrey Harley Mewton. Mewton and Grounds became known as Australia's leading advocates of modernism in house design. Together they produced prize-winning modernist designs for the 1934 Melbourne Centennary Homes Competition. Grounds eventually moved on to designing homes solo. He explored the Colonial Revival style, which inspired his works such as Lyncroft (1935) and the Chateau Tahbilk Winery (1936). In the late 1930s he travelled back to England to work with Australian architect Raymond McGrath on projects in Welwyn City. He returned to Melbourne in 1940, designing flat-roofed buildings with open floor plans, the most notable being the elegant Clendon Flats in the stripped Neo-Georgian style. During the Second World War he designed buildings for the Royal Australian Air Force. By 1948, Grounds was back to designing houses, including the Henty House (1953), also known as the Round House for its circular floor plan, the Leyser House (1952), triangular in plan, and his own home, Grounds House (1954), which consisted of a square floor plan with a central circular courtyard and won the 1954 Victorian Architecture Medal. From 1948 until 1952 he taught at the University of Melbourne architecture school. In 1953 he established a partnership with Frederick Romberg and Robin Boyd, which lasted almost six years. Grounds' architectural theme of geometric forms carried through into his later work, including the Sidney Myer Music Bowl (1957), the Shine Dome (1959) of the Australian Academy of Science, the National Gallery (1968), and the Arts Centre Melbourne (1984).

Most recognised buildings:

- Lyncroft, Mornington Peninsula, VIC, 1935
- The Chateau Tahbilk winery, Strathbogie Shire, VIC, 1936
- Ramsay House, Mt Eliza, VIC, 1937
- Leyser House, Melbourne, VIC, 1952
- The Henty House (Round house), Mornington Peninsula, VIC, 1953
- Grounds House and flats, Melbourne, VIC, 1954
- Sidney Myer Music Bowl, Melbourne, VIC, 1957
- Shine Dome, Australian Academy of Science, Canberra, ACT, 1959
- National Gallery of Victoria, Melbourne, VIC, 1968
- Blackwood Hall, Monash University, Melbourne, VIC, 1971
- Wrest Point Hotel Casino, Hobart, TAS, 1973
- Baker Library, Bacchus Marsh, VIC, 1979
- Penders Holiday Retreat/ the 'Bran'/ Myers House, Tanja, NSW, 1980
- John Medley Building, Melbourne, VIC, 1981
- Arts Centre, Melbourne , VIC, 1984

Kenneth Ross. Courtesy Philip Goad

Myer House (1954), Mt Eliza, Victoria

John Gollings

Featherston House (1969), Melbourne, Victoria

Robin Boyd

Robin Boyd (1919–1971) was one of Victoria's most prominent architects of the post-war era. He was a leader in Melbourne's modern architecture movement and left his mark as an author, public educator, and critic, and was a spokesman for architecture and the built environment in Australia. His writings encouraged good design and a broader public understanding of its benefits. Boyd studied at Malvern Church of England Grammar School in Victoria until 1936 and thereafter began to work for prominent architect and businessman Kingsley Henderson. In the evenings he studied at the Royal Melbourne Technical College (now RMIT University). From 1938 until 1940 he studied at the University of Melbourne Architectural Atelier. Boyd's literary and critical abilities became evident in his earlier writings and editorial work for *Lines*, the annual magazine of the Victorian Architectural Students' Society, which was relaunched in 1937. In 1939, Boyd became the founding editor of *Smudges*, an unbiased monthly architectural newsletter which awarded monthly 'Bouquets' and 'Blots' for the best and worst buildings of each month. His first designed building to be constructed was a studio for his cousin in Murrumbeena, Melbourne, built in 1938. In 1942, Boyd joined the Australian Imperial Force where he continued to write about architecture for *SALT*, the army's newsletter. In 1945, he designed houses with Francis Richard Bell and Kevin Harry Pethebridge, including his own home in Camberwell, Victoria. He became a registered architect in 1946 and started his own practice in 1947, focusing on designing single-family houses. In the same year, he wrote his first book, *Victorian Modern: 111 years of modern architecture in Victoria*, a history of modern architecture in Victoria. He also won the coveted Robert and Ada Haddon Travelling Scholarship in 1948 which later took him overseas. As a response to the housing crisis following the Second World War, he designed The House of Tomorrow, which sought to address the need for affordable and well-constructed homes. His design was exhibited at the 1949 Modern Home Show at the Royal Exhibition Building in Melbourne. Between 1947 and 1953 he wrote weekly articles on architecture for the Melbourne-based newspaper *The Age*. His second book, *Australia's Home: Its Origins, Builders and Occupiers* was published in 1952. In 1953, Boyd joined the architects Roy Grounds and Frederick Romberg to form the partnership Grounds, Romberg & Boyd. Here his main focus remained but was not limited to designing houses. In 1955, Boyd designed the Peninsula House on behalf of Consolidated Homes Industries, and many variations of the design were built later. He left Australia in 1956 for MIT in Boston, US, where he spent some time as visiting professor and wrote articles for the US Journal *Architectural Forum*. These writings later informed another popular publication of his, *The Australian Ugliness* (1960). His most celebrated work, Walsh Street House (Boyd House II), in Melbourne's suburbs, is a contemporary house which Boyd designed for his family in 1957. Over the course of his career, Boyd worked on roughly 200 houses, characterised by controlled materiality and a conscious engagement with the natural landscape and neighbouring buildings.

Most recognised buildings:

- Arthur Boyd Studio, Melbourne, VIC, 1938
- Edith Boyd House, Burwood, VIC, 1939
- Boyd House I, Camberwell, VIC, 1947
- Fenner House, Canberra, ACT, 1953
- Hilary Roche House, Deakin, ACT, 1954
- Myer House, Mt Eliza, VIC, 1956
- Domain Park Flats, Melbourne, VIC, 1962
- Baker House, Bacchus Marsh, VIC, 1966
- Featherston House, Melbourne, VIC, 1969
- Churchill House/Winston Churchill Memorial Trust, Canberra, ACT, 1971

Robin Boyd's Walsh Street House (1959), Melbourne, Victoria

John Gollings

John Gollings © Penelope Seidler

Waverley Civic Centre (1984), Melbourne, Victoria

iStock (chameleonseye)

Riparian Plaza (2005), Riverside Centre (1986), Brisbane, Queensland

John Gollings

Berman House (1999), Joadja, New South Wales

Australia's Influential Modernists

Harry Seidler

Harry Seidler (1923 -2006) is one of the most admired architects of Australia's modernist movement and was the first in the country to incorporate Bauhaus principles. His ability to integrate art and modern technology is most celebrated in his Rose Seidler House (1950), among his residential works, and in his Australia Square (1967), among his commercial works. Seidler was born in Vienna, Austria, and lived there until the age of 15 when his family escaped Nazi-occupied Austria for England. There, he spent some time studying at Cambridgeshire Technical School. During the Second World War he was interned for 17 months as an enemy alien and transported to Canada. He was eventually released on parole to study architecture at the University of Manitoba, Winnipeg, graduating with a bachelor degree in architecture. Soon afterwards, he won a scholarship to study at the Graduate School of Design at Harvard University, US, where he studied the principles of the Bauhaus under leaders of the movement, Walter Gropius and Marcel Breuer. In 1946, he undertook a design course at Black Mountain College, North Carolina, under the artist Josef Albers. He then worked as chief assistant to Marcel Breuer in New York City from 1946 to 1948. Seidler's parents moved to Australia during this time and were eager for him to join them, but as modernism was flourishing in New York City at the time, Seidler declined their invitation until he received a commission to design their home in Sydney. Seidler jumped at the opportunity and accepted the commisison before first spending a few months in Rio de Janeiro, Brazil, working in the office of Oscar Niemeyer, a key figure in the development of modern architecture and expert in free-flowing concrete forms. He arrived in Sydney in 1948, at the age of 25, and completed the Rose Seidler House by the time he was 27. Modernism had not yet reached Australia and the design for the modernist home attracted a new list of curious clients who wanted something just like it. He went on to design more modern houses including the Rose House (1950) and the Marcus Seidler House (1951). As Seidler's reputation grew, his work began to take on larger forms which encouraged new ways of building. Seidler married fellow architect Penelope Evatt in 1958, and by 1963, he had established the practice Harry Seidler & Associates. Seidler is recognised for his contributions to architecture in Australia throughout his career as a designer, lecturer, teacher, writer, and supporter of the arts. He has received numerous awards, including the honour of being made a Life Fellow (1970) and receiving 50 awards from the Royal Australian Institute of Architects (RAIA). Five of these were Sir John Sulman Medals, four were Wilkinson Awards, and in 1976 he won the Gold Medal. In 1987, he was awarded the Companion of the Order of Australia, Australia's highest honour.

Most recognised buildings:

- Rose Seidler House, Sydney, NSW, 1950
- Marcus Seidler House Sydney, NSW, 1953
- Julian Rose House, Sydney, NSW, 1954
- Blues Point Tower, Sydney, NSW, 1962
- Muller House, Port Hacking, NSW, 1966
- Australia Square, Sydney, NSW, 1967
- Harry and Penelope Seidler House, Killara, NSW, 1967
- Edmund Barton Building, Canberra,1974
- MLC Centre, Sydney, NSW, 1977
- City of Monash (former Waverley Civic Centre), Melbourne, VIC, 1984
- Lakeview Townhouses, Canberra, 1984
- Hannes House, Sydney, NSW, 1986
- Shell, Melbourne, VIC, 1989
- Riverside Centre, Brisbane, QLD, 1986
- Grosvenor Place, Sydney, NSW, 1991
- QV1, Perth, WA, 1991
- Horizon Apartments, Sydney, NSW, 1998
- Berman House, Joadja, NSW, 1999
- Riparian Plaza , Brisbane, QLD, 2005

Max Dupain, © Penelope Seidler

Max Dupain, © Penelope Seidler

Sunlight and Architecture

Harry Seidler (1959)

Light makes it possible for us to see, but sunlight lends drama to what we see.

Sunlight is probably the most powerful design element in architecture. It imparts emphasis and an additional constantly changing element – that of shade and shadow, which bring out the true nature of form and texture.

Solid form is accentuated and added to by the shadow it casts which recalls its design form. Hollowed out form – negative space – becomes significant in sunlight. Spidery elements, adjuncts to buildings and sculpture, increase the interest of their own forms by the complex pattern of their shadows, which are in themselves a new pattern form which must be considered as an integral part of the elements that cast them.

Australia is a country of much sunlight and it seems logical and fitting that its architecture should be one that makes a feature of sunlight both from a practical as well as an aesthetic point of view.

The practical considerations are well known. It should go without saying that unprotected large glass areas facing the sun are a menace. Let us repeat that one should never use large glass areas on the East or West unless protected by scientifically designed sun-control devices, otherwise a hot-box will be the result. All sun-protection devices must be outside the glass to be effective. The North is the ideal exposure. There the sun is above and can easily be shaded by a roof overhang, awning type projection, or horizontally fixed or moveable louvres to stop the high summer sun and allow the lower rays of the winter sun to come in and help heat the interior.

Many devices have been used effectively on the difficult orientations, East and West, which admit low rays of the rising and setting sun. The one giving fully effective control of sun and light intensity on the interior are moveable vertical louvres made of various light-weight materials such as aluminium, wood, etc. These installations are costly and not always desirable. Very close to ideal conditions can be obtained by the use of

Top left:
Kalowski House, Dover Heights, Sydney, architect: Harry Seidler, 1958

Left:
Office Building in Sydney, architect: Harry Seidler, 1956

Max Dupain, © Penelope Seidler

Max Dupain, © Penelope Seidler

Left:
Amenities and Workshop Building, Banksmeadow, architect: Harry Seidler, 1955

various types of grilles, placed outside the glass. These can be of pre-cast concrete, terracotta, etc., and the possibilities of design variation are limitless and a great deal of experimentation can well take place in this field. Design for climate both physical and aesthetic can be the key to good building which thus becomes truly a part of its environment.

Much modern art and modern architecture have been concerned with visual contrast – opposition, i.e., sun and shadow. The oscillation between light and shade gives richness to building in contrast to the sterile glassy flatness which is all sun, or all shadow, lacking that so necessary visual contrast. Much recent building, mainly in the field of office buildings, has copied the American trend of mass-produced 'curtain' walls. These were designed mainly for cold climates, and all countries that have a high degree of industrialisation and production of mechanical equipment. Here such buildings are feasible only through the use of oversized highly expensive air-conditioning systems. In such buildings, that quite blatantly expose their sheer glass faces in all directions, it is necessary to keep the interior fully closed by venetian blinds which negate all the advantages of glass. The result is that we get the glass box with an air-conditioning system using up enormous power, and additionally the electric light burning inside on a sunny day because the blinds must always be kept fully shut. What a price to pay for keeping up with the New York skyscrapers! It seems a hollow victory to be able to copy this overseas design tendency, and aside from the well-known and unsolved problem of leakage occurring through these curtain walls.

Instead, by using our common sense and inventiveness, should we not exploit the necessity of climate and create a richness of façade that deals with the sun and produces visually far more satisfactory results? The problem is to live with the sun and get its benefit when we want it, and yet control it completely.

In Colonial times people were far more aware of this problem, and many traditional examples of Australian architecture are proof of this. The deeply cut sculptural façades and detail, the verandahs and overhangs are proof of sensitive good design of that period.

Present day routine work sidesteps the issue by producing a solid brick building with as few openings as possible. This seems reasonable climatically, but surely unacceptable structurally and aesthetically. This and the complete insensitivity of such buildings to architectural detail, such as outside plumbing pipes in hard relief under strong sun as a façade feature, must give way to an architecture that brings together the practical considerations of climate with today's aesthetic intention in a happy marriage.

John Gollings

The Marie Short Farmhouse (1974), Kempsey, New South Wales

John Gollings

Simpson-Lee House (1993), Mount Wilson, New South Wales

Bill Peterson

The Arthur Boyd Education Centre (1999), Riversdale , New South Wales

Australia's Influential Modernists
Glenn Murcutt

Glenn Murcutt (1936–) is Australia's most internationally acclaimed architect who has received 25 Australian architecture awards, including the Australian Institute of Architects Gold Medal. His international awards include the Gold Medal of the Royal Australian Institute of Architects (1992), the Alvar Aalto Medal (1992), the Pritzker Prize for Architecture (2002), and the Australian Institute of Architects Gold Medal (2009). Murcutt was born in London, England and spent the early years of his childhood living in New Guinea with his Australian parents. During these early years he lived in an elevated timber house with a low pitched corrugated-iron roof and louvered shutters. In 1941, his family moved back to Australia. Murcutt went on to study architecture at the Sydney Technical College. He gained experience in his student years working for Neville Gruzman, Levido & Baker, and Allen & Jack. After graduating in 1961, he moved to the United Kingdom to work with Ian Fraser & Assosciates and spent some time travelling through Europe where his love for vernacular architecture grew. He returned to Sydney in 1964 and worked for the firm Ancher, Mortlock, Murray & Woolley before starting his own practice in 1969. In 1973 he undertook a three-and-a-half month world tour through Mexico, the US, and Europe. It was through this trip that he developed a sensitivity to architecture's relationship with site, views, light, and climate which formed his approach to domestic architecture. He went on to create works inspired by Mies van der Rohe, designing for example the minimalist Laurie Short House (1973) and Marie Short Farmhouse (1974). He responded to climate conditions using steel and open-plan designs and emphasised the mediation of sunlight through louvres and flat-roofed verandas. He defined corrugated iron as a symbol of Australian identity and celebrated the material along with his ethos of '[touching] the earth lightly', a metaphor for his understanding of the relationship between buildings and the landscape. He continuously implemented his design principles in his works, including the Magney House (1984), Simpson-Lee House (1993), Marika-Alderton House (1994) through to his most recent work, the Walsh House (2005). These drew international attention which led to numerous publications of his extensive work as a critic, lecturer, and teacher worldwide. He continues as sole practitioner and professor at the University of New South Wales Australia. In 2016 he was appointed Chair of the Pritzker Prize Jury.

Most recognised buildings:

- Laurie Short house, Sydney, NSW, 1973
- Marie Short / Glenn Murcutt House, Kempsey, NSW, 1974
- Nicholas House, Mount Irvine, 1980
- Museum and Information Centre, Kempsey, NSW, 1982
- Fredericks / White house, Jamberoo, NSW, 1982
- Magney house, Bingie Bingie, NSW, 1984
- Done house, Sydney, NSW, 1991
- Raheen (Pratt Family Wing Addition), Kew, VIC, 1992
- Simpson-Lee house, Mount Wilson, NSW, 1993
- Marika-Alderton House, Eastern Arnhern Land, NT, 1994
- Bowali Visitor Information Centre, Kakadu National Park, NT, 1994
- Douglas and Ruth Murcutt House, Woodside, NT, 1996
- The Arthur Boyd Education Centre, Riversdale , NSW, 1999
- Kangaloon House, Kangaloon, 2001
- Murcutt-Lewin House and Studio, Mosman NSW, 2003
- Walsh House, Kangaroo Valley, 2005
- Moss Vale Education Centre (University of Wollongong), Moss Vale, NSW, 2007
- Australian Islamic Centre, Newport, VIC, 2016

Bowali Visitor Information Centre (1994), Kakadu National Park, in collaboration with Troppo Architects

Luke Durkin

A Lucky Country

John Gollings

Australia is a 'lucky country', wrote historian Donald Horne in 1964. This was not praise but a cynical critique of mediocrity and provincialism. In 1960, architect and writer Robin Boyd published *The Australian Ugliness*, criticising the country's lack of design style and Australians' slavish imitation of American 'featurism'. The underlying tension between provincialism and derivative design ideas on the one hand, and original, Australian design thinking on the other remains a quandary for contemporary architects. Our luck as a society is, in fact, due to middle-of-the-road complacency deriving from continuous stable government, relatively homogeneous wealth, and a benign climate. Since European settlement in 1788 – and despite the frontier wars and the violent displacement of the native people, the Aboriginal Australians, from their lands – we have been a nation of remarkable racial integration and tolerance. Geographically Australia was also lucky. Until 1788 it was an unpolluted paradise. For 70,000 years, the entire island continent was under the stewardship of Aboriginal people. Largely nomadic, with a sophisticated culture and social structure and deep spiritual connection to the country, they actively managed the land using fire. They sourced their food and medicine from nature. They neither industrialised, settled, nor built permanent structures. The influence of Aboriginal values on modern Australian culture is marginal, not mainstream, and is mostly discerned in attitudes towards sustainable land-management practices and in the arts. Aboriginal values are barely discernible in Australian architecture – except in the work of Gregory Burgess and perhaps Glenn Murcutt and Troppo, with their organic forms, lightweight construction, and use of natural materials. However, the Wrightian organic school in its current manifestation – centred on sustainability and connection to place – is a strong tendency, and it coincides with Aboriginal sensibilities about the land.

This organic tendency is one of three strands I identify to explain current Australian architecture. The other two are based on international modernism and on expressionism. It is not surprising that the history of Australian architecture is one of derivations and transformations of imported building types and styles. Among the early convict arrivals was Francis Greenway who was appointed government architect. The era was Georgian. Greenway designed the first colonial civic buildings, and the early settlers built Georgian cottages, mansions, and townhouses, adapting them to the climate by adding verandas imported from colonial India to provide shade. The 1850s gold rush contributed impressive, solid, European civic and residential townscapes, especially in Victoria, including remarkably intact regional cities like Bendigo and Ballarat. In 1901, Australia became a federation of states. A corresponding architectural style of the

Worn Gundidj Visitor Centre (Robin Boyd, 1969), Towerhill, Koroit, Victoria.

time, Federation, was a particularly Australian rendering of Arts and Crafts. The Arts and Crafts tendency was amplified when Walter Burley Griffin and his wife Marion Mahony Griffin, devotees of Frank Lloyd Wright, won the design for the new national capital, Canberra, in 1911. Their work was a synthesis of Wright's Prairie School and Arts and Crafts. Other notable Australian Arts and Crafts exponents include Harold Desbrowe-Annear in Victoria and Robin Dods in Queensland, whose influences were European rather than American.

Between the two world wars, another heavily American-influenced style, Art Deco, came to Australia. International modernism appeared in the 1930s. It had two sources: refugees from Europe, and international publications on modernism that were avidly read in Australia. Prominent exponents were Stephenson & Turner (trained at the Architectural Association in London after the First World War), who imported European modernist ideas. Based in Melbourne, they became the largest firm in Australia, notable for hospitals and public buildings. Hugh Buhrich and Harry Seidler, immigrants from Europe, brought modernist values to Sydney. In Brisbane John Dalton developed a modern regionalism. Modernism also arrived from the United States. Bates Smart McCutcheon's 1955 ICI House in Melbourne shares the International Style language of SOM's Lever House in New York of 1952. Curiously, the only building form developed in Australia conspicuously lacks any architectural design: the rational, modest and featureless L-shaped house on a quarter acre allotment. Tens of thousands were built after the Second World War when materials and money were short and families were large.

From the 1970s onwards, as Australians grew wealthier, residential tastes trended to faux Palladian villas dependent on air-conditioning to be habitable. A lack of originality in Australian architecture was troubling to the post-war baby boomers. They were the beneficiaries of decades of peace and economic growth – and also the dismantling of the International Style. By the 1970s, when the baby boomers came of age, postmodernism briefly promoted a doctrine of historicist eclecticism that made expressionism respectable again. There are three design tendencies that I identify in Australian architecture: the organic school, an architecture that responds to environment and place; international modernism, essentially the Sydney School; scenographic expressionism, principally in Melbourne. The organic school incorporates (but not necessarily at the same time) natural and lightweight materials, climatic imperatives, regional values, dissolution of barriers between interior and exterior, and mystic geometries. In Queensland: Rex Addison, Donovan Hill. In New South Wales: Walter Burley Griffin and Marion Mahoney Griffin's work in Castlecrag, Peter Muller, Bruce Rickard,

Nishi Building (Fender Katsalidis Architects, 2013), NewActon, Canberra, ACT

John Gollings

John Gollings

Buhrich House II (Hugh Buhrich, 1972), Castlecrag, New South Wales

Neville Gruzman, Ancher Mortlock Woolley, Richard Leplastrier, Glenn Murcutt. In Victoria: Robin Boyd, Graeme Gunn, Kevin Borland, Peter McIntyre, Greg Burgess, Alastair Knox, Rodney Eggleston (March Studio). In South Australia and Northern Territory: Troppo Architects. The enduring legacy of the International Style is rationalism. Form follows function, but with local idiomatic twists and undogmatic poetics. In Queensland: Lindsay and Kerry Clare. In New South Wales: Ken Woolley, Harry Seidler, Alex Popov, Richard Francis Jones. In Victoria: Bates Smart McCutcheon, Neil Clerehan, Denton Corker Marshall, Sean Godsell. Scenographic expressionism has thrived in Melbourne as a grab-bag of styles. Peter Corrigan – architect and set designer – led the pack; his followers include Ashton Raggatt McDougall. There was also Daryl Jackson, Peter McIntyre, Philip Cox, Nonda Katsalidis, Cassandra Fahey, Dylan Brady, Jackson Clements Burrows, Angelo Candalepas, John Wardle. In New South Wales: Durbach Block Jaggers. This results in a Jencksian categorisation of styles but it serves to distinguish the major tendencies evident in contemporary Australian architecture. The three tendencies are not rigid: they all intersect to greater or lesser extent. And the list of architects commended here is far from complete.

John Gollings

Dome House (McBride Charles Ryan, 2005), Hawthorn, Victoria

Hotel Lobby and Nishi Grand Stair Interior
(March Studio, 2014), NewActon, Canberra, ACT

John Gollings

Sydney

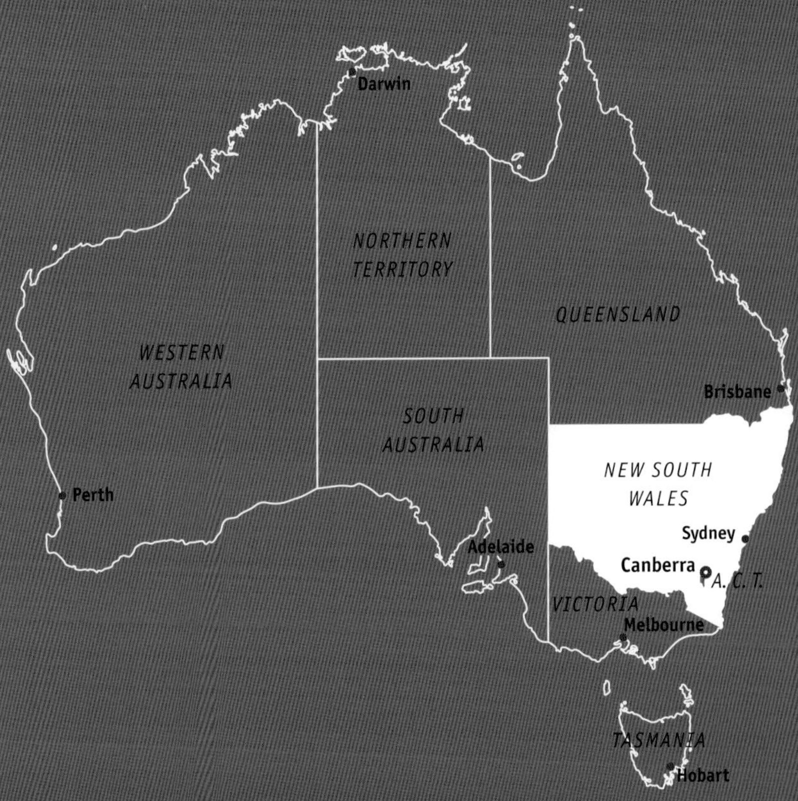
Darwin
NORTHERN TERRITORY
QUEENSLAND
WESTERN AUSTRALIA
SOUTH AUSTRALIA
Brisbane
NEW SOUTH WALES
Perth
Sydney
Adelaide
Canberra
A. C. T.
VICTORIA
Melbourne
TASMANIA
Hobart

A
Sydney
012
015
018
021
022
024
025
016
005
035
031
017
008
006
026
034
033
004

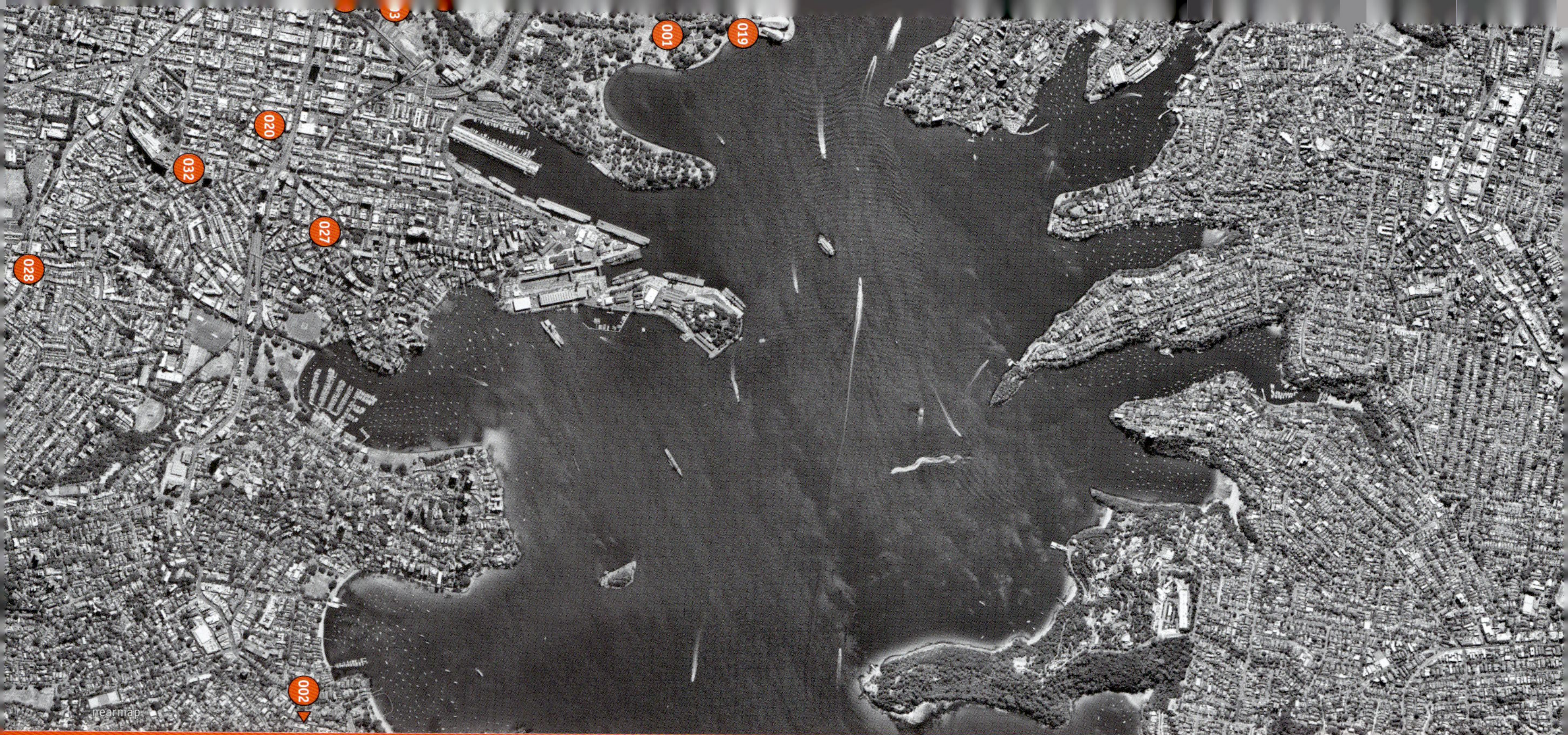
001
019
020
032
027
028
002
nearmap

Sydney

A trip to Australia wouldn't be complete without a visit to the internationally admired Sydney Opera House. This celebrated symbol of Australia has undoubtedly put Sydney on the map as the most remarkable city in Australia. Sydney is the capital city of the state of New South Wales and is located on Australia's eastern coastline surrounding the world's largest natural harbour, Port Jackson. The city was officially founded by Captain Arthur Phillip on his arrival in 1788 which brought the First Fleet of convicts to Botany Bay. Not long after, the fleet moved to the more desirable Port Jackson location that is Sydney Cove. It was here that Sydney, the first European settlement in Australia, was established. With convict transportation eventually coming to an end and the discovery of gold in the mid 19th century, the city began to grow rapidly, transforming from a colonial frontier to the major cultural and economic gateway to Australia that it is today. By the turn of the 20th century it had inherited the title of Australia's largest city from Melbourne. Since its discovery, the city's population has grown to an estimated 5.25 million (2016), establishing Sydney as Australia's largest city and one of the most multi-cultural cities in the world. The youth of this vibrant city is evident in the international influences of its architecture. Prominent styles include Neo-Gothic (Government House), Neo-Classical (State Library

Aerial view over Sydney's city centre nestled between the harbour and surrounding suburban neighbourhoods. Right page, centre: *505 George Street* by Christoph Ingenhoven, Sydney's soon-to-be tallest residential tower with a height of 270 metres.

of New South Wales), and Romanesque (Queen Victoria Building), stemming from the old Colonial, Victorian, Federation, Inter-War, post-war, and late twentieth century periods. Sydney is one of the top tourist destinations in the world and Australia's most celebrated city with its rich blend of natural landscapes complemented by remarkable architecture, from the twentieth century Sydney Opera House, Sydney Harbour Bridge, and Sydney Tower to more historic buildings such as the Government House and St Mary's Cathedral. The combination of these structures form exciting settings that attract millions of visitors annually. Milestones for the City of Sydney include hosting the 2000 Olympics as well the establishment in 1850 of the University of Sydney, Australia's first university, which is recognised as one of the world's leading universities today. The Great Depression and the Second World War led to a housing shortage in the late 1940s. Regarding the cost of housing, Sydney has been ranked as the world's second most expensive city to live in (2017) after Hong Kong. Suburbs such as Point Piper, Darling Point, Cremorne Point, and Bellevue Hill are consistently regarded as the most expensive to live in. Fortunately natural beauty can be found at no charge on Sydney's white sandy beaches, the most visited of which is Bondi Beach. The sparkling harbour and adjoining mountainous landscape are only a short trip from the city. *SZ*

Government House

001 A

Macquarie Street
James Bloodsworth (1788), Edward Blore (1845)
1788, 1845

It was in 1788 that Sydney's first Government House was built following the British settlement. This building, influenced by the Georgian style, was designed by convict James Bloodsworth, Governor Phillip's Superintendent of Tradesmen. Despite its simple, symmetrical, two-storey design with hipped roofs, its architecture was incredibly elaborate for that time in Australia. The original building was located on Bridge Street and served as the political and social hub of the colony for many years until the decision was made to tear down the dingy structure and relocate the governor's residence to Macquarie Street, closer to the Royal Botanic Gardens. Construction began in 1836 and ended in 1845. From this point onwards, the house served as the official residence and office of 27 different governors, starting with Sir George Gipps, the ninth governor of New South Wales. It was eventually opened to the public in 1996, but it recommenced its role as the governor's official place of residence in 2013 and has been occupied

iStock (davidf)

by the 38th Governor of New South Wales, David Hurley, since 2014. The remarkable castled sandstone towers and medieval features of the building's exterior were influenced by the Gothic Revival style, which the architect Edward Blore, already renowned at the time of the building's design, frequently used. *SZ*

Australia's first government building to be built, circa 1809

Macquarie Lighthouse

Old South Head Rd
Francis Greenway (1816), James Barnet (1883)
1816, 1883

002 A

The Macquarie Lighthouse is Australia's first lighthouse and remains operational today. It is located approximately two kilometres from the entrance to Sydney Harbour. The area has been used as a navigational base since 1791. A flagstaff was erected in 1790, followed by a tripod-mounted iron basket in 1793. The lighthouse was designed by convict architect Francis Greenway and completed in 1816. Its soft sandstone structure began to deteriorate not long after it was completed, and the decision was made to replace the tower with a new structure, which was completed in 1883 and stands today. The architect James Barnet designed the tower in such a way that it would bear close resemblance to the original tower, although the crown and the lantern room were increased in size to accommodate larger equipment. *SZ*

Left: the original and new Macquarie Lighthouse standing side by side, 1883

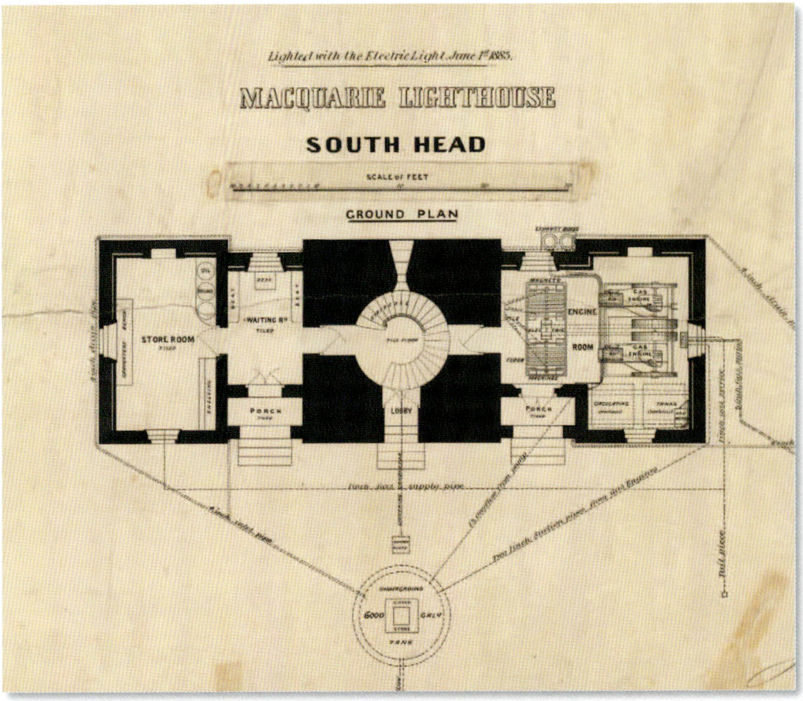

Ground floor plan, Macquarie Lighthouse, 1883. Architect: James Barnet

iStock (zetter)

Darren Foreman

« St Mary's Cathedral 003 A

St Mary's Road
William Wardell, Hennessey & Hennessey
1851, 1928 -

The mid 19th century St Mary's Cathedral was sadly destroyed by a fire in 1865. Construction of the current building began shortly afterwards and was ongoing for over 100 years. The architect William Wardell designed the church with English gothic influences, which in turn helped make the cathedral become one of Sydney's most recognised and significant historic buildings. Wardell died before he could see the completed building, as construction took such a long time. The architects Hennessey & Hennessey were responsible for the project from 1899 onwards. It was opened in 1928, still only partially completed. A series of steps leads to the cathedral's main entrance, which was oriented to the south due to the slope of the site. The weathered sandstone exterior is enriched by the rose windows and pointed arches. The plan resembles those of conventional English cathedrals, with a cruciform shape and two towers, one placed where the nave crosses the transept, and another at the main entrance. Inside, the central nave features high-reaching buttresses that separate the two stone aisles. The decoratively carved ceiling and stained glass illuminate the interior spaces and direct the eye to the cathedral's pitched roof. *SZ*

≽ Main Quadrangle Building 004 A

University of Sydney
Edmund Blacket, James Barnet
1859 -

The University of Sydney, founded in 1850, is Australia's first university, and its campus continues to grow with the addition of contemporary buildings. A group of Gothic Revival buildings fill the centre of the campus, forming the Main Quadrangle. This quadrangle comprises a series of two-storey sandstone wings that contain the Great Hall, MacLaurin Hall, the Faculty of Arts office, and the Nicholson Museum. The Main Quadrangle Building is a crowd pleaser, attracting many *Harry Potter* fans due to its resemblance to the series' fictional Hogwarts School of Witchcraft and Wizardry. The building's construction started in 1854 at the eastern end and continued for over 100 years, with development of the southern end beginning in the early 20th century. The quadrangle was inspired by Neo-Gothic principles, of which the Great Hall, which opened in 1859, is a perfect example, with its pointed arches, steep-sloping roofs, and elaborate carvings. Contributing architects included Edmund Blacket and James Barnet. Walter Liberty Vernon stepped in at a later date with his design for the MacLaurin Hall, completed in 1909. Vernon also drew on gothic styles, as evident in the steep copper roof featuring extravagant metal lanterns. *SZ*

Daniel Neubauer

The Main Quadrangle Building is a crowd pleaser for fans of the *Harry Potter* series due to its resemblance to the famous Hogwarts School of Witchcraft and Wizardry.

Daniel Neubauer

flickr (trufru)

General Post Office

1 Martin Place
James Barnet
1874

005 A

Angus Fraser

Sarah Zahradnik

Sydney's General Post Office (GPO) is New South Wales's finest example of Victorian Italian Renaissance style architecture. This grand building was designed by colonial architect James Barnet. His design drew on the styles of late-Medieval and Renaissance Italy. Sydney's first General Post Office, located on George Street and designed by Francis Greenway, proved to be too small and was later demolished to make way for the current GPO. In 1865, Barnet presented a proposal which linked George and Pitt Streets, with a public colonnade to front a large public space. This public space would later be named Martin Place. After a lengthy construction period, the post office building was opened in 1874. Further works continued, including the extension of the post office onto Pitt Street (completed in 1885), the clock tower (1891), and addition of a fifth storey (1899). The original George Street clock was disliked as it only had a single face not visible from George Street. It was replaced with the present-day three-faced projecting clock. An open arcade wraps around the ground-floor façade of this remarkable building. This arcade consists of polished monolithic columns, domical vaults, and carved capitals based on similar materials. The façade is made of Pyrmont stone. Symmetrical bays face Martin Place with end pavilions. An enormous clock-and-bell tower rises up to a height of 64 metres from its centre. *SZ*

The façade of the General Post Office, circa 1900

Sydney Town Hall

006 A

483 George Street
J H Willson (1884),
Thomas Sapsford, John Hennessey (1889)
1884,1889

Sydney Town Hall has been the heart of the city since it was first opened in 1880. It was the most renowned and innovative building of its time with its highly lavish design and neo-classical features. The heritage-listed building's high Victorian interiors contain state-of-the-art venue spaces: the Vestibule and Centennial Hall. The Vestibule was the first of the two spaces to be completed and features an elegant elliptical dome made of some of the earliest Australian stained glass with a glorious crystal chandelier hanging from the centre. The Centennial Hall features an acclaimed grand organ that stretches twenty-five metres along the entire length of the western wall. The hall is decked with rich stained-glass windows, a colourfully adorned ceiling, and twelve enormous marble pillars at the corners. J H Willson was the architect behind the design of the first stage of this building, completed in 1884. The next stage was carried out by the architects Thomas Sapsford and John Hennessey, whose design included the significant west extension and the grand hall. To this day, the Town Hall remains the most ornate late-19th-century civic building in the country. *SZ*

Ian Armstrong

Jasmine Deng

State Library of NSW

» Culwulla Chambers

007 A

67 Castlereagh St

Spain, Cosh & Minnett

1911

At the time of its completion, in 1911, Culwulla Chambers was the tallest building in Sydney's city centre. Major technological advances in steel construction and fireproofing made it possible to construct the building with a height of 50.25 metres. However, the building was at the centre of much controversy due to its height, which far exceeded any of its surrounding buildings. As a result, the city's planners introduced the Height of Buildings Act of 1912 (NSW), which restricted building heights to a maximum of 45.72 metres. This law stayed in place until 1957, when it was revoked. Culwulla Chambers remained the tallest building in Sydney's central business district until 1961 when the AMP Building was constructed on Alfred Street with a height of 117.3 metres. The historic significance of the Culwulla Chambers stems not only from its height but also because it serves as a fine example of the Federation Free Style. The architecture firm Spain, Cosh & Minnett designed the twelve-storey office building to be made of reinforced concrete with highly aesthetic detailing. Brick and stone claddings are combined to create a linear formation and distorted neo-classical features. *SZ*

Sarah Zahradnik

Front elevations

Hideya Hamano

Queen Victoria Building

455 George Streets
George McRae
1898

008 A

Daniel Neubauer

The atmospheric Romanesque style architecture of the Queen Victoria Building, more commonly referred to as QVB, marks the junction of George, Market, York, and Druitt Streets. The grand building was designed by George McRae during the recession in the late 19th century. It was the only major city building under construction in 1898 providing work for unemployed craftsmen, stonemasons, plasterers, and stained-window artists. The building was completed in 1898 and originally accommodated entertainment halls, cafés, offices, warehouses, and shops. The building was remodelled in an Art Deco style in the 1930s, when the Sydney City Council was its main occupant. The building was threatened with demolition from 1959 to 1971. In response, a major restoration project was launched to refurbish the entire building, which was eventually reopened in 1986. Inside, the stained glass, the ornamental copper elements, and the detailing of the arches, pillars, balustrades, and flooring impart an exuberance to the space. But the main feature of the interior is undoubtedly the prominent central glass dome with the original 19th century staircase situated below. *SZ*

Daniel Neubauer

Thorsten Rust

Thorsten Rust

≈ Hyde Park Barracks Museum 009 A
Queens Square, Macquarie St
Francis Greenway
1819, 1991

The historically significant Hyde Park Barracks is listed on the UNESCO World Heritage list, being one of world's most important cultural heritage sites with a compelling history. This colonial building was the first of the convict barracks to be constructed in the colony and the centre of colonial convict administration in Australia. Commissioned by Governor Lachlan Macquarie, it was built with convict labour and was intended to increase the productivity of the convicts residing within. The building also accommodated immigrant, elderly, and deprived women and later served as an office for government and administration. Convict architect Francis Greenway received a full pardon for his Georgian style design of this three-storey building, with its refined façade and large shingled roof. It was completed in 1819 and redeveloped into a museum in 1991 by Tonkin Zulaikha Greer Architects, who adopted a strict approach to the conservation and interpretation of its complex, historical layers. The original surfaces were conserved, while non-original surfaces were either repainted with colours similar to the original ones or left neutral. All new work is clearly distinguishable and has a deliberately strong architectural character to bring the present and past together. *SZ*

» Anzac War Memorial 010 A
Liverpool Street, Hyde Park
Charles Bruce Dellit
1934

One of Australia's many war memorials, the commemorative Anzac War Memorial sits alone beside the pool of reflection in Sydney's Hyde Park. It was designed by Australian architect Charles Bruce Dellit as a place to remember the First World War. The idea of creating a space of remembrance came about after the 1915 Gallipoli campaign and the monument was officially opened in 1934. The exterior was decked with several ornaments, relief panels, and monumental figures, depicting military personnel, sculpted by English artist George Rayner Hoff. The harmony between the sculptures and the cladded granite structure with its setbacks, buttresses, stepped roof, and large stained-glass windows is an admirable example of Art Deco architecture. *SZ*

Jasmine Deng

Sydney Harbour Bridge from the north side, showing the completed arch, 1930

Fiona Moore

Sydney Harbour Bridge

011 A

Sydney Harbour Bridge
Dr J J C Bradfield, NSW Department of Public Works, Dorman Long and Co
1932

Undeniably one of Australia's most photographed landmarks, the Sydney Harbour Bridge was completed in 1932 after a long eight-year construction period. It is known to locals as 'the coathanger', given its arched form. A general design for the bridge was developed by John Bradfield and the NSW Department of Public Works and later handed over to the firm Dorman Long and Co for construction. The steel arch bridge is the world's largest of its kind, with a height of 134 metres from top to water level. Eight traffic lanes and two rail lines run in each direction along the bridge, which spans a distance of 504 metres. The arched structure is made up of two 28-panel arch trusses which vary in height and are supported at each end by large steel pins that allow for expansion and contraction caused by changes in temperature. BridgeClimb, an organisation established in 1998, allows many eager visitors to traverse the catwalks and climb the stairs and ladders to experience the panoramic views from the top of this famous monument. The south-eastern end of the bridge holds an exhibition space and the popular Pylon lookout, which offers visitors a 360-degree view over the harbour. *SZ*

The series of steel arch trusses which support the arched structure of the Sydney Harbour Bridge

011 A

Ida Jarosova

Rose Seidler House » »

012 A

71 Clissold Rd, Wahroonga
Harry Seidler
1950

Marcell Seidler

The first house completed by Seidler was for his parents. He created a hollowed-out square plan exposed on all sides, with the living area and sheltered terrace opening out towards the north – the preferred orientation – and also offering a view of the valley. The living and sleeping areas are separated by a central family room that can either be connected to the alcove-like bedrooms or incorporated into the living space by a dividing curtain. The rectangular mass of the building is hollowed by the open central terrace and the adjacent two-storey well that vertically pierces through the building, allowing light to penetrate into the otherwise dark centre. From the rectangular structure, 'tentacles' reach out and anchor it into the surrounding land, the stone retaining walls, the ramp leading to the garden, and the louvre fence shielding the drying yard. In 1988, the house was conditionally gifted to the Sydney Living Museums and opened to the public in its original furnished condition. *PA*

Julian Rose House

013 A

Wahroonga*
Harry Seidler & Associates
1954

The Julian Rose House, like the Rose Seidler House, is raised off the ground to take advantage of the valley view to the north. The structure, with diagonal tension bars exposed inside and outside, resembles a bridge with both ends suspended in midair, giving it a striking, sculptural appearance. The ground floor is mainly open, with a small central studio including a utility and shower room clad in brick and a double carport under the west end, which contains the living room above. The second floor is compactly arranged with one bedroom, a bathroom, and the kitchen, dining room, and living room all lined up back to back from east to west along an inset, continuous terrace that is 2.5 metres wide. The terrace overlooks the northern view down to the valley and avoids direct sun. It is separated from the interiors by sliding glass doors. *VB*

* Private residence not open to public

Max Dupain, © Penelope Seidler

sydneylivingmuseums.com.au

George Williamson House 014 A

65 Parriwi Rd, Mosman*

Harry Seidler & Associates

1954

The Williamson House double garage with its distinctive double-arc roof complements the surrounding hilly shoreline and alludes to Oscar Niemeyer's Pampulha Belo Horizonte, Brazil, of 1943. The house is on top of a precipitously sloping rocky site with panoramic views over Middle Harbour, toward the northeast. The three-level house has its interiors mainly on the middle floor – one level down. The structure's top level is aligned with the street. All rooms – living room, dining room, a small bedroom, and a master bedroom – are in-line and positioned toward the view. All rooms except a small bedroom have full-height glass sliding doors leading to shaded recessed terraces. A study, kitchen, two bathrooms, and dressing area are positioned on the street side and all have ribbon windows for privacy and cross ventilation. *VB*

* Private residence not open to public

Max Dupain, © Penelope Seidler

≫ Blues Point Tower

015 A

14 Blues Point Rd
Harry Seidler & Associates
1962

Blues Point Tower is located on a harbourside peninsula on Sydney's Lower North Shore. Australian architect Harry Seidler designed the residential tower in the post-war modern style, with an arrangement of façade elements in a scintillated pattern inspired by his former ex-Bauhaus teacher Josef Albers. Blues Point Tower was included in the North Sydney Council's heritage list in 1993. Seidler believed that the structure's reinforced concrete and brick-infill walls were a more climate-friendly alternative to the more conventional glazed façades. Strips of high horizontal windows line the dining and bedroom areas and full-length glass doors open from the primary living spaces to French balconies. The 78.3-metre-high apartment building accommodates 144 apartments. The heavy concrete tower was Australia's tallest residential building until 1970. *SZ*

Max Dupain, © Penelope Seidler

Australia Square

016 A

264 George St
Harry Seidler & Associates
1967

Designed by Harry Seidler, the elegant Australia Square Tower is an icon of Australian architecture – an icon that established new principles in commercial design and construction. Its distinctly circular design with a large public plaza at ground level was the first of its type to be constructed in Australia. Surrounded by activity, this public open space sits raised above street level and forms a surpsingly pleasant hub with cafés, water fountains and artwork. At the time of its completion in 1967, it became Sydney's first skyscraper and the world's tallest lightweight concrete building. The pre-cast façade, an admired structural innovation, was designed by one of the world's leading engineers, Pier Luigi Nervi. Its repetitive floor plan and cast-in-situ core significantly accelerated its construction time and set a benchmark for office tower design. *SZ*

Max Dupain, © Penelope Seidler

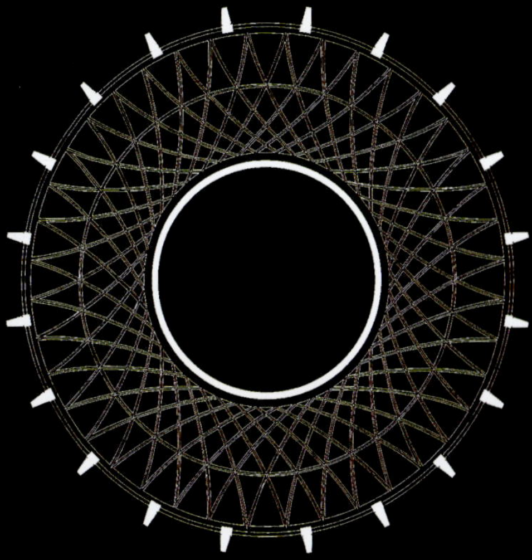

Harry Seidler & Associates

Alex Proimos

Sydney Tower 017 A

100 Market St

Donald Crone and Associates

1981

Reaching a total of 309 metres in height, Sydney Tower is the city's tallest tower soaring high from its Market Street location and can be seen from afar. Designed by Australian architect Donald Crone, it is rated to be one of the safest buildings in the world, capable of withstanding earthquakes and extreme wind conditions. Forty-six individual barrel units form the shaft of the tower, which supports the golden turret above. A gantry crane was used to hoist the barrel units on top of one another. The spire on top was erected after the tower structure was completed. *SZ*

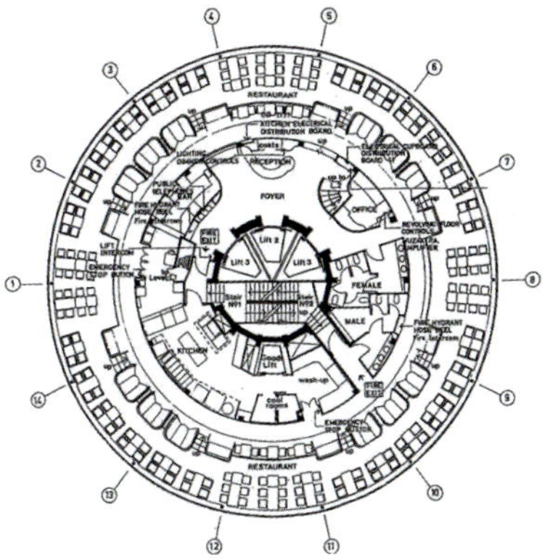

Level 03 Floor Plan

Sirius Building 018 A

48 Cumberland St, The Rocks

Theodorus (Tao) Gofers

1980

A rare example of the brutalist architectural style, the Sirius building is a social housing complex. It was designed by former Housing Commission architect Theodorus (Tao) Gofers who incorporated spaces for communal activities in his design to encourage interaction between residents. The success of the public housing development is built on the union of both private and public spaces throughout the site, in courtyard spaces, entrances, corridors, and the rooftop garden. The complex offers a total of 79 apartments, one to three storeys in height and with one to four bedrooms. Its grey concrete façade is made of repeated geometries that have been stacked on top of one another and modestly stagger and protrude. Although the building has been refused a heritage listing since its opening in 1980, it is indeed an unofficial landmark in The Rocks neighbourhood, a popular locality on the southern shore of Sydney Harbour. Its prime location, directly adjacent to Circular Quay, has fuelled the controversial dispute, ongoing since December 2015, regarding plans to demolish the brutalist-style public housing building and to redevelop the site with luxury apartment blocks. *SZ*

iStock (JohnCarnemolla)

Sydney Opera House

019 A

Bennelong Point
Jørn Utzon
1973

The Sydney Opera House is an admirable example of how a single building has the potential to transform an entire nation. Australia's symbolic architectural landmark, the Sydney Opera House is a world-class performing arts centre situated on the divine Darling harbour-side setting. This freestanding structure was built on a site which has been considered sacred to the local Gadigal people for thousands of years and is the most recognised twentieth century building in Australia to date. The architect, Denmark's Jørn Utzon, won the 1957 international competition to design a 'national opera house' for Sydney's Bennelong Point. Utzon's vision of a sculptural, curved building sitting on the harbour triumphed over more modernist rectangular and cubed forms. His design comprised a spherical solution inspired by the organic and natural form of shells. The result was an elegant structure designed with remarkable technical complexity, presenting a picturesque approach to the unique topography of the site. Its iconic form consists of a large, red, 'rock-like' granite platform. This platform anchors the sail-like roof, made from several pre-cast vaulted shells, which were glazed with ceramic white tiles and interconnected with one another. The engineering of this challenging roof resulted in a prolonged 16-year construction period beginning in 1959 and ending in 1973. Utzon was forced to resign as leading architect in 1966 after disputes on designs, schedules, and

iStock (Siwawut)

iStock (simonwoolley)

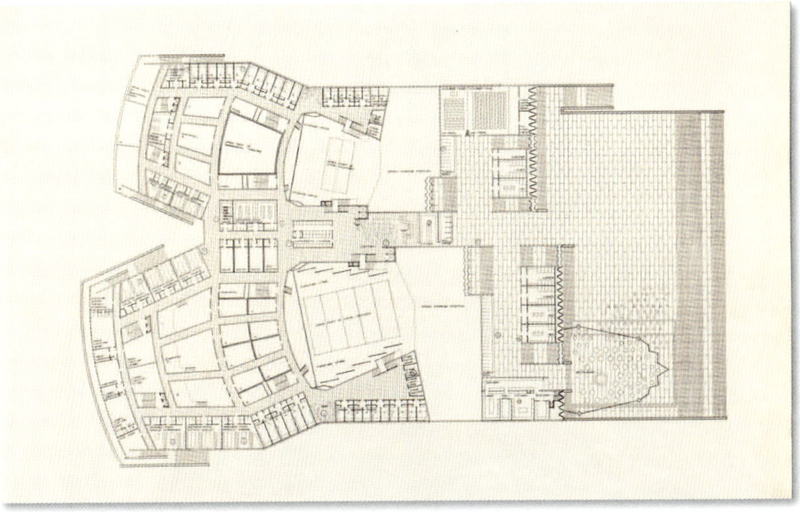

Level 01 Floor Plan

cost estimates with the Minister of Works, Davis Hughs. In spite of many protests by locals, Utzon was not reinstated. Architect Peter Hall was appointed in his place to design the interior of the Opera House. It wasn't until 1999 that Utzon was reengaged to develop a set of design principles intended as a permanent reference for all future changes to the building. Since its completion, glazed openings have been added along the western edge with wide colonnades to provide shading. The various terraces surrounding the building serve as platforms on which visitors can enjoy panoramic views of the harbour. Inside, the building comprises two main halls that sit beside one another and are accessed via an almost 100-metre-wide monumental staircase. The building contains a concert hall, opera and drama theatres, an auditorium, a playhouse, and a studio. The Sydney Opera House received international architecture's highest honour, the Pritzker Prize, in 2003 and was the youngest building ever to be included in the UNESCO World Heritage list in 2007. This list recognises the building as one of the most outstanding places on Earth amongst architectural greats such as the Taj Mahal, the Ancient Pyramids, and the Great Wall of China. The Sydney Opera House is not only a cultural icon, it is also a timeless precedent standing for ingenious design. *SZ*

flickr (Cyradis)

019 A

iStock (DuncanSharrocks)

John Gollings

Horizon Apartments (1998), Sydney.

Horizon Apartments

020 A

184 Forbes St
Harry Seidler & Associates
1998

The Horizon is a forty-three-storey apartment tower located in the residential area of Darlinghurst in East Sydney. A prominent landmark clearly visible from the city and the harbour, the building is shaped to maximise sweeping harbour views centred on the Sydney Opera House. Constructed over five levels of underground parking for 500 cars set apart from the tower, the complex comprises low-rise, split-level town houses along the perimeter, a small lawn, a 25-metre-long swimming pool, and a tennis court. In 1999, Seidler received his fourth Wilkinson Award from the Royal Australian Institute of Architects for the Horizon, which was to be the last major project award given to the architect.

When proposed, the building provoked controversy and protests by area residents fearful that it would be vastly out of scale with the surrounding low-rise houses. The project's site was exempted from strict neighbourhood height restrictions because it was owned by the federal government. Seidler calmed these fears by proving that the tall tower would be less of an obstruction to views than a building half its height and twice the footprint that would cast a much broader shadow.

Centrally located two-bedroom apartments on the middle floors and three-bedroom dwellings on the upper floors, as well as penthouses on the top two floors – all facing the harbour – are planned so that their living and bedroom spaces are equal in size. This allows the apartments to be interchangeable in plan, resulting in alternating even and odd floor balconies that not only contribute to a dynamic image for the tower but also create double-height spaces over the balconies of the units. All apartments are united by a continuous ribbon of tinted windows – floor to ceiling in the living rooms and partial in the kitchens and bedrooms. Glass parapets on the balconies are extended below as solid partial walls to strengthen their deep cantilevers and to act as sun shields for lower floors. The entrance hall of the Horizon is tiled in black marble and features a large, multicoloured, commissioned wall mural by Sol LeWitt centred on the entry. This is the only area of the building dominated by a splash of colour in an otherwise controlled palette of white and grey complemented by glass surfaces. Glazed, shared entrances for the complex's town houses are also used by their residents as small lobbies where personal artworks and other possessions can be displayed. *VB*

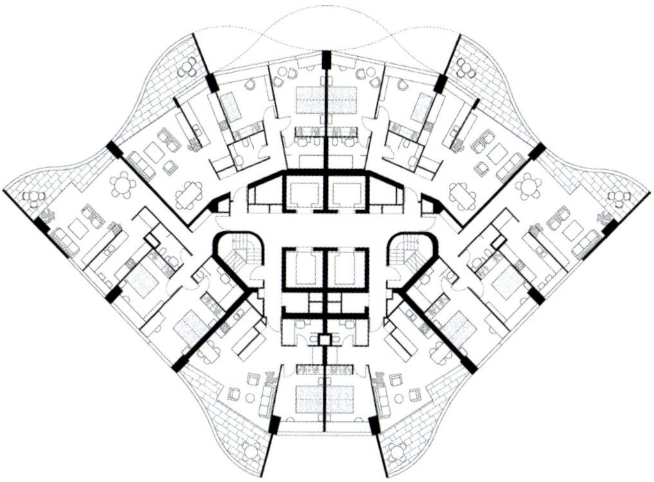

Harry Seidler & Associates

Typical Floor Plan, Horizon Apartments. The plan divides the floor space evenly between living and bedroom areas, making these interchangeable.

022 ANZ Stadium
Allianz

iStock (stellalevi)

David Clark

Kokkai Ng

« Sydney Hockey Centre 021 A

Shirley Strickland Avenue,
Sydney Olympic Park
Ancher Mortlock Wooley
1998

Sydney's premier hockey centre was completed in 1998 and lies within the large sports and entertainment complex Sydney Olympic Park. It is a multi-use sporting complex with a seating capacity of close to 4,000 visitors and an overall capacity of 8,000. Temporary grandstands were added for the 2000 Olympic Games and accommodated up to 15,000 spectators. The stadium itself has two fields, one for training and another for competitions. The firm Ancher Mortlock Wooley designed the main grandstands roof to be supported by a high mast, eliminating the need for columns and allowing for unimpeded views onto the pitch. *SZ*

≈ ANZ Stadium 022 A

Edwin Flack Avenue,
Sydney Olympic Park
Populous, Bligh Lobb Sports Architecture
1999

The multi-purpose ANZ Stadium was completed in 1999 in preparation for the 2000 Olympic Games. It is situated in Sydney Olympic Park alongside other sports buildings. It was designed in a joint venture collaboration between Populous and Bligh Lobb Sports Architecture to accommodate 118,000 viewers during the Olympics with the possibility of reducing the capacity to 85,000 viewers afterwards. As a result, the stadium has been ranked one of the most environmentally sustainable stadiums worldwide. Its circular floor plan and moveable seating tiers allow spectators to get closer to the action while providing maximum flexibility. *SZ*

Anthony Browell

Anthony Browell

Cook and Phillip Park Aquatic and Fitness Centre

023 A

4 College Street

BVN Architects

1999

The Cook and Phillip Park Aquatic and Fitness Centre is a major civic design project encompassing a sports and aquatic centre, a car park, a series of urban spaces between St Mary's Cathedral and the Australian Museum, and Sydney's first new park in over 100 years. The site, originally a park divided by two busy roads with a privately owned bowling club, became a unified 4.5-hectare public amenity. The park provides the city with a continuous stretch of accessible green spaces. The Aquatic and Fitness Centre includes three swimming pools, gyms, cafés, community facilities, and multi-use sports courts. A formal square water garden and terraced public spaces provide further urban amenity, with the civic square of the cathedral extended, without diminishing the importance of Hyde Park. The building layout responds to two main grids – the CBD grid running parallel to College Street and that of the former East Sydney grid, which is at a five-degree angle. Addressing the steep sloping site, a series of terraces that link the urban park and the building have been created. There are intentionally few buildings on each terrace, responding to a need for varied public spaces within the CBD. The space successfully serves many users, from school children and churchgoers to office workers. *PA*

John Gollings

St Patrick's Cathedral

024 A

1 Marist Place
MGT Architects, Romaldo Giurgola, Guida Moseley Brown Architects
2003

The site of St. Patrick's Cathedral has been integral to the history of the Catholic Church in Australia since the 1820s. The original cathedral was destroyed by fire in 1996, leaving only the masonry walls standing. MGT Architects, with Romaldo Giurgola, were commissioned in 1997 to undertake the restoration and design of a new cathedral complex on the original site. Giurgola focussed on the restoration of the original cathedral while designing functional and structural alterations of the now Blessed Sacrament Chapel. This redesign includes a new extension, accommodating 800 seats for those attending mass. Other additions include a new entry plaza, cloister garden, parish hall, and improved parking. *SZ*

John Gollings

Patrick Bingham Hall

Scots Church Redevelopment

025 A

44 Margaret St
Tonkin Zulaikha Greer Architects
2005

Won as the result of a limited design competition, this project explores the redevelopment of the disused heritage-listed Scots Church in Sydney's CBD. The project involves the conversion of the former church building and its airspace into residential units with some commercial uses at the lower levels. A stratum containing the original church auditorium of 2,500 seats has been retained by the church and restored (as a separate commission). The new development utilises the original support structure and references the neo-gothic massing of the original design, abandoned during the Great Depression. To achieve a maximum number of high-quality apartments, a system of two-level units was developed with corridors and lift access at every second floor. The whole building is within a 45° sloping height-limit plane, which preserves solar access to Wynyard Park south of the site. The elevation created by the sequence of double-storey apartment boxes continues the proportions of the perpendicular gothic façade below, emphasising its verticality and creating a dynamic silhouette. Evocative roof forms are developed as a series of sky follies leaning over each of the rectilinear 'towers', with the northernmost looking towards the harbour. The double-storey façade spaces enhance views to the sky and the city. Integrating natural ventilation, openable sliding doors, and shading elements, the attached winter gardens function as an acoustic buffer and a passive solar system to allow daylight to penetrate deep into the apartments. The new towers use sandstone colours to connect to the restored stone base, as well as expanses of seamed zinc and brilliant glazing. The interplay of solid and light, zinc and glazing combined with the irregular rhythm of coloured glazing panels, blinds, and shutters, creates an elevation that reflects the vitality of the urban setting. *PA*

Michael Nicholson

Dirk Meinecke

Ian Thorpe Aquatic Centre

026 A

456 Harris St
Harry Seidler & Associates
2007

The Ian Thorpe Aquatic Centre, named in recognition of the Olympic swimming champion, was built in Ultimo under the City of Sydney planning policy to provide community-based facilities in strategic municipal precincts. The result of a design competition held in 2001, construction began in 2005 and was completed in 2007. The building is crowned with a wave-shaped roof that rises from the Darling Harbour elevation towards the Harris Street ridge. The expressed steel roof structure recalls the character of Darling Harbour and resolves itself with a colonnade of shaped concrete piloti columns on Harris Street complementing other iconic buildings in this precinct such as the Powerhouse Museum. The built form addresses the hierarchy of Harris Street as the primary urban axis, the main 'boulevard' for Ultimo, and William Henry Street as a primary view corridor. This results in a non-symmetric, dynamic resolution to the principal corner of the site. Clear glass walls to the east and west façades also reinforce important visual links towards the city skyline, not only for swimmers inside the facility but also through the building from Harris Street. This transparency establishes a dialogue between the activities of the aquatic centre and Harris Street, and by extension, the community. The curved form of the roof is also recalled in the free-form shapes of the protruding amenity pods and the leisure pool in contrast to the otherwise controlled rectilinear form of the three-storey building. The high spatial volume was appropriately provided over the main pool with the lower space over the smaller pools. The entry was deliberately compressed to heighten the experience of the grand space to the pool concourse. The high end walls to the north and south were glazed with U-profile glass panels to economically resolve the large spans. This glass is frosted to provide a sense of enclosure, a steamy bathhouse feel, yet a hint of what lies beyond. After dark the building glows like a lantern. The glass walls to the pool concourse are flushed with tempered air from linear floor grilles to avoid condensation. The aquatic centre incorporates a pedestrian link, with lift service, through the northern edge of the site from Harris Street to the Pyrmont Street public domain through to Darling Harbour. The Heritage Pump Station is treated as a freestanding element within this domain, overlooked by the café and recreation terraces and fitness centre revealing the activity within. *PA*

Peter Bennetts

Anthony Browell

5–9 Roslyn Street

027 A

5–9 Roslyn St, Potts Point
Durbach Block Jaggers
2009

5–9 Roslyn Street, in the suburb of Potts Point, is a triangular site, less than 200 square metres in size. The rounded end looks directly onto a small public space. The shape of the site exaggerates perspective, the tiny footprint amplifies the perception of height. The firm Durbach Block Jaggers designed the building with a new take on thick masonry walls, small detailed windows, and overhanging cornices typical of the area. The cornice is exaggerated to overhang the street, to suggest a room. The fine steel-lined windows are slightly offset and casually misaligned. The awning splits to mark individual entry points on the street. From the street, it seems an ephemeral version of the neighbourhood buildings, the rhythm held by the openings as the wall recedes. Then, at the corner the building shifts to being strongly surfaced, curving in two directions, becoming a peninsular of moulded light. The surface of crackled tiles, a mixture of gloss and matt, white and biscuit, reflects and refracts the surroundings. An exotic rooftop garden of frangipani trees and seasonal plants is framed in the sky through buckled openings. The softly modulated interior of the restaurant accommodates the shifting geometry of the site, uses of the room, and its services. The palette of timber, off-white concrete, graded textiles, and delicate white furniture gives the room a calm and slight remove from the intensity of its urban setting. Solid masonry walls provide insulation from outside temperatures, while windows with recessed reveals provide natural light without excessive heat gain. High floor-to-ceiling heights admit plenty natural light in winter while excluding sun in summer and contribute to the volume and efficiency of natural ventilation. Opening sections in the windows reduce a deep street awning on the north side and shade the full-height glazing of the restaurant. A roof garden provides insulation and contributes to the greenery of Kings Cross. *PA*

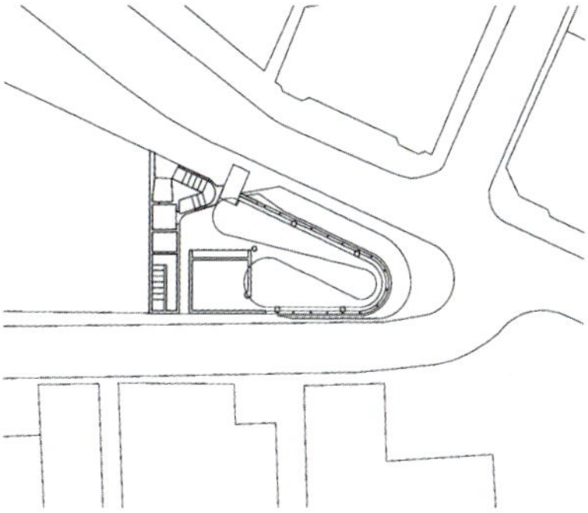
Site Plan

Julia Charles

Brett Boardman

Paddington Reservoir Gardens 028 A

251–255 Oxford St, Paddington
Tonkin Zulaikha Greer Architects, JMD Design
2009

When TZG and JMD were commissioned to convert the Paddington Reservoir into an urban park, the general expectation was that the site would be capped off and a brand-new arrangement built on top. However, the architects were captivated by the possibilities of revealing the 19th century structures as a ruin through which members of the public could wander, taking in the dramatic spaces and play of light across the remnants of historic walls and vaults. Listed as a site of state heritage significance,

Brett Boardman

the Paddington Reservoir was originally constructed in two stages, completed in 1866 and 1878. The water chambers were built below street level with a grassed park above, opened to the public in the 1930s. The operational life of the reservoir ceased in 1899 and the site was used as a workshop and garage until 1990, when roof collapses forced its closure. An accessible sunken garden and pond, surrounded by a raised precast concrete boardwalk, has been inserted within the conserved ruin of the western chamber of the former reservoir. The edges of the ruin are contained by concrete up-stands in such a way as to amplify the distinctive curved characteristics of the original brick vaults. The eastern chamber has been conserved, stabilising the brickwork and forming the base for the new landscaped park above. Two lightweight roofs float above the reservoir, signalling the main entry points to the park. The lightness of the roofs acts as a counterpoint to the solid earthiness of the masonry vaults, while there is a whimsical reference to the older masonry mortar joints in the staggered pattern of the metal grid. A restricted pallet of three materials was utilised; steel, aluminium, and concrete were chosen as contemporary partners for the historic brick, cast iron, and timber. This quality, crucial to sustaining the memory of the original purpose of the structure, is softened by the status given to the planting and also by the overt invitation, implicit in the walkways, to explore the whole park. *PA*

Australian architects are in tune with their projects' environments

The firm Tonkin Zulaikha Greer Architects has a special interest in public spaces, public buildings, and 'edge' architecture, often providing buildings with roles and uses outside their traditional functions. The practice takes the intersection of cultural values and architecture as a springing point for their design philosophy. The firm's architectural works bring surprising diversity to the completed projects, with an on-going sense of exploration and discovery. They are constantly and thoughtfully grounded in appropriateness and sustainability.

What differentiates architecture in Australia from international architecture?
We have a short immigrant history and a long and ancient indigenous history, often in conflict, hopefully coming into an alignment to inspire place and climate-specific design. Contrary to popular belief, architecture in Australia is highly urbanised and not rural. The warm climate invites Australians to the periphery of their buildings where they spend time in the 'third room' – that ambiguous indoor/outdoor space. And despite a long-standing 'cargo cult' of imported architecture, regionally relevant and identifiable approaches to our design have evolved.

What role do current architectural trends play in your design approach?
We're enthusiastic about the new authenticity, the 'realness' of architectural materials: 'what you see is what you get.' Our modernist beliefs have always been manifested in authentic and enduring materials and a respect for function and structure in all our work, and unite with a more historically inspired respect for context and continuity.

Where do you find your inspiration?
We are motivated by the evolution of the city. Our architecture is rooted in the past and its programmes project into the future. As our buildings are seated in their

Peter Tonkin, Brian Zulaikha, and Tim Greer

urban context, they immediately take part in an architectural 'continuum' – that ever-changing story of how citizens explore and inhabit their city. Meanwhile, in our projects in more open landscapes, we are concerned largely with the sustainability of organic systems, and with understanding these before designing the architectural interventions.

Which Australian buildings do you most admire and why?

Tim Greer: The Sydney Opera House (Jørn Utzon) and Melbourne's Eureka Tower (Fender Katsalidis Architects), for their original and perfectly appropriate architectural gestures to completely different contexts.

Peter Tonkin: We are currently conserving Ken Woolley's 1960 Mosman House – a pioneering investigation of open-plan living, expressed through rugged, unfinished materials and shifted modules, and eloquent of its respect for the Sydney bush. Francis Greenway's 1819 Hyde Park Barracks defined a city scale for the colony, with a sophisticated materiality and proportion, economically and elegantly fulfilling its public role.

Brian Zulaikha: I love the Sydney Harbour Bridge, designed by consultant structural engineer Ralph Freeman for the bridge builder Dorman Long with architect Thomas Tait of JJ Burnet and Partners, and the Sydney GPO designed by colonial architect James Barnet. Both structures enhance and contextualise their locations.

What could the rest of the world learn from Australian architecture?

In general, Australian architects are in tune with the environments of their projects, urban or rural. Historic buildings are treasured and integrated into renewal projects, leading to richer surroundings. In spite of the growing amount and complexity of the planning and building regulation in Australia, there are still opportunities for the architect to express originality and freshness, even personality.

Michael Nicholson

Portico Scots Church, Sydney

Brett Boardman

Garden House 029 A
6 Cowper Wharf Rd,
Woolloomooloo
Durbach Block Jaggers
2011

Level 01 Floor Plan

Julia Charles

On a wider than normal site, Garden House was built in an almost Tuscan part of Sydney. Established gardens surround gracious houses with a generous veranda, traditional roof lines, and materials. The house is sited to hug the sloping rear boundary, orienting to the northern sun and a new garden with established trees. The firm Durbach Block Jaggers designed the house with a simple L-shaped plan that both contains and extends into the stepping garden. An internal garden court is hidden in the depth of the plan, bridging between the floors and inverting the line of inside and outside. Governed by a height covenant, the roof parapet line is fixed and straight. The first floor houses the private spaces of the house, with a slightly compressed floor-to-ceiling height. These private spaces have precise and figured openings in the continuous brick façade. The mass of the first floor rests on the lightest of support systems, improbably hovering over the ground level. The underside of this looping façade tilts and lifts, admitting light and views to the ground-floor public rooms through clerestory glazing. The brick façade is given a fabric-like quality through its pattern, texture, and treatment. The edges of shadows are slightly corrugated by the pattern while strong sunlight flickers cinematically on the surface through the day. The woven brick surface contrasts with the glazed set render of the ground floor. *PA*

Julia Charles

1 Bligh Street

030 A

1 Bligh Street
Architectus, Ingenhoven Architects
2011

Hans Georg Esch

Architectus and Ingenhoven Architects have created a highly sustainable office tower on a site bound by Bligh, Bent, and O'Connell Streets. The design was developed with four critical considerations: view, public space, work environment, and green building. Located at the centre of the 'valley' created by the Macquarie Street ridge and the tall buildings, the site is highly visible in its context when viewed from the harbour. These most prominent of views are a key asset on which the form of the building has drawn. Views along Bligh and O'Connell Streets to the city and a view over Bent Street to the harbour have also been a direct influence on the position and orientation of the elliptical form. This is combined with the main entrance location to provide a strong address for the building. By shifting the axis of the building's form to align with the grid to the north, views toward the bridge and the harbour

are opened and the square of Farrer Place is more clearly defined. The ground plane is given over to public use and the slope of the site is celebrated with a sweeping curve around the O'Connell Street corner. Broad curving steps rise to the winter-garden level and provide a place to sit. The work environment is designed around the principles of flexibility, efficiency, communication, transparency, and a high level of indoor environment quality. A naturally ventilated glass atrium running the full height of the building enhances connectivity and access to natural light and features break-out spaces with access to fresh air. The entire lobby is naturally ventilated with in-slab heating and relief-air cooling to temper conditions during the very cold and warm days. The building's six-star Green Star rating score is the highest awarded in NSW and includes the maximum allowable five points for innovation in categories such as environmental design initiative and exceeding Green Star benchmarks. Key sustainability innovations include the double-skin façade, naturally ventilated atrium, 40 per cent recycled concrete, 90 per cent steel with 50 per cent recycled content, FSC certified timber, recycled timber, solar cooling, trigeneration, black water treatment, rainwater harvesting, and sewer mining. *PA*

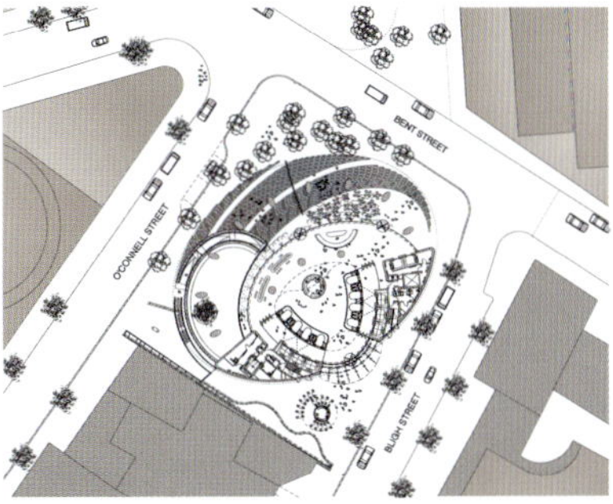

Site Plan

J.P.Morgan
STREET

Westfield Sydney

031 A

Pitt St & Market St
John Wardle Architects, Westfield Design & Construction
2012

This commercial development comprises three major parts. The reconfiguration of three separate and outdated retail buildings into an integrated six-level retail centre anchors the overall project. The retail plan and internal design of this podium is by Westfield, and the external façade has been designed by JWA. The refurbishment of an existing commercial building and the addition of a new thirty-storey office tower complete the project; both are designed by JWA. To bring together these disparate elements and to form a coherent whole required a suite of ideas convincingly stitched together. Individual high-profile retail tenants make separate architectural statements at the lower levels of the podium. Around them, there is white glass along with green zinc panels displaying a vertical, leaf-like pattern. Punctuating this pattern and identifying key entry points are sculptural black zinc and concrete cowls with picture windows framed within. A glass canopy, with an expressive tensile-rod support system, appears to be stitched to the main façade and separates the changeable tenanted space below from the more stable architectural elements above. The existing commercial office building has extremely large floorplates with limited floor-to-floor heights. The design carves four new atrium spaces into the floors to improve natural light and ventilation. The external envelope is subtly realigned and replaced with a vertically expressed glass curtain wall of two colours that connect to form an interlocking pattern that can be read at an urban scale. The existing Centrepoint tower and its strong circular geometry and cable structure is a dominant element both at street level and within the context of the skyline. The existing Skygarden commercial tower to the north, with its rectangular floorplate, is a considerable vertical face and edge condition. The new floorplate profile for 85 Castlereagh Street is an elliptical shape designed to maintain important vistas to the Centrepoint tower from the north-west and the Pitt Street mall. When compared to a conventional rectangular floorplate, the ellipse allows improved view lines around it from various vantage points whilst being a complementary form for the radial Centrepoint tower structure. The tower's shape is formed by the extruded ellipse sliced clearly at its top to sit within Sydney's sun access plane, and at its base where an oblique cut opens up toward the shuttle lifts from the commercial entry lobby below. The effect at the base is to create a dynamic curving edge to the curtain wall, not dissimilar to the circular rim of a spinning coin caught mid rotation. The inclined elliptical roof plane is incised with a series of troughs, required for servicing and cleaning, which form a strong graphic addition to the Sydney skyline. *PA*

Trevor Mein

John Gollings

Kinghorn Cancer Centre

032 A

370 Victoria St, Darlinghurst
BVN Architects
2012

The Kinghorn Cancer Centre brings together the Garvan Institute of Research and St Vincent's Hospital facilities into one cohesive and interactive environment. The brief was to create a nurturing non-hospital setting that facilitates collaborative research between scientists, clinicians, and patients to deliver personalised medicine and to advance research through rapid translation to the clinic. Filled with natural light, timber finishes, and landscaping, the building is organised into functional zones, with the sequence of spaces moving from service core to laboratory, to write-up space, to meeting rooms, to the public atrium where all activity is visible to anyone entering the building. The design of the atrium encourages the trans-disciplinary exchange of culture and information. Externally, each of the façades discreetly addresses the different functional and cityscape requirements of the building. In a first for Australia, the Kinghorn Cancer Centre research laboratories use natural ventilation and mixed mode servicing to avoid the need to separate the spaces into compartments, further encouraging collaboration. *PA*

John Gollings

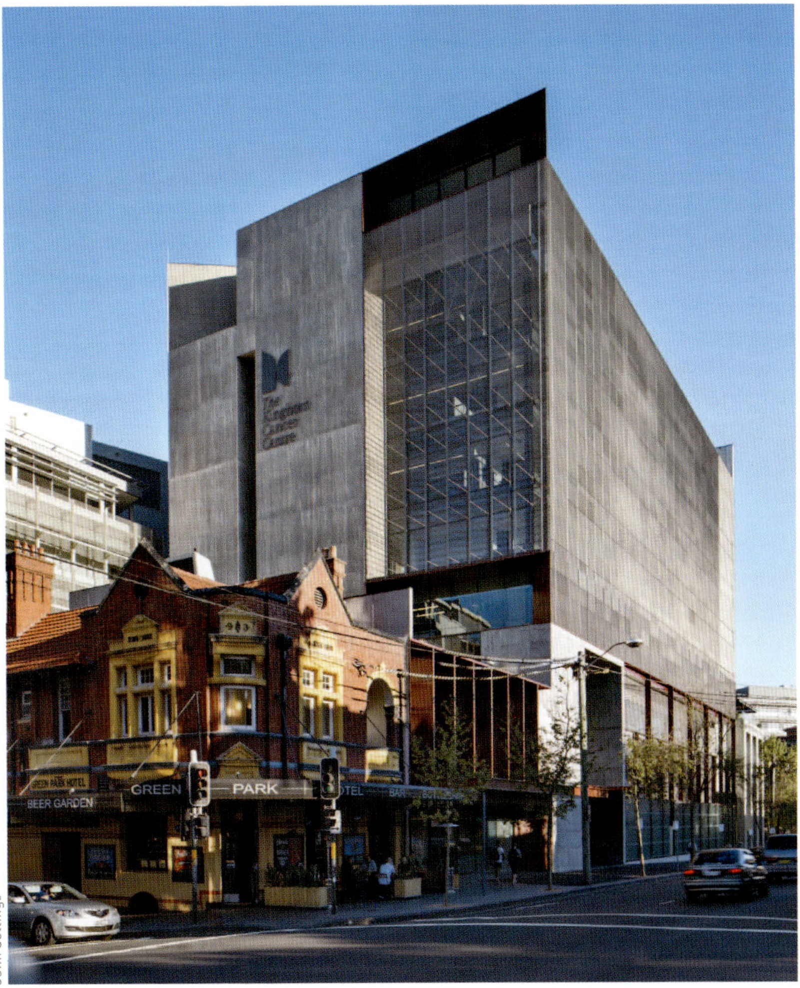

John Gollings

Richard Glover

Faculty of Engineering and Information Technology

033 A

University of Technology
Denton Corker Marshall
2014

The new Faculty of Engineering and Information Technology engages with its urban context and conveys the University of Technology's position at the intersection of creativity and technology. On a prominent urban site, the building creates a gateway to the university's revitalised city campus and the southern end of Sydney's CBD. Fourteen levels, plus four below ground, accommodate state-of-the-art lecture rooms, academic offices, seminar rooms, teaching and research laboratories, a student union, food and recreation areas, along with bicycle and car parking. The building is expressed as a singular sculptural object, setting it apart from the more traditional architectural expression of its neighbours and from proposed towers at the Fraser Broadway Development opposite the site. Four tilted and skewed plates envelope the building's volume. The plates are made of aluminium sheets perforated in a pattern derived from the binary code for 'University of Technology Sydney Faculty of Engineering and Information Technology'. 'Gills' creased into the surface of each plate punctuate the façade, visually reinforcing the sense of plate as skin and symbolically allowing the building to breathe. The faculty's collaborative learning culture materialises in the ultra-thin crevasse-like atrium which links all teaching, learning, and social spaces. It's a dynamic space occupied by open stairs, random bridge links, and lounges for informal encounters, with circulation along its edges. The raw aesthetic achieved internally with materials such as off-form concrete and Corten steel engenders a warehouse quality, aligning the faculty with environments favoured by the creative industries. Offering naturally lit access through the building at ground level, the crevasse directly links the university to the local neighbourhood. The interior architecture has an innovative pedagogical approach and a technology-rich environment at its core, which aims to support student needs and future industry trends. The latest in cutting-edge technology includes robotics, computer- and human-centred design labs, and a 3D data visualisation facility, the Data Arena – the most advanced research facility of its type in Australia. An extensive range of environmentally sustainable design initiatives makes a substantial contribution to achieving best-practice standards in the faculty accommodation. *PA*

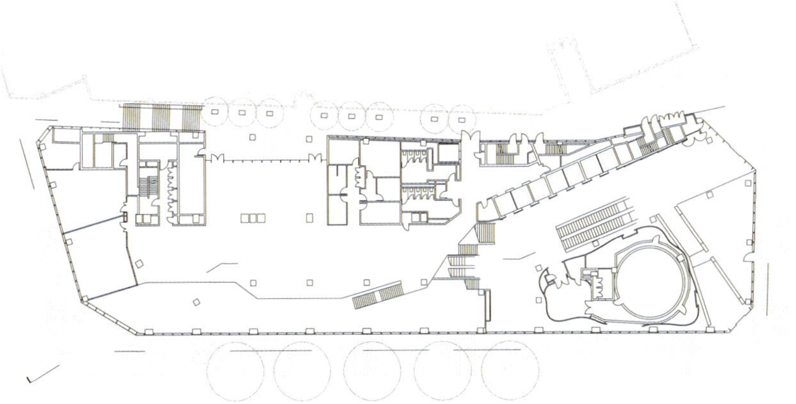

Level 01 Floor Plan

Richard Glover

Michael Nicholson

Dr Chau Chak Wing Building

034 A

University of Technology
Frank Gehry, DJRD
2014

As the first Australian building designed by Frank Gehry, the Dr Chau Chak Wing Building is a flagship project of the University of Technology Sydney's (UTS) $1.3 billion City Campus Master Plan. The building, located at UTS's City campus in the inner-city suburb of Ultimo, Sydney, provides learning, research, and office space for up to 1,600 students and staff in the UTS Business School. It also features extensive public spaces, including two cafés, across its 11 occupied floors. Gehry Partners, with DJRD as executive architects, designed the building from the 'inside out' in order to create internal spaces that inspire real and relevant research and learning outcomes. The unique exterior of the building combined with its thoughtful interior are a manifestation of the creative thinking that underpins the teaching and research undertaken by the Business School and, more broadly, the university. Adopting the metaphor of a treehouse, the design allows students and staff to undertake quiet, focused work in offices and other rooms in the building's 'branches' and then meet in formal and informal social spaces in the 'trunk', including student lounges, cafés, and general teaching spaces along with more specialised learning areas such as the oval classrooms, collaborative theatre, and auditorium. Occupying the building's atrium void are the two oval collaborative classrooms which have been designed in the fashion of a bird's nest with a series of large laminated timber beams providing a character-defining sculptural form within the building's foyer. Supplementing the building's vast number of formal and informal learning spaces is the circulatory nature of the building which makes prominent use of stairways to move people through it. The most striking of these is the polished stainless steel staircase, which lends a sculptural focal point to the main lobby and reflects the movement of both people and ideas. *PA*

Michael Nicholson

Waterfront Pavillion

035 A

2 Murray St, Sydney
FJMT
2015

Anchored to the South Wharf of Sydney's Darling Harbour, the Australian National Maritime Museum's Waterfront Pavilion was built to mark the centenary of the First World War and commemorate 100 years of service by the Royal Australian Navy. The purpose of this museum pavilion building is to serve as a transitional space for visitors from the waterfront dock onto the two naval vessels HMAS Vampire and HMAS Onslow. The pavilion was built on a narrow, existing wharf structure and to a tight budget. The central design question was: what should be the character of such a 'building' over the water of Darling Harbour, sitting tightly between two of the most significant Australian naval vessels? The design seeks to bring the narratives of war to life and to enliven the visitor's relationship with the vessels, waterfront, and broader museum precinct. The articulated façade of the pavilion complements the scale, form, and colour of the vessels as well as the broader marine environment. The Waterfront Pavilion offers a dynamic, immersive experience and is an elegant, integrated addition to the Harbour precinct. The suspended tube 'hovering' over the wharf creates space at the wharf level in which visitors can move around and experience the edge, where the vessels meet the water. The tube appears to 'float' in the air between the vessels floating in the water. This tube was then formally shaped and profiled in relation to the natural movement of visitors from the dockside up into the building, through the portals and gangways onto the vessels. The pavilion is further shaped by the primary forms of the adjacent vessels themselves, the conning tower of the submarine, and the bridge of the destroyer, creating central formal distortions. These distortions are then transformed into large glazed portals that frame lateral views onto the vessels. The interior of the pavilion is evocative of the interior of the naval vessels or of an industrial shed: hardy, rough, and adaptable, with sheet vinyl floors, insulated aluminium walls, and industrial suspended fans. A lack of preciousness invites later adaptation and evolution for future curators and visitors. *PA*

Brett Boardman

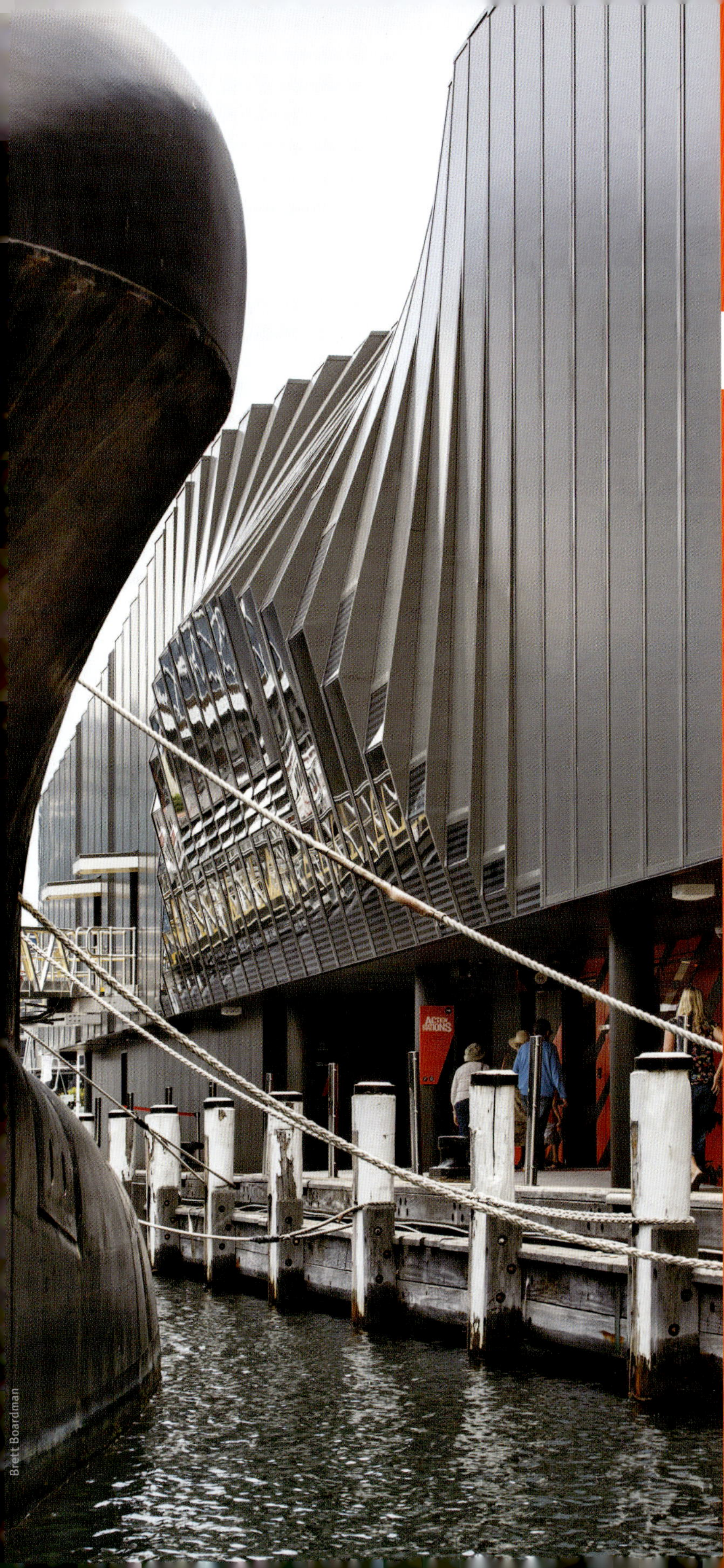

Brett Boardman

Canberra

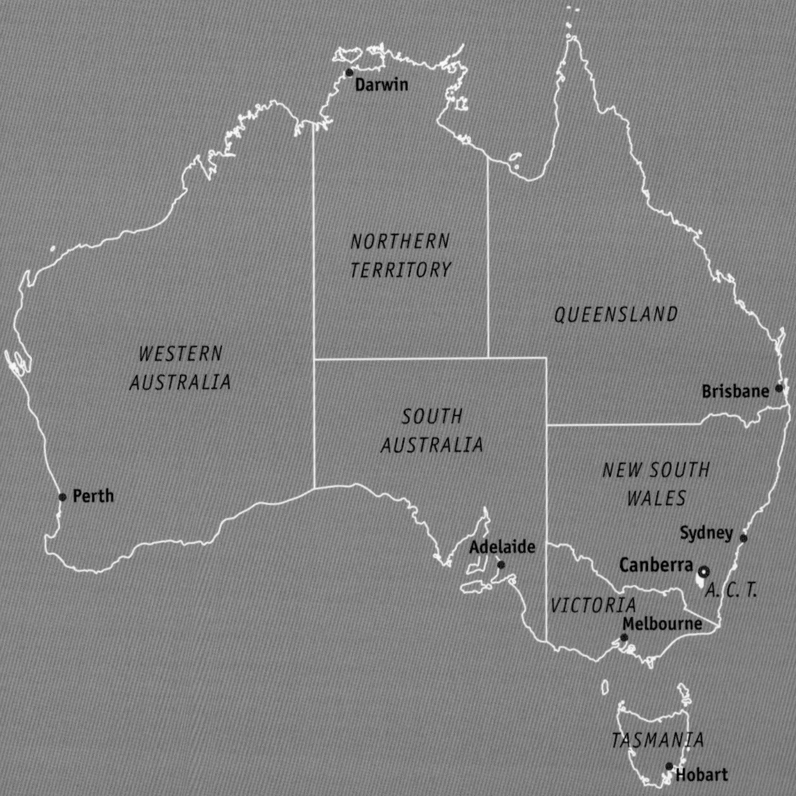
Darwin
NORTHERN TERRITORY
QUEENSLAND
WESTERN AUSTRALIA
Brisbane
SOUTH AUSTRALIA
NEW SOUTH WALES
Perth
Sydney
Adelaide
Canberra
A. C. T.
VICTORIA
Melbourne
TASMANIA
Hobart

B
Canberra
048
045
055
056
057
041
042
059
044
040
060
053
051
038
050
037
047
054

043
046
036
039
058
nearmap

Canberra

Canberra, Australia's capital city, is the country's seat of government and political hub. After much debate on whether the capital of Australia should be Sydney or Melbourne, a compromise decision was reached to establish the Australian Capital Territory, measuring 372 square kilometres and occupying the state of New South Wales. After the location for this new capital had been selected, an international design competition was held in 1911 to design a new city masterplan. American architects Walter Burley Griffin and his wife Marion Mahony Griffin were the winners with their 'City Beautiful' and 'Garden City' design principles inspired by the natural landscape of the site. The sophisticated and systematically arranged design for the city of Canberra was implemented in 1912. The heart of this plan is the Parliamentary Triangle, a government precinct focused around a central triangle derived from the axial arrangement of a hexagonal web of roads which interlink with one another. This precinct incorporates government buildings on terraces, the peak of which is the Parliament House

Aerial view over the city's iconic Parliamentry Triangle and Lake Burley Griffin from Black Mountain lookout

iStock (zetter)

which overlooks the artificial Lake Burley Griffin. Named after Walter Burley Griffin himself, this lake is the centrepiece of the city's masterplan, which stretches from east to west and divides the city in two. A fusion of civic and residential buildings encompass this lake, including national monuments and educational institutions amongst government buildings. The National Library of Australia, the National Gallery of Australia, the National Museum of Australia, the National Carilion, and the High Court of Australia can all be found along this lake-side setting. Many mid-century residential houses designed by renowned Australian architects such as Harry Seidler, Robin Boyd, and Roy Grounds reveal themselves amid suburban neighbourhoods. With over eighty embassies and high commissions located in this city, the suburb of Yarralumla makes for a scenic drive past traditional and modern architecture from many countries. Summits such as Black Mountain and Mount Ainslie are also noteworthy locations for architectural appreciation contributing impeccable views over the city. *SZ*

Nation Archives of Australia

The Lodge, private residence of the Prime Minister of Australia, Adelaide Avenue, Deakin, under construction, late 1920s

Kingston Powerhouse

036 B

11 Wentworth Ave, Kingston
John Smith Murdoch
1915

The Kingston Powerhouse is listed on the country's heritage register as Canberra's first permanent public building to have been constructed. At the time of its completion in 1915, it was considered to be the most modern powerhouse in Australia. Since then, it has frequently been closed and reopened. It sits in the Kingston suburb with solid walls of concrete and a terracotta-tiled gabled roof. The industrial building was designed by architect John Smith Murdoch with strong neo-classical influences. It plays with three volumes of different heights: a three-storey Boiler Bay, a two-storey Engine Bay, and a single-storey Economiser Annexe. *SZ*

« The Lodge

037 B

5 Adelaide Ave, Deakin
Oakley & Parkes
1927

The Lodge has served as the permanent private residence of the prime minister of Australia since its completion in 1927. Oakley & Parkes Architects designed this respected residence with great attention to symmetry and Georgian detailing, overall in the inter-war Georgian Revival style. This historically significant building is two storeys in height with a rendered-brick exterior and a slated, hipped roof. Porches are perched at the corners of the façade and surrounded by wrought-iron balusters. Inside, American Colonial characteristics are evident in the stained plywood detailing and the grand staircase at the entrance hall. *SZ*

iStock (Daniel)

Old Parliament House 038 B

18 King George Terrace, Parkes

John Smith Murdoch

1927

The prominent Old Parliament House sits at the base of Canberra's Parliamentary Triangle and was designed by Walter Burley Griffin, the same architect who designed the city. The old federal building opened in 1927 after four years of construction. It was operational until 1988 after which parliament was relocated to the New Parliament House on the top of Capital Hill. Nowadays the heritage-listed building houses the Museum of Australian Democracy and also hosts temporary exhibitions, lectures, and concerts. John Smith Murdoch, at the time the chief architect of the Commonwealth of Australia, designed the landmark government building with functional planning and material simplicity. Its powerful double-height white façade comprises a terraced roof structure and is cladded in brick interrupted by arched bronze windows. The interior contains two generous courtyard spaces and the historically significant Kings Hall, the House of Representatives chamber, the Senate chamber, a library, and a dining room with joinery all made from Australian timber. *SZ*

Joy VanBuhler

Jason Tong

Sherman S. L. Yip

Sarah Zahradnik

Australian War Memorial

039 B

Treloar Cres, Campbell
John Crust & Emil Sodersten
1941

A nationally recognised paradigm of civic architecture, the Australian War Memorial sits dignified at the end of Anzac Parade with its inter-war Art Deco style design in honour of those who served in the First World War. An international design competition was held for the memorial in 1926, and two designs were short-listed – those by John Crust and Emil Sodersten. The two architects amalgamated their designs into one, incorporating Crust's cloisters and Sodersten's grand Byzantine dome structure. The Great Depression played a large role in drawing out the construction period to twelve years, from 1929 to 1941. The sandstone-cladded masonry building contains the Commemorative Courtyard, the domed Hall of Memory, the Tomb of the Unknown Australian Soldier, and the Pool of Reflection. The Commemorative Courtyard is an open, linear space with set-back loggias along the two longitudinal sides. The loggias frame the Pool of Reflection and the Roll of Honour, allowing visitors to view the list of names of Australians who died during the war. The alignment of the courtyard with the monumental Anzac Parade is intended to establish a cognitive link between the two spaces. Beneath the centrally placed dome of the Hall of Memory sits the Tomb of the Unknown Australian Soldier, a space for silent contemplation. The hall's superb Art Deco interior features stained-glass windows and a mosaic cupola. The Anzac Hall is an exhibition pavilion designed by the respected architecture firm Denton Corker Marshall. It was completed in 2004 and has further enhanced the presence of the memorial. SZ

Oscar Gruno

Simon Hukin

National Film and Sound Archive (NFSA) 040 B

McCoy Circuit, Acton
William Hayward Morris, Robert Casboulte
1930

The National Film and Sound Archive (NFSA) is Australia's major 'living' archive which is responsible for the development, preservation, maintenance, promotion, and housing of the national collection of audiovisual materials. Planning of the NFSA building originally began in 1925 by architects of the Commonwealth Department of Works and Railways. Walter Hayward Morris, one of the Federal Capital Commission's architects, eventually took over the process and the building was completed in 1930. The building was initially occupied by the Institute of Anatomy until the Australian Government announced that the building was to become the NFSA's national headquarters and the archive was formally opened in 1984. A grand example of both late 20th century Stripped Classicism and 1920s Art Deco, the building has gained a reputation for being the most beautiful Art Deco building in Canberra and the site was listed on the Commonwealth Heritage register in 2004. True to its style, it features a horizontal skyline, large columns, and a central main entrance between the vertical bays of its symmetrical façade. Inside, its U-shaped floor plan is complemented by detailed decorative geometric and angular elements, representative of Art Deco design. Although most of the building's original fabric and architectural detailing remain intact, the building's formerly more conservative garden is no longer in sight. Moreover, the building was extended in 1999 when the NFSA began to grow and expansion was necessary. A large annex was added in 1999 to house specialist audio and technical laboratories as well as administrative offices. *SZ*

« ANU School of Music 041 B

William Herbert Place
Daryl Jackson, Evan Walker
1970

ANU's formally bold heritage-listed School of Music building displays cubist influences and was designed by architects Daryl Jackson and Evan Walker. The building's six levels are made up of predominantly white off-form concrete walls, framing and floors with minimal glazing, and a metal deck roof. Public and administrative areas have been placed in acoustically sensitive performing and teaching areas on the lower levels in order to serve as a barrier against noise. Inside lies Llewellyn Hall, a 1,400-seat concert hall that hosts events for the entire city. *SZ*

⌄ ANU School of Art 042 B

2 Childers St
Cuthbert Whitley, E.H. Henderson (1939), Daryl Jackson, Evan Walker (1981)
1939, 1981

Sitting within the Australian National University (ANU) campus, what is today the Canberra School of Art was originally designed as a high school in the early twentieth century. A centrally placed clock tower breaks the long symmetry of the façade, inspired by both inter-war Art Deco and inter-war Stripped Classicism. Architects Daryl Jackson and Evan Walker redeveloped the axial building in 1981 with extensions to the southern wing. Additional spaces were added along the axis with fully glazed walls that open onto the courtyard spaces. *SZ*

Sarah Zahradnik

Sarah Zahradnik

» National Gallery of Australia 043 B

Parkes Pl E, Parkes
Edwards Madigan Torzillo and Partners
1982

The striking National Gallery of Australia was opened in 1982 after fourteen years of construction. Its lake-side location sits at the base of the Parliamentry Triangle across the High Court of Australia. In 1968 a design competition was held and the architectural firm Edwards Madigan Torzillo and Partners was announced as the winner. Senior architect Colin Madigan was the lead designer of this dynamic, sculptural building, which integrates the environment and meets functional requirements. The gallery has a floor area of 20,573 square metres, of which 7,000 square metres are reserved exclusively for use as exhibition space. Its geometric form is mainly made of reinforced concrete with a bush-hammered finish. *SZ*

» Shine Dome (Australian Academy of Science) 044 B

15 Gordon St, Acton
Roy Grounds of Grounds, Romberg & Boyd
1959

A notable example of structuralist architecture, the Shine Dome was Canberra's first-ever building to be added to the National Heritage List for its architectural significance. A limited design competition was held, which was won by renowned Australian architect Roy Grounds. Completed in 1959, it is one of his most iconic buildings and was admired for its futuristic arcaded dome shape, structural complexity, and innovative use of reinforced concrete and copper cladding. The concrete dome, 47 metres in diameter and 75 millimetres in thickness, was the largest to have been built in Australia. The circular floor plan was inspired by the surrounding site conditions and this shape is repeated throughout the design.

A circular moat surrounds the building while also serving as a ring beam. The circular voids at the base of the building create light pockets which allow natural light to enter the internal space. The interiors consist of earthy tones: brown brick and vertical timber-batten walls, terrazzo and carpet floors, and custom furniture made of Australian timbers and designed by furniture designer Fred Ward. *SZ*

Sarah Zahradnik

Ryszard Stelmachowicz

iStock (Phillip Minnis)

» Telstra Tower

045 B

100 Black Mountain Dr, Acton
Department of Housing and Construction
1980

Located in the Black Mountain Nature Reserve, the Telstra telecommunications tower, formerly Telecom tower, is locally referred to as the Black Mountain Tower and stretches high over its mountain summit. The Department of Housing and Construction was in control of the design for the 195-metre-high concrete structure, completed in 1980. Canberra's television and broadcasting services are transmitted via the tower's telecommunications facilities. It also provides visitors with a souvenir shop, café, an indoor observation deck, and outdoor lookout platforms which offer spectacular panoramic views over the city and surrounding landscape. *SZ*

Sarah Zahradnik

«» The National Carillon

046 B

Aspen Island, Kings Park
Cameron, Chisholm & Nicol
1970

A national monument, the National Carillon is a musical instrument housed within a bell tower that stands isolated in Aspen Island off of Lake Burley Griffin. A gift from the British government, it is an architectural landmark which commemorates the 50th anniversary of Canberra as Australia's national capital. The 50-metre-high tower was designed by the architecture firm Cameron, Chisholm and Nicol and contains a total of 55 bronze bells whose musical chiming can be heard all the way from Canberra's Parliamentary Triangle and suburbs. *SZ*

Sarah Zahradnik

» Callam Offices

047 B

13 Easty St, Phillip
John Andrews
1981

Construction of the Calum Offices, designed in the late-twentieth-century structuralist style, was completed in 1981. The Australian architect behind this remarkable structure is the internationally admired John Andrews. Andrews designed the perimeter of the large-scale office building to be entirely supported by suspension cables which extend diagonally from above the roof in a triangular form. The innovative interior of the office complex demonstrates a modern architectural theme with its planned distribution of modular office pods. *SZ*

Flickr (martin)

flickr (Nicholas Cull)

flickr (Alex Proimos)

« GIO Stadium

048 B

Battye St, Bruce
Philip Cox & Partners
1977

The GIO Stadium, originally referred to as Bruce Stadium, sits beside the Australian Institute of Sport Arena in Bruce. It is a modern state-of-the-art sport arena and is primarily used for soccer and rugby events. It was designed as the National Athletics facility in the early 1970s for the Pacific Conference Games by the architects Philip Cox and Partners. Cox and Partners have continued to be involved in the renovations and redevelopment of the facility since its 1977 completion. It originally had a seating capacity of 8,000 spectators. In 1985, it was expanded from the then 16,000 seating capacity to 25,000, making it Canberra's largest sports building. *SZ*

^ High Court of Australia

049 B

Parkes Pl, Parkes
Edwards Madigan Torzillo & Briggs
1980

The High Court of Australia is a perfect example of late-modern brutalist architecture at its finest. With its bold geometric spaces, concrete mass structure, and internal layout it is both asymmetrical and functional. A national design competition was held in 1972 and architectural firm Edwards Madigan Torzillo and Briggs took home the gold. Since its 1980 completion this monumental building has continued to receive awards such as the 2007 RAIA National 25 Year Award for Enduring Architecture, awarded by the Australian Institute of Architects. It has also been listed on the National Heritage Register and the World Register of Significant 20th Century Architecture. *SZ*

Aerial view over Capital Hill with the spectacular New Parliament House

050 B

John Gollings

PhillipMinnis

istock (Colin and Linda McKie)

New Parliament House

050 B

Parliament Dr
Mitchell Giurgola and Thorp, Guida Moseley Brown Architects
1988

An icon of Canberra, the magnificent New Parliament House building has been home of the Australian Parliament and seat of government since its completion in 1988. An international design competition was held to design the government building which Mitchell/Giurgola & Thorp Architects (MGT) won. The core group of architects at MGT who worked together on the winning design has evolved into Guida Moseley Brown Architects. The design for the Federal Parliament building provides 300,000 square metres of space to accommodate offices as well as parliamentary and ceremonial functions. It is situated on a 32-hectare site at the midpoint of the Parliamentary Triangle, Capital Hill. The complex brief required the design of a building capable of accommodating the functions of Australia's democratic government system and of standing as a visual symbol of that democracy. The result is a space that also encourages public access and involvement while responding to climatic conditions and the surrounding landscape. The building's curved walls push out, reinstating the radial avenues of Walter Burley Griffin's 1912 masterplan as the primary axes of the city. Integrated into this design is the focal point of the façade, a large flag mast which rises from the centre of the structure and land axis. A large mosaic designed by Aboriginal artist, Michael Nelson Jagamara, is embedded into the forecourt. Its design reflects Australia's ancient beginnings. A great veranda greets visitors at the main entrance with its opulent white marble cladding on the façade walls. Marble is carried into the interior space of the main foyer's staircase. The flooring and the columns, cladded in pink and green, reference the colours of the two parliamentary chambers – the House of Representatives Chamber and the Senate Chamber – which sit on opposing wings and are inspired by the Australian landscape. A large venue space called the Great Hall spreads over two levels that can be accessed centrally. This space is covered in timber and tapestry designed by renowned Australian artist Arthur Boyd in collaboration with the Victorian Tapestry Workshop. Further on is the Members Hall which lies in the centre of the parliament house directly below the flag mast. *SZ*

John Gollings

Ryan Wick

National Library of Australia

051 B

Parkes Pl W

Walter Bunning, T.E. O'Mahony.
1968

The elegant National Library of Australia is the country's main storehouse of documentary heritage. The freestanding building is located at Parkes Place, next to Lake Burley Griffin. Prior to its official opening in 1968 the library's collection was spread across several buildings within the city. Architects Walter Bunning (of architectural firm Bunning and Madden) and T.E. O'Mahony designed the building in the late-twentieth-century Stripped Classicism style. The 47,000-square-metre building is spread out over eight levels supported by a 16 × 8 grid of columns. The architects emphasised the columns, making the outer columns a prominent feature of the façade's perimeter. The exterior is cladded in light marble, with granite, bronze, slate, and copper, and features a copper roof. The interior includes many reading rooms and collection spaces which have been finished in fine Australian timbers and feature heritage furniture designed by Fred Ward and Arthur Robinson. Above the library's main entrance is a copper bas-relief sculpture created by sculptor Tom Bass. *SZ*

Kit Carruthers

» Commonwealth Place

052 B

44 Parkes Place, Parkes
Durbach Block Jaggers with Sue Barnsley Design
2014

Located inside the Parliamentary Triangle and beside Lake Burley Griffin, Commonwealth Place covers both outdoor and indoor space. The project, spanning architecture and landscape architecture, comprises a public gathering area, an exhibition hall, offices, and a restaurant. Inside the exhibition hall (formerly the Gallery of Australian Design) is the National Capital Exhibition, an attraction that relays the story of Canberra as the capital of Australia. The sloping roof of the exhibition building and that of the restaurant opposite form a concave, grass-covered public square measuring around 100 × 50 metres. A rounded metal balustrade surrounds the edges of the roofs. The paved path across the square connects with a passage through the higher ground behind. This sleek walkway is made up of Australian stone – the high walls are clad in sandstone and the floor is bluestone – and its mirror-covered ends are glazed. The path leads to Reconciliation Place. Behind that is Old Parliament House, which appears to stand in the middle of the green concave square when seen from the other side of Lake Burnley Griffin. *DP*

Nick D

« National Museum of Australia

053 B

Lawson Crescent, Acton
Ashton Raggatt McDougall, Robert Peck von Hartel Trethowan
2001

The audacious National Museum of Australia sits on the edge of Lake Burley Griffin on an 11-hectare site. Its eye-catching design was created by architects Ashton Raggatt McDougall and Robert Peck von Hartel Trethowan, who won the 1997 International Design Competition held to design the museum building. The architects gave the museum a postmodern style, uncommon at the time for traditional museum buildings, in an attempt to reflect the diversity of the collection exhibited within. The building's exterior is clad in anodised aluminium panels and patterned concrete. Its main design feature is a large coloured loop, referred to as the Uluru line, intended as a tribute to Australia's famous Ayers Rock. The loop begins as an entrance canopy and rises up to form a 30-metre-high curve which then ends in a wide footpath. Colour is used extensively throughout the building, based on a vibrant palette of crimson, orange, bronze, gold, black, and silver. The museum is accessed through the main hall, a curved open space with plentiful natural light, which leads to gallery spaces spread out on three levels. Inside, the building offers 6,600 square metres of exhibition space and consists of various individual spaces that join together like a jigsaw puzzle. These pieces form a semicircle around the Garden of Australian Dreams, a large sculptural landscape. *SZ*

Bird's-eye view over the eccentric roof of the National Museum of Australia sitting on the edge of Lake Burley Griffin

053 B

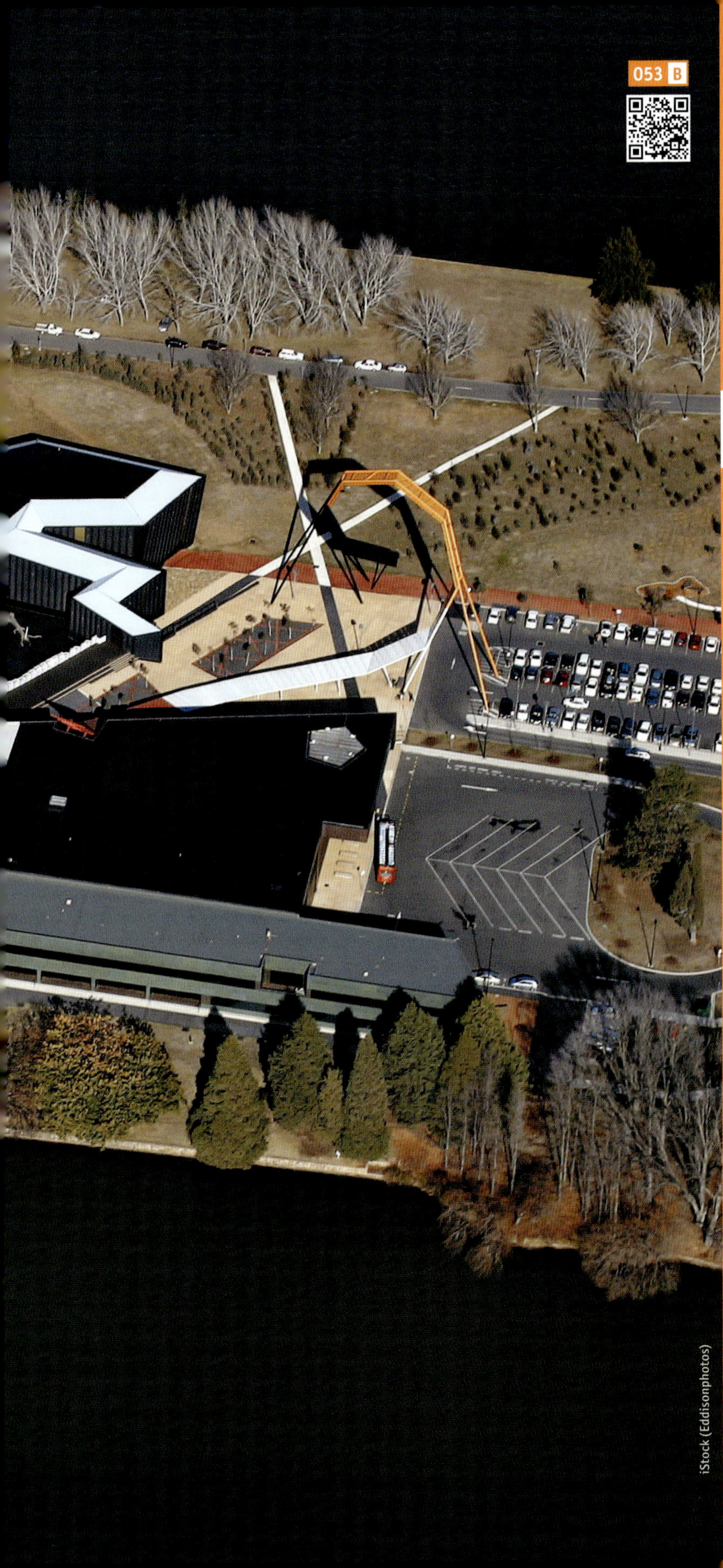

iStock (Eddisonphotos)

John Gollings

John Gollings

Botswana High Commission

054 B

130 Denison St, Deakin
Guida Moseley Brown Architects
2010

The Botswana High Commission presents architecture of contemporary character that incorporates references to traditional forms and crafts of Botswana. The building frontage consists of carefully composed brick walls in which the architects inserted a 'break' to clearly mark the entrance. A special reformation of the sloping roof allows a large amount of daylight to enter this public space. The street-facing side of the building is marked by a distinctive and colourful brickwork design derived from traditional patterns found in Botswana's famous woven baskets. The floor plan enables the public to easily access the various spaces created for conferences, receptions, and cultural performances without disrupting the secure working areas. There are two major spaces that can be easily accessed by visitors and dignitaries. The larger of these, a 'freestanding' hall, has a form evoking the organically formed traditional dwellings and meeting places of the Tswana people. The hall has an independent identity and opens onto a private garden characterised by native Australian plants similar to those found in Botswana. The offices are aligned along the primary brick walls and look out onto the street, while the passages and common-use spaces overlook the garden court and offer far-reaching views, serving as informal gathering spaces for staff and visitors. The glazed circulation walls and the High Commissioner's office are curved to provide a distinctive character to the interior spaces. They give shape to the garden, while also complementing the unique form and independent character of the hall. *PA*

John Gollings

National Arboretum Canberra 055 B

Forest Drive, Molonglo Valley

Tonkin Zulaikha Greer Architects

2013

TZG, in association with landscape architects Taylor Cullity Lethlean, won an Australia-wide competition for the National Arboretum, on a 290 hectare site of bushfire-damaged land north of Canberra's Lake Burley Griffin. The Arboretum is a collection of 100 forests, each home to a single internationally endangered species. The species are chosen from the many thousands that are threatened worldwide, and curated according to colour of foliage, pattern of bark/leaf, filigree of branches, scent and texture, and suitability to local growth conditions. By the opening of the Arboretum to commemorate Canberra's centenary in February 2013, 96 of the 100 forests have been planted, complemented by a major Visitor Centre, the Margaret Whitlam Pavilion, a regional Playground, and the first of the many gardens planned for the site. A full road and pedestrian circulation system are operational, and a site-wide interpretation strategy underlines the project's long-term ecological benefits. *PA*

John Gollings

≈ Village Centre 056 B

National Arboretum Canberra
Tonkin Zulaikha Greer Architects
2012

The refined Village Centre is the main point of arrival for the National Arboretum Canberra and provides a full range of visitor facilities to complement the outdoor experiences of the Arboretum. The Centre's architecture develops the long-standing tradition of significant garden buildings as transparent enclosures with dramatic internal volumes and a strong sense of indoor-outdoor connection. Importantly, the strong presence of the building acts as a focus for the Arboretum while the trees are immature. The exterior of the building is a sculptural form in the site's rolling topography, contrasting low stone-clad wings with a high arching roof clad in weathered zinc, the form of which is inspired by the fronds of the adjoining forest of Chilean Wine Palms, and by the ribbing of many tree leaves. The interior subtly recalls the branched forms of mature trees. Carefully sited below the ridgeline, the building forms a unified composition with Taylor Cullity Lethlean's dramatic sculpting of the site's Central Valley, the Event Terrace, and the small Pavilion, now under construction and a counterpoint to the Village Centre. From the car park, visitors enter the Arboretum through the new building, passing through the dramatic Entry Cutting formed through the ridgeline knolls, planted with forests of white-flowering crepe myrtle. The heart of the building is its main vaulted space, which flexibly accommodates a range of functions, including exhibitions, events, retail, a café, and programmed activities. The dramatic, low-energy timber structure was fully computer dimensioned and prefabricated in Tasmania and quickly erected on site. The choice of timber reduces embodied energy by nearly 90 per cent compared to steelwork, and the stone walls have an equally low energy profile. *PA*

Sarah Zahradnik

John Gollings

John Gollings

Margaret Whitlam Pavilion

057 B

National Arboretum Canberra
Tonkin Zulaikha Greer Architects
2013

The Margaret Whitlam Pavilion is located on the south-western tip of the U-shaped Events terrace, looking across the future grassed Amphitheatre to the Visitors Centre and out to the Central Valley and the city of Canberra beyond. Its axis aligns with the Captain Cook water jet, continuing Griffin's structuring of the city by focal radiating axes. The building is kept below the landscaped ridge to the west, so that it is subordinate to the landform, whilst its roof shape is a defined curve in contrast to the rolling topography of the site. The pointed curve of the roof will be an emphatic pause in the sweep of the Arboretum's landscape in this precinct, and a dramatic statement when viewed from the main car entry adjoining Tuggeranong Parkway. The building includes a main internal space suitable for functions of up to 120 people, including cocktail parties, weddings, dinners, music, and other performances and ceremonial events. The space opens eastwards to an outdoor terrace projecting over the lip of the slope, and north and south to smaller linking terraces, each with fully openable glass doors. The eastern terrace captures a panorama of the city and its surrounding mountains, with the sweep of the lake and the Parliament flagpole as a focus. The structure is an innovative prefabricated arrangement of steel beams and insulating composite panels, clad externally in zinc, matching the ribbed roof of the Village Centre to the north. *PA*

Interview

Harold Guida

Sieglinde Whittle

Guida Moseley Brown Architects is an architectural, interior design, and urban design firm operating an international practice from Australia's national capital. The firm has extensive experience in major public buildings, educational and research facilities, large-scale residential developments, a range of commercial and corporate projects, and urban design and master planning. Central to their design approach is the understanding and appreciation of place. They aim to respond to a variety of environmental, cultural, social, and historical factors in order to discover an independent and unique expression in each project. It is their belief that a comprehensive and sensitive engagement with the sense of place leads to successful, aesthetically durable, and intelligent design solutions.

What differentiates architecture in Australia from international architecture?
Australian architectural history contains a series of unique vernacular styles, approaches, and typologies that are specific to different regions and continue to be explored and developed by contemporary practitioners. From the Victorian row houses to the Queenslander home through to the re-interpretation of the industrial shed, Australian architects are re-inventing prevailing typologies and building upon a strong cultural legacy. The different climates and topographies across Australia drive many of these different approaches, with different cities developing their own unique design responses and identities. Australian architects, while practising locally, are cognisant of contemporary international ideas, and in some cases, these are reinterpreted in response to local environments and implemented through a uniquely Australian material sensibility.

What role do current architectural trends play in your design approach?
Our design approach for each project evolves from a series of different concerns, centred around a philosophy of sensitive, transformative engagement with place. These factors include an appreciation of history, context, environment, functional

Architecture as a philosophy of sensitive, transformative engagement with place

Paul Mutton

John Guida

and social programming, and how geometric, atmospheric, and material concepts will coalesce into a unique architectural identity. While we do not consciously aim to implement current trends in architecture, our work exists in dialogue with other historical and contemporary projects and ideas, in particular where related to our focus on sustainability and the exploration of new materials and emerging construction technologies.

Where do you find your design inspiration?
We analyse project drivers such as brief, context, and cultural issues, from which an idea or a series of parallel concepts emerge as a means to organise and give expression to a specific project. These ideas can arise from site topography, cultural and social narratives, research into building performance, and geometrical concepts.

Which Australian buildings do you most admire and why?
The Sydney Opera House is an incredible project, from its original concept through to its integrated structural and material resolution. The building has an audacity that makes it both an icon and a timeless piece of 20th century architecture. On a different scale we appreciate the strong body of Australian residential architecture and the ways in which it provides a unique interpretation of modernism. In particular the Hugh Buhrich House II has a combination of rawness and precision, executed with a very original expression. Contrasting with that, the Roy Grounds House in Toorak and Robin Boyd's Wash Street House are also seminal Australian works, each highly finessed in their interpretation of an Australian way of living. Beyond this we also appreciate the historical buildings and urban design of Australia's development during the 1800s and early 1900s, which are unique to each city and town. These include the great stone buildings and laneways of Melbourne, the giant wharf sheds in Woolloomooloo, Sydney, and the Art Deco buildings of Canberra.

What could the rest of the world learn from Australian architecture?
It could be said that Australian architects are great assimilators, in the sense that they are able to draw upon a variety of international and local influences and produce a balanced, multifaceted architecture. In particular Australian architects are able to engage with broader international movements and ideas, while satisfying the often-competing local demands related to sustainability and market-driven design and while still being imbued with a unique Australian material aesthetic.

Canberra International Airport 058 B

Pialligo Avenue
Guida Moseley Brown Architects
2013

In 2005 Guida Moseley Brown Architects won a design competition for the new Canberra Airport. The project involved the master planning of the 17 hectare site and detailed development of a domestic and international terminal complex to completely replace the existing airport buildings and operations. The terminal is designed to service up to eight million passengers per year across twelve domestic gates, two international swing gates, ten passenger boarding bridges, and fourteen Boeing 737-800 compliant parking bays. The new complex has been designed to contribute to the formal identity of the national capital. The airport, as a major 'public building', can be viewed and accessed along a landscaped axial roadway, like other major public buildings in Canberra. Two car-park structures flank the axis and offer direct access to the terminal at the ground and second levels, virtually eliminating conflicts between pedestrians and vehicles. The central axis of the landscape visibly continues through the terminal and is marked by a three-storey atrium with shaded skylights. The central atrium incorporates the security check area and continues to the external wall of the terminal on the air-side, with full-height glazing overlooking take-offs and landings and the landscape beyond. The terminal comprises three floors with a partial basement. An elevated road leads directly to the upper-level drop-off and departure areas, with a ticketing hall, baggage drop areas, and related facilities. Arrival facilities are located on the ground floor, overlooking the landscaped gardens and providing access to the baggage claim area, an enclosed taxi waiting area, and a bus and vehicle pick-up zone. The positioning of the new buildings, the character of the visible landscape, the lighting, and the architectural form of the building's elements are intended to provide a welcoming sense of identity and enable easy wayfinding. *PA*

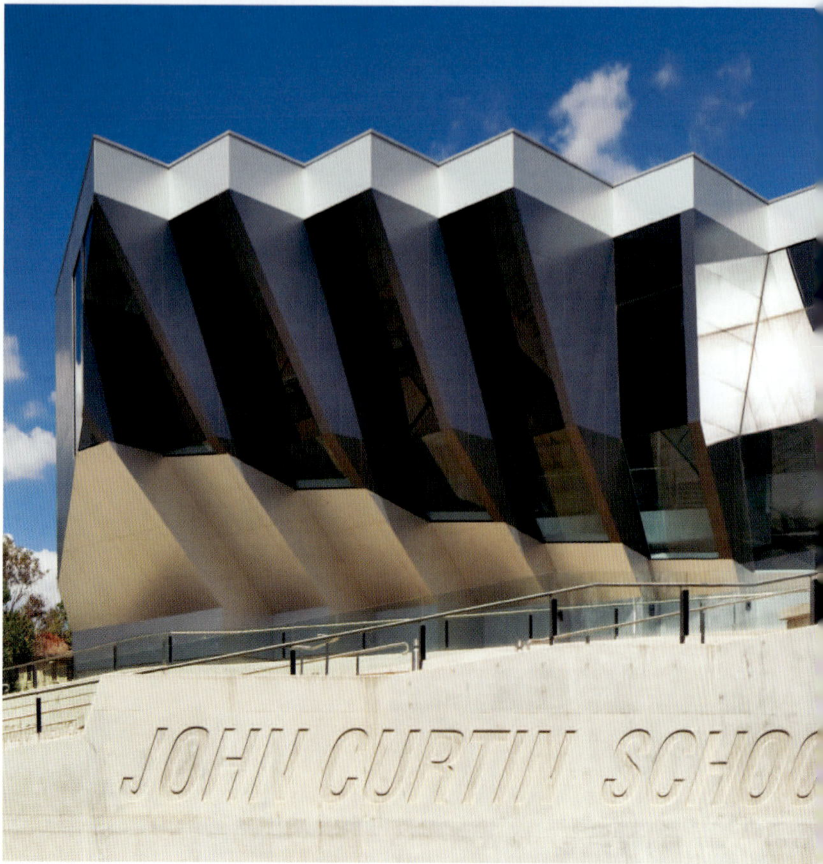

John Gollings

John Gollings

John Curtin School of Medical Research

059 B

131 Garran Road, Acton
Lyons
2009

Opened in 2009, the John Curtin School of Medical Research at the Australian National University is an institutional building designed by Australian architecture firm Lyons. On the outside, the front side of the fan-like folded façade is made up of angular glass panels and steel. This staggered form adds to the visitor's experience of movement while approaching the building's main entrance via the long, stepped plaza that is integrated into the landscape. Digitally rendered concrete with impressions of molecules and DNA strands wrap around the building envelope. Intended to bolster interactivity and collaboration, the research facility's interior offers open-plan offices, exhibition spaces, support spaces, shared laboratories, and a 200-seat public lecture theatre. *PA*

iStock (Kokkai Ng)

John Gollings

Nishi Building

060 B

25 Edinburgh Ave, Canberra
Fender Katsalidis
2013

The fourth and final major stage of the NewActon precinct is Nishi. A highly distinctive landmark on the Lake, Fender Katsalidis worked with Japanese architects Suppose Design Office to create an iconic and eclectic mixed-use building for Canberra. The development contains 220 exquisitely designed apartments, an eight-screen cinema, and an award-winning boutique hotel and restaurant. The office component is cohesively integrated into the project and houses the Department of Industry and Science and legal firm Clayton Utz. With its stunning design and cultural offerings, Nishi is the centrepiece of Canberra's NewActon precinct. Every aspect of Nishi's originally Japanese-inspired design has been reconsidered so that tenants can benefit from its innovative solar heat retention principles. Nishi delivers an extraordinary six-star Green Star 'as-built' rating, in addition to an eight-star NatHERs rating, which was achieved by creating a building that responds to the surrounding environment. A sustainable Australian-timber-louvered façade provides shading to limit solar gains, and the largest field of photovoltaics in Australia is housed on the roof. The building's designs also include a sewage recycling plant, low-energy fixtures and fittings, and lighting which responds to available daylight. The Molonglo Group, the developers of the precinct, very much wanted the building to be the best possible embodiment of the values they hold dear. Those values include the imperative of environmental sustainability, the desire to create a pocket of urbanity, tolerance, inclusiveness, and richness in Canberra, and their love of the immersion of daily life in a milieu of culture and stimulation. The main entrance to Nishi Residential, opposite the linking stair, was also part of March Studio's brief. Outside is a canopy which shrugs off its weight with flowing timber recalling the Commercial Lobby. The entrance airlock is lined on two walls and ceiling with what could be steel punch cards for an ancient mainframe. Filling the gaps punched in these steel sandwich panels are amber marbles, thick glass which filters the light and warms the space. The directionality of the commercial lobby is mirrored here, in the lines of punched holes on wall and ceiling, which scatter across the rear wall and flow into the stacked timber of the Hotel Hotel library. *PA*

John Gollings

John Gollings

Hobart and Surroundings

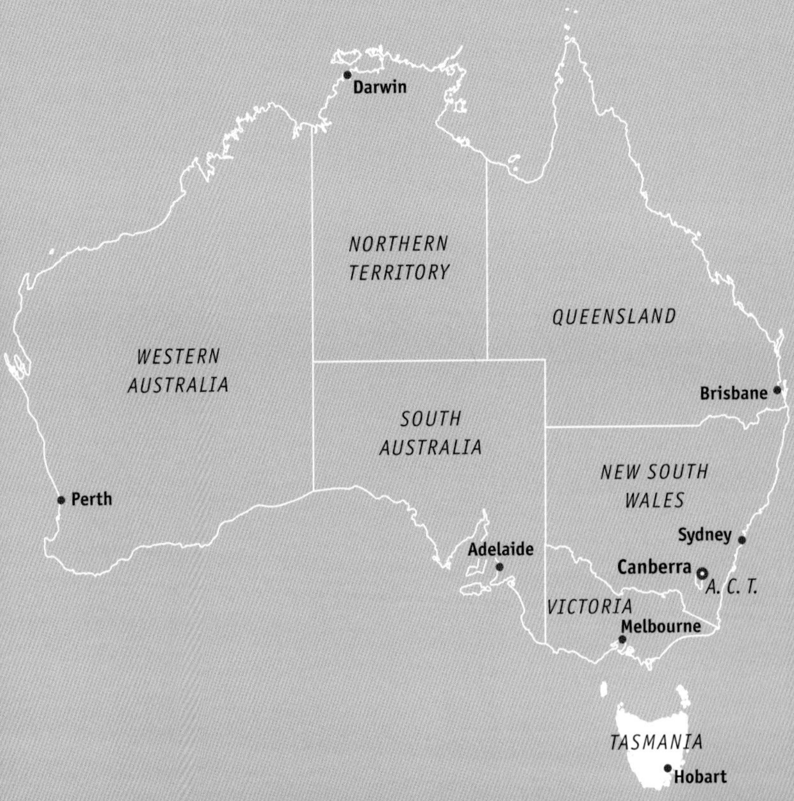
Darwin
NORTHERN TERRITORY
QUEENSLAND
WESTERN AUSTRALIA
Brisbane
SOUTH AUSTRALIA
NEW SOUTH WALES
Perth
Sydney
Adelaide
Canberra
A. C. T.
VICTORIA
Melbourne
TASMANIA
Hobart

C
Hobart
082
085
069
Bass Strait
TASMANIA
Devonport
Launceston
080
088
089
081
Hobart
079
061

077
075
065
062
078
086
074
076
071
064
073
070
063
072
066
068
067
087
nearmap

Hobart and Surroundings

The city of Hobart is the heart of the small island that is Tasmania, located 240 km off the south-east corner of mainland Australia. The city lies on the shores of the Derwent River in close proximity to Mount Wellington. This unique setting has led to the city's height restrictions and resulted in Hobart's large number of low-rise buildings. The first sighting of Tasmania was reported in 1642 by Dutch explorer Abel Janszoon Tasman, who named the island Anthoonij van Diemenslandt after the Governor of the Dutch East Indies, who had sent Tasman on the voyage. The name was later shortened by the British to Van Diemen's Land and remained as such until 1855. The isolated land had been inhabited by Aboriginal Australians for around 35,000 years before British settlement. It wasn't until 1804 that Hobart was officially founded by the British as a penal colony, making it the second oldest capital in Australia after Sydney. It is the second-least populated city in Australia with a population of 227,000 inhabitants. With the well-preserved Port Arthur Historic Site approximately 100 km south-east of Hobart and only a short ferry ride away,

Hobart is a mecca for tourists wanting to see the heritage ruins and restored buildings of the once convict site that dates back to the 1830s. Pre-dating the Port Arthur site is Hobart's own Penitentiary Chapel. Another historic building nearby is the Grand Theatre Royal, one of Australia's oldest working theatres. Government architects such as John Lee Archer and William Porden Kay played a significant role in the formation of Tasmania's first public buildings, including Hobart's Parliament House and Government House. Post offices were among the first buildings developed in each new town and colony and an important part of Australian life from the early colonial period, given their role as the only means of contact between Australia and Britain for much of the 19th century. Aside from the Georgian style colonial architecture Tasmania flaunts architectural styles including but not limited to Gothic Revival, Greek Revival, Renaissance Revival, and Italianate. Hobart Harbour is a perfect spot to take in Tasmania's fine blend of heritage buildings, scenery, and culture with harbour views. *SZ*

Port Arthur Historic Site
Arthur Hwy, Port Arthur
British Empire
1830–1877

061 C

Located 100 kilometres southeast of Hobart lies the UNESCO World Heritage-listed Port Arthur Historic Site, which was the centre of the convict settlement in Australia between 1830 and 1877. It was named after Sir George Arthur, the disciplinarian governor of that time. The American War of Independence led to the deportation of British convicts to Australian colonies and the establishment of the Port Arthur site, which was much larger in its heyday, serving as the main settlement location for convicts in Tasmania and housing over 30,000 convicts in 1847. Convicts serving life sentences remained in Port Arthur even after convict transportation had ended and were eventually transferred elsewhere in 1877 upon closure of the site. Aside from correctional facilities, the site also includes many industrial buildings from when it operated as an industrial manufacturing camp for timber, ships, shoes, and bricks. Today it is an open-air museum, popular among tourists, exhibiting the restored remnants of over 40 Georgian-style buildings that sit within the unique landscape. The main buildings include the Commandant's House, the round Guard Tower, the church, the Shipwright's House, the Clerk of Work's House, the Hospital, the Commandant's Office, the Magistrates House, the Medical Officer's House, and the Model Prison. *SZ*

nearmap

iStock (roboriginal)

Sarah Zahradnik

« The Tench

062 C

Brisbane and Campbell Sts
John Lee Archer
Early 1830s

The Penitentiary Chapel, more commonly referred to as 'The Tench', was completed in the early 1830s to serve as a place of religious worship for the increasing number of convicts arriving during this period. However, this building was not such a holy space: it was designed to contain cells for solitary confinement beneath its floor. Over 50,000 convicts experienced this form of incarceration at this prison. Irish Architect John Lee Archer designed this 'religious' structure in the shape of a cruciform. After the transportation of

convicts came to an end, the site was reinstated as the Hobart Town Gaol, and portions of the chapel were converted into two Supreme Courts. *SZ*

Theatre Royal

063 C

29 Campbell Street, Hobart
John Lee Archer
1837

A state treasure, the Theatre Royal is a performing arts venue and the oldest continually operating theatre in Australia. With the rapid expansion of the colony, Hobart's business leaders gathered to establish a permanent theatre for the community. Peter Degraves, founder of Cascade, Australia's oldest brewery, designed the building with Government Architect John Lee Archer. The theatre building was opened in 1837 and has since undergone considerable refurbishment and restoration, including the addition of a gallery space and new detailing to the auditorium. The building was under severe threat of demolition in the 1950s, which prompted Gwen Friend and her partner Fifi Banvard to establish a permanent theatre company in Hobart and reclaim the Theatre Royal building for its original purpose. The pair rented the space from the National Theatre and Fine Arts Society (NATFAS) and used their own private funds to refurbish the theatre's interior, thus securing the future of the Theatre Royal. *SZ*

Tasmanian Archive and Heritage Office

≈ Parliament House
064 C

1 Salamanca Pl, Hobart
John Lee Archer
1840

Tasmania's sizeable Parliament House is within walking distance from Salamanca Place, where a famous weekly market is held. Originally designed by John Lee Archer to serve as a customs house, the building's design is representative of colonial style architecture with Georgian influences. Predominantly constructed by convicts, it was opened in 1840 and was occupied by the Customs Department until 1905. In 1940 the building was converted to include an Assembly Chamber and Members' Lounge. Additional work was carried out in 1980 to make room for a Parliamentary Library, Committee Rooms, and other facilities. *SZ*

≈ Queen Mary Club
065 C

143 Macquarie St, Hobart
James Blackburn
1843

The Queen Mary Club of Hobart building was formerly The Bank of Australasia. It was established in 1910 as a residential Social Club for Ladies, which included around 100 members. The building, designed by colonial architect James Blackburn, was completed in 1843. The heritage building received a Mercury award in 1964 and was regarded as the best restored and preserved building on the National Trust Register. Since its completion, its freestone structure has suffered much deterioration due to the build-up of salt, which has resulted in ongoing restoration works to maintain the building's original integrity. *SZ*

stors.tas.gov.au

Barry LB

C

Government House

066 C

7 Lower Domain Rd, Hobart
William Porden Kay
1857

Tasmania's first Government House was built in 1817, but the government soon relocated to the Queens Domain site, as the original building was deemed unsatisfactory. The new government building was completed in 1857, and Sir Henry Fox Young became the first governor to occupy the residence, which today is considered to be one of the best of its kind in the Commonwealth. Designed by colonial architect William Porden Kay, it is a fine example of the neo-gothic style and one of the largest residences in this style in Australia. The building was constructed with local sandstone and timber and features a slate roof and exceptionally carved interior features including bas-relief sculptures. *SZ*

Image of the house, from *The Cruise Round the World of the Flying Squadron 1869-1870*

Flickr (Heather)

iStock (slovegrove)

» Hobart Gas Company

067 C

2 Macquarie St, Hobart
Unknown
1854

The Hobart Gas Company, established in 1854, is located on the corner of Hobart's eastern edge. It was formerly responsible for manufacturing coal gas and gasworks and distributing these throughout Hobart. As demand for electricity grew, the company's building was expanded in 1894 to make room for an electric power station. It was after this addition that the building's distinctive brick chimney was erected. After the dependence on coal dropped in the 20th century, the gas company eventually closed, and its building has since been renovated to house a restaurant, convenience store, bottle shop, and offices. *SZ*

» Royal Engineers Building

068 C

2 Davey St, Hobart
Roger Kelsall (Enginner)
1847

Completed in 1847, Tasmania's Royal Engineers building is located in Hobart neighbouring the Hobart Gas Company. It was constructed in the Georgian standard to house the headquarters for the Royal Engineers. Its symmetrical two-storey exterior is made of solid sandstone brick and several tudor style pitched roofs which vary in scale and orientation. The building's Gothic Revival style was uncommon in this period and is owing to engineer, Roger Kelsall, who was one of the many engineers responsible for the design and construction of infrastructure within the colony in the 19th century. *SZ*

« North Hobart Post Office 069 C

412 Elizabeth Street,
North Hobart
19th century

The North Hobart Post Office is an exemplary landmark building reminiscent of the Australian Federation style architecture combining Edwardian, Queen Anne, and Arts and Crafts styles. It is a symbol of North Hobart and still serves its original purpose as a post office. The colourful two-storey brick exterior sits within the wide Elizabeth Street setting amongst other 19th century Colonial, late Victorian, Federation, and Inter War buildings. *SZ*

Royal Engineering Building with Hobart Gas Company's brick chimney in front

iStock (David Lade)

Hobart Town Hall 070 C

50 Macquarie Street, Hobart
Henry Hunter
1866

Declared as a public holiday, the day the Hobart Town Hall's foundation stone was laid in 1864 was a time of celebration and excitement which marked the progress of Hobart City. Another public holiday was declared in 1866 upon the town hall's completion. Prior to then the Hobart City Council had occupied the ballroom of the Government House. Prominent colonial architect Henry Hunter designed the sandstone building with classical influences, which can be seen in the building's considerable symmetry and elaborate detailing. The main entrance flaunts a triple-arched portico. Its interior features a grand J.W. Walker & Sons (London) organ which at the time of its installation, in 1870, was considered to be the second largest in the southern hemisphere. It remains regarded as one of Australia's finest historical pipe organs. The Town Hall building originally accommodated the police force and magistrates' court, which was later replaced by the Lord Mayor's reception room in 1912. From that year onwards, the building was primarily occupied by the local city government. Nowadays, this major civic building of Tasmania can be hired out for events including balls, receptions, meetings, courtroom finished. *SZ*

iStock (ClaudineVM)

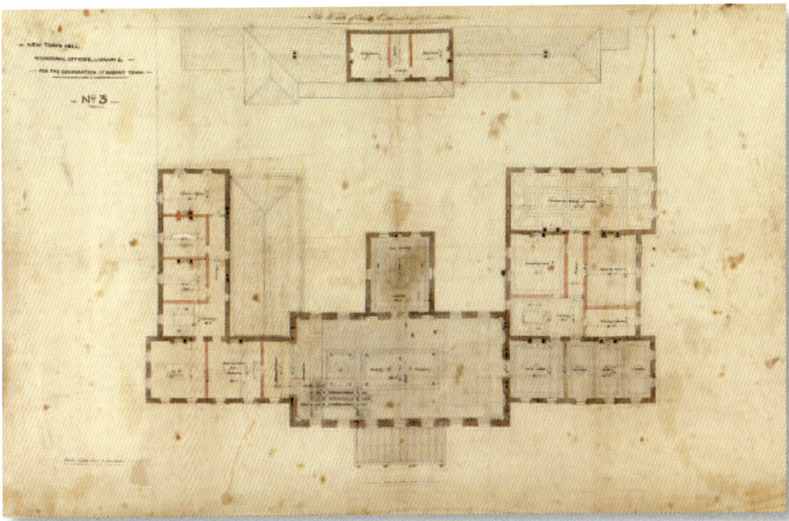

Tasmanian Archive and Heritage Office

Floor Plan of Hobart Town Hall, designed by architect Henry Hunter

Sarah Zahradnik

« General Post Office 071 C

9 Elizabeth St, Hobart

Alan Cameron Walker

1905

Postal services were of high importance in Australia during the early colonial period, as they offered the only means of contact with Britain. Listed on the Commonwealth Heritage List, the monumental Hobart General Post Office (GPO) has sat boldly perched on the corner of Elizabeth Street and Macquarie Street since its completion in 1905. Local architect Alan Cameron Walker designed the headquarters for Tasmania's postal services with strong Edwardian Baroque principles. The large clock tower was an addition funded by the citizens of Hobart. *SZ*

» State Offices Building 072 C

10 Murray Street, Hobart

D. Hartley Wilson & Bolt

1966

The State Offices Building was completed in 1966 and sits on a recessed stone plinth on a sloped site in close proximity to the Parliament House. The building comprises three storeys below street level and fifteen storeys above. Its glazed cubic façade is framed by an in-situ-concrete grid made up of columns and beams which extend around the perimeter's edge. Tasmanian architects D. Hartley Wilson and Bolt designed the building with the aim of responding to the historic surroundings through the classical distribution of its structural elements. *SZ*

≈ Hydro Electric Commission Building

073 C

16 Elizabeth St, Hobart
A & K Henderson & Partners
1940

Sitting on the corner of Davey Street and Elizabeth Street is the prominent Hydro Electric Commission Building (HEC Building), once the headquarters of the state's largest 20th century corporation. At the time of its completion, in 1940, the six-storey building was one of the first multi-storey structures to be built in Hobart. Architects of the Melbourne-based firm A & K Henderson & Partners designed the modern building as a representation of the new age of electricity. Inspired by the street-corner location of the site, they gave the building a distinct Art Deco style through several features: a corner entrance, vertical accents on the façade, a stepped building volume, and ornamental high-relief sculptures depicting electrical insulators. The building is made of stone-coated masonry walls with polished granite at the base. The Hobart City Council has occupied the building since the mid 1990s. *SZ*

Sarah Zahradnik

Sarah Zahradnik

Colonial Mutual Life Building 074 C
18 Elizabeth St, Hobart
Hennessy & Hennessy
1936

The Royal Australian Institute of Architects has included the grand Colonial Mutual Life Building on its list of notable twentieth-century Tasmanian buildings. This inter-war building features characteristics of Stripped Classicism and Art Deco as well as traces of the Gothic Revival, with sculptural elements in the form of gargoyles. The building was designed by the Sydney-based architectural firm Hennessy & Hennessy and opened in 1936. The seven-storey building, used commercially, is cladded in stone and multi-coloured roof tiles. *SZ*

Masonic Temple 075 C
3 Sandy Bay Rd, Hobart
Albert Lauriston Crisp
1938

An admirable example of stripped classical style architecture, the Masonic Temple stands unobtrusively in its Sandy Bay setting in Hobart and serves as an office and meeting space for the Hobart Masonic Lodge. The architect Albert Lauriston Crisp created the design, incorporating elements of both Art Deco and Egyptian styles. The composition of the double-height symmetrical mass is made of light-coloured brick, which is banded horizontally and also articulated vertically into three bays, the central one of which frames the main entrance of the building. *SZ*

Supreme Court of Tasmania

076 C

5 Salamanca Place, Hobart
Peter Partridge
1970s

The Supreme Court Complex, situated on Salamanca Place, is a worthy example of public architecture. It consists of two entities, divided by a large plaza that opens up a diagonal thoroughfare between St David's Park, Parliament Square, and the Sullivans Cove waterfront. Cladded in traditional sandstone, the two volumes sit elevated on a slate podium integrated within the landscape. The Department of Public Works collaborated with architect Peter Partridge to design the building, combining classical design principles with a brutalist materiality. Completed in the 1970s, the complex was recently awarded the 25 Year Award for Enduring Architecture: an apposite selection, given its aesthetic and material durability. *SZ*

Barry L B

Wrest Point Hotel Casino

« Wrest Point Hotel Casino

077 C

410 Sandy Bay Rd, Hobart
Roy Grounds
1973

Standing tall over the city of Hobart, the iconic Wrest Point Hotel Casino was the first legal casino to be established in Australia. The land beneath the hotel was purchased by a local, Arthur Drysdale, in the 1930s, but it wasn't until 1973 that the hotel was opened by Australia's oldest operating hotel group, Federal Hotels, and put on the map for tourists. The landmark 17-storey octagonal tower with its revolving restaurant at the top level was designed by Roy Grounds, one of Australia's leading architects of the modern movement. It remains the tallest building in Hobart to this day and was listed on Hobart's Heritage Register in 2015. *SZ*

» Dorney House

078 C

22 Gardenia Grove, Sandy Bay
J. H. Esmond Dorney
1978

Included in the Tasmanian Heritage Register, Dorney House is a important modernist work, built on the remains of Fort Nelson, a fort that stood from 1909 until 1949. The architect J. H. Esmond Dorney bought the site in 1949, and over time constructed three houses there. Only the last, from 1978, remains (bush fires destroyed the others). On steep terrain high above Sandy Bay, the house is open to the landscape: large windows under roof vaults with thin steel columns provide all-round panoramic views. Inside, there is built-in furniture, such as the 'fire pit'. Owned by the City of Hobart, the house is open to the public. *DP*

City of Hobart

Ray Joyce

City of Hobart

Peppermint Bay

079 C

3435 Channel Hwy, Woodbridge
Terroir
2003

Hard to miss, the Peppermint Bay Building is a modern bistro that offers a picturesque stop just 40 kilometres south of Hobart. Designed by Hobart-based architecture group Terroir, the uniquely shaped building accentuates the superb views over Peppermint Bay and is approached from a car park entrance atop a small cliff. The building's exterior materials comprise a folded grey metal roof which crowns the complex glass walls whilst the warmer interior is made up of timber and concrete surfaces complemented by slivers of light entering from the window openings. *SZ*

Sarah Zabrodnik

Brett Boardman Photography

Brett Boardman Photography

The Forest Eco Centre

080 C

Scottsdale, Tasmania
Circa Morris Nunn Architects
2010

Circa Morris Nunn Architects have executed a new, sustainable ecological vision with their design for the Forest EcoCentre. This building houses the new interactive forest interpretation centre and offices of Sustainable Timber Tasmania, formerly Forestry Tasmania, a government forest management enterprise. The building's design presents a clean, green image to the public and is at the same time a highly energy-efficient ecological building. It is a conservatory, housing an interpretative display on the ground floor and offices of Sustainable Timber Tasmania in the form of upper-level platforms within the large internal volume. The architects developed the outer form of the building in line with the client's wish of reducing the overall wall surface area to a minimum (to reduce heat gain and loss). As such, it has a round shape as opposed to a square one. The building volume is tall, allowing the stack effect to bear out and form natural zones of warmer and cooler air inside the building. The designers manipulated these areas, producing a building that is energy efficient throughout the year to the greatest extent possible with current technology. They aimed to achieve energy efficiency as much as possible using completely natural processes, integrating plants and trees that act as bio mediators inside this microclimate. Laminated beams, made of radiata pine, form the exposed structure: they are used as conical struts externally and as post-and-beam supports for the upper floors internally. The walls are formed with two layers of transparent polycarbonate sheets, which contribute to the internal greenhouse effect yet have twice the insulation capacity of glass. The roof is in the form of a woven membrane. Its support structure is composed of stainless-steel wires laced together, forming a double spiral pattern that exactly represents the mathematical progression known as the Fibonacci numbers. The form of the double spirals is exactly the same as the one found in the seeds of radiata pine cones. *PA*

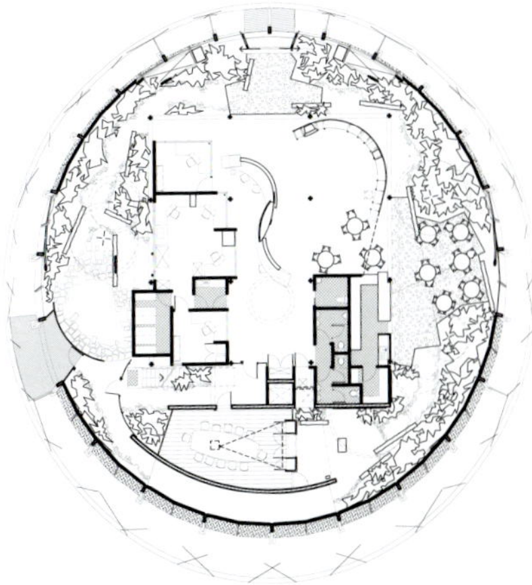

Saffire Resort

2352 Coles Bay Rd, Coles Bay
Circa Morris Nunn Architects
2010

081 C

The site of the Saffire Resort is located at Coles Bay on the east coast of Tasmania and overlooks Great Oyster Bay, the Hazards, and the Freycinet Peninsula. The architects' brief was to create an intimate luxury resort, with 20 private suites, that would be a destination in its own right and mainly cater to inbound interstate or international guests. It was to provide for and possibly create a new high-end tourist market in the state. Also important to the client was that the project have an iconic, highly recognisable form that would also relate to the natural site. Although the resort is located within what is extensively a natural native coastal landscape, the project site was scarred from its previous use as a disused caravan park. The project became as much about repairing the site and interpreting its unique qualities as it was about creating a new space. The resort maintains an organic relationship with the site and is evocative of coastal forms. However, the form also works with the programmatic requirements of the brief. Essentially, the main resort building (or Sanctuary) is entered from the tail; inside, it opens onto a large volume that provides a panoramic view of the Hazards and Great Oyster Bay. The reception lounge is on this level; the mid-level contains bar, restaurant, and lounge areas; and the lowest level houses a gallery, board room, and day spa. Undercover walkways link the reception building to the suites. The Hazards are a dominant feature of the site, and the architecture deliberately blocks and reveals views throughout the visitor's entire journey. One of the main challenges of the design was to reconcile the client's (and market's) perception of luxury with elements of the unique Tasmanian context. The view is an important part of this, but the materials, colours, scale, and form also contribute strongly. Materials were selected to work on many levels: to meet pragmatic requirements (relating to built form, availability, and remote construction), to evoke particular aesthetic associations (vernacular style, natural context, and luxury expectations), and to mediate space and volume. The choice of materials was complemented by a colour palette that was sampled from a close examination of the surrounding landscape. Furthermore,

George Apostolidis

the grandness of the main resort building, which responds to its wider context, is counteracted by a more personal and intimate scale in the suites. Where possible, issues relating to sustainable design were considered. However, sustainable design was also weighed against the issues that arise when constructing on a remote site and against market expectations for luxury resorts (both in material selection and building services). A major consideration for the project was water usage in what is typically a drought-affected area. New rain water-collection and storage infrastructures were built (off site) as part of the project for use by the development and the nearby township as well as sewage treatment facilities. Rainwater from roofs is also collected and re-used in the reflection pools, and water-efficient devices were specified. Another important factor, due to the predominantly cool climate and south-facing orientation of the site, was heating the resort. All buildings are well insulated, and high-performance glazing was installed. Energy-efficient water-heating and air-conditioning systems were used. *PA*

George Apostolidis

Museum of Old and New Art 082 C
655 Main Rd, Berriedale
Fender Katsalidis
2011

Undoubtedly a highlight of any visit to Tasmania, the Museum of Old and New Art (MONA) is embedded into its rocky surroundings on a clifftop just outside of Hobart. This award-winning architectural masterpiece, completed in 2011, was designed by renowned architecture firm Fender Katsalidis. It is best reached by a ferry. Upon arriving at the museum, visitors are confronted with a long set of steps – 99 to be exact – which leads to the top of the building. Visitors then arrive at a series of smaller structures: a semi-covered pavilion space, and a terrace framed by a distorted reflective surface. From this point onwards, visitors experience the sheer scale of the exterior, which has been incorporated unobtrusively and inconspicuously into its landscape setting. A work by the painter and sculptor Anselm Kiefer needed a particular space in which to be displayed, and two buildings by Roy Grounds were already standing on the site. This led to the decision to build the museum underground. The underground structure makes a clear distinction between interior and exterior. The exterior mainly consists of zinc panels, steel, and concrete, while the interior presence is amplified through the detailed use of lighting, raw materials, and a central, spiral steel staircase that connects three gallery levels. *SZ*

C

flickr (Russell James Smith)

Shearers' Quarters 083 C

North Bruny Island*

John Wardle Architects

2011

Shearers' Quarters is located on Waterview, a historic farming property built on North Bruny Island in the 1840s. The property is a working sheep farm of 440 hectares that has been operated by the Wardle family for 14 years. The family's priority to date has been the rejuvenation of the landscape with over 150 hectares reserved for conservation purposes and over 6,000 indigenous trees planted. The Shearers' Quarters is located on the site of the old shearing shed that was destroyed by fire in the 1980s. The building sits as a companion building to the existing historic cottage. It has been designed to house shearers, the family, friends, and JWA staff on annual tree planting weekends and retreats. It contains a large living/dining/kitchen area, small bathroom and laundry, two bedrooms, and a bunkroom. The plan form transforms along its length to shift the profile of a slender skillion at the western end to a broad gable at the east. This exposition of the two primary forms of agricultural structure allows the plan to align exactly with both the fall of the land to the south and the line of the original residence along its north. The inset veranda on the northern elevation shifts the alignment with the ridge to line exactly with the veranda of the original house to the east. This transformation in plan also allows for the building to broaden at its eastern end to contain the living area and open towards the ocean view. A singular palette of materials has been used: corrugated galvanised iron to the exterior, and timber internally. The building has a small footprint of 136 square metres and is nestled low along the gully to shelter from prevailing winds. Openable vents and louvres allow for controlled cross ventilation during summer. Double glazing and high-performing

Trevor Mein

insulation on the floors, walls, and ceiling reduce heat loss during the winter months. There has been extensive use of recycled materials: timber flooring, apple-box timber walls, and the chimney bricks. All rainwater is collected and used for drinking, toilets, and showers. All waste water is treated on-site and used to irrigate a small native plantation. Water is solar heated, and there is a wood heater to respond to year-round occupation. Working as both architect and client this project presented an opportunity for John Wardle to explore a series of architectural ideas without significant time constraints, but with a direct sensitivity to the project budget. *PA*

* Private residence not open to public

Trevor Mein

The Glenorchy Arts and Sculpture Park, GASP!

084 C

Brooker Highway, Elwick Bay
Room 11
2011

GASP! is a major new public walkway by room11 architects. Elevated, elongated, and arcing, it forms an extended line, three kilometres long, embedded in the landscape of River Derwent. It is built over the water and delicately touches the land at the river's inlets that occur naturally. The project was conceived as a community park, offering an arts programme as well as a play space for young children. The walkway is not only a novelty structure traversing the bay; it also strategically removes pedestrians from the adjacent Brooker Highway. Away from the growl of the traffic, pedestrians can appreciate the landscape for what it is. The structure of the walkway is simple and restrained. Timber decking and railings are finished in black, with the exception of the inner faces of the balustrades, which are individually highlighted. The tones shift across the colour spectrum, and the effect is either subtle or striking, depending on whether one is walking upon it or driving past it. The Grove Pavilion is located where the arc briefly touches back on land. It is carefully sited between mature existing trees. It is a low and long structure, built to line the overarching curve of the walkway, and provides shelter for those who wish to rest and view the texture of the water and the distant edges of the river. *PA*

Benjamin Hosking

Benjamin Hosking

The vital, experimental immediacy of Australian architecture

Thomas Bailey

Thomas Bailey is founding director of Room11 architects, a firm with a special geographical focus on Tasmania and Victoria. It has been said that Bailey's sensitivity to, and preoccupation with, the superlative Tasmanian landscape typifies his work. The list of notable buildings includes Lighthouse, Shutter House, D'Entrecasteaux House, the public walkway GASP!, and his own residence Little Big House. Bailey has received a large number of awards for his architectural works. He lives and works in Hobart.

What differentiates architecture in Australia from international architecture?
Australia is a continent with an ancient landscape and some relatively new cities. The southern hemisphere creates some very specific climatic conditions. It is difficult to speak too emphatically about the architectures that develop upon it. We operate at a southern edge, on the isle of Tasmania. It is cold. It snows. It has a small population and economy. It is, however, quite extraordinarily beautiful. The rewards of practice are profound.

What role do current architectural trends play in your design approach?
Very little I hope. We are products of the world and as such are influenced by all contemporary phenomena. Architecture should answer to a greater agenda if possible. Some elements of this agenda are periodically fashionable.

Where do you find your design inspiration?
The landscapes and climate for each project as well as local materials and client needs all feed the process and inspire the resulting architecture.

Which Australian buildings do you most admire and why?
I enjoy the freshness of much of Harry Seidler's work. The Sydney Opera House is of course a part of our consciousness and much of Glenn Murcutt's works set a different agenda for architecture in Australia and continues to influence our work.

What could the rest of the world learn from Australian architecture?
In comparison to Australian architecture, there is a thin, vital, experimental immediacy to much of our work which is not common for a great deal of European architecture.

Lighthouse, residential home in South Hobart

Benjamin Hosking

Shutter House, overlooking the Huon River in Southern Tasmania

Benjamin Hosking

D'entrecasteaux House, Apollo Bay, Bruny Island

Lookout House

085 C

Port Arthur*
Room 11
2013

Lookout House is a residential home positioned on a previously cleared site with views towards Tasman Island and the Southern Ocean beyond. This project takes the farmhouse typology and transforms it into a hybrid courtyard house. Visitors enter through a covered threshold, experiencing views into the treed courtyard and the sea beyond, before venturing into the main living space where the full panorama unfolds. Three gable-roof extrusions define particular functions within each with particular relationships to the courtyard and specific views to the surrounds. The extruded form pushes beyond the building envelope providing covered outdoor living spaces. *PA*

* Private residence not open to public

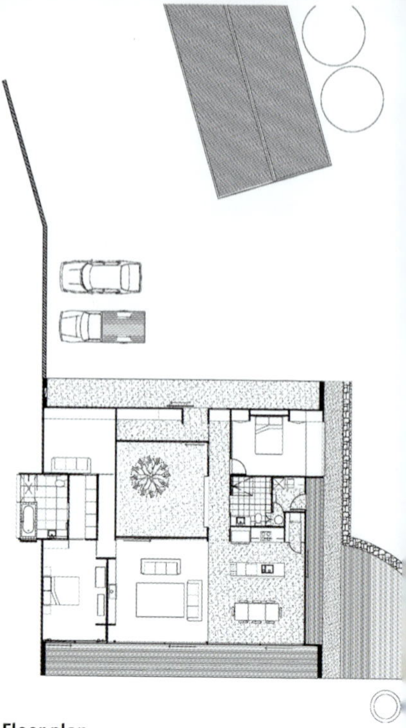

Floor plan

Ben Hosking

Ben Hosking

Tasmanian School of Business and Economics 086 C

57 Grosvenor St, Sandy Bay, Hobart
Hayball
2015

In 2013, the University of Tasmania embarked on the revitalisation and consolidation of its southern campuses. A key project at the Sandy Bay campus was the relocation of the Tasmanian School of Business and Economics to a refurbished wing of the more centrally located Centenary Building. The new location offers a postgraduate suite, new Harvard-style lecture theatres, a Technology Enhanced Active Learning space, and an informal learning area with a mix of spaces for students to pass time, socialise, eat, and conduct private study: learning pods, open lounge, booths, bench seating, and group rooms. The space also includes a café. The new location of the TSBE also houses offices for services relating to the school and its students. The building had been constructed in 1990 and was no longer serviceable, requiring refurbishment. Challenges included introducing lecture theatres and community spaces into the partially underground location. The architects aimed to ensure that the new spaces feel alive and fresh. A structurally challenging cantilevered steel and glass balcony at the building's highest level offers a stunning view of the university oval and Derwent River. *PA*

Institute for Marine and Antarctic Studies Building, University of Tasmania

087 C

20 Castray Esplanade, Battery Point
John Wardle Architects, Terroir
2013

Located on Princes Wharf No 2 in Sullivans Cove, the new building for the Institute for Marine and Antarctic Studies (IMAS) at the University of Tasmania (UTAS) stands proud as a genuine contribution to the civic and economic life of the state capital. Forty per cent of Australia's marine science research is undertaken in Tasmania and much of this state's considerable activities in marine and Antarctic science now take place in this building. The form of the new building harks back to other structures on the cove floor, past and present. The fenestration is designed to provide a level of permeability that is appropriate for this building, which is publicly accessible on all sides. The IMAS has been designed as a shed, but it is a shed with a difference. It adopts the extruding gable-roof form often found in historical models of sheds. But it is raised above the cove floor, making the ground level very transparent. This transparency reveals the activities of the institute's researchers and students to the public and clearly states the purpose of the building. A gallery, theatre, and conference spaces give an additional public face to the institute. The shed form is sliced open on the western end to further reveal the activities inside and to emphasise the continuous roof and wall form that wraps the interior spaces at the upper levels. The slight downwards fold in the roof combines with the oblique angle of the slice to open up the western end of the building toward Salamanca Place. Inside, various functional spaces are arranged along the length of the building. Laboratories are located to the south, and offices and write-up spaces to the north. In between, there are formal and informal meeting spaces as well as voids, allowing greater collaboration among researchers and students. This is an innovative approach to the often traditional laboratory typology and is intended to foster a collaborative culture between the many stakeholders at IMAS. In keeping with the greater vision for a sustainable future, the new building is heated and cooled by water drawn from the Derwent River. This river is a core element of the prominent site selected by the UTAS and represents the single most significant opportunity to reduce energy consumption. *PA*

Leigh Woolley

Adam Gibson

Pumphouse Point

088 C

1 Lake St Clair Road
Cumulus Studio
2014

Pumphouse Point, located just inside the Tasmanian Wilderness World Heritage Area, was originally constructed as part of Tasmania's hydroelectric scheme and has been unused for over 20 years. The redevelopment involved the adaptive reuse and refurbishment of two existing, heritage-listed, off-form concrete Art Deco buildings – the Pumphouse and the Shorehouse – into a wilderness retreat. The Pumphouse, a three-storey building originally constructed in the 1940s to house pump turbines, sits on Lake St Clair at the end of a 250-metre concrete flume which is its only connection to land. The Shorehouse, located at the start of the flume on the edge of the lake, was constructed at the same time and accommodated offices and a maintenance workshop for the turbines. Eighteen new guest suites have been inserted within the existing concrete building envelopes. Only minimal work has been done to the exterior of the buildings. This was a deliberate measure to maintain the high heritage value of the existing buildings and to emphasise the contrast between the new interiors and the exterior. The approach to the Pumphouse, surrounded by mountains and water, heightens the anticipation and sense of arrival. Guests pass through solid metal doors into the entry foyer – an intermediate zone through which guests are brought gently into the comfort of the suites from the rawness of the wilderness outside. The twelve studio-sized suites run lengthways down the two outer wings, leaving the central core devoted to communal lounge areas on each level, open at both ends so that the sight-line that begins from the flume continues through the building. *PA*

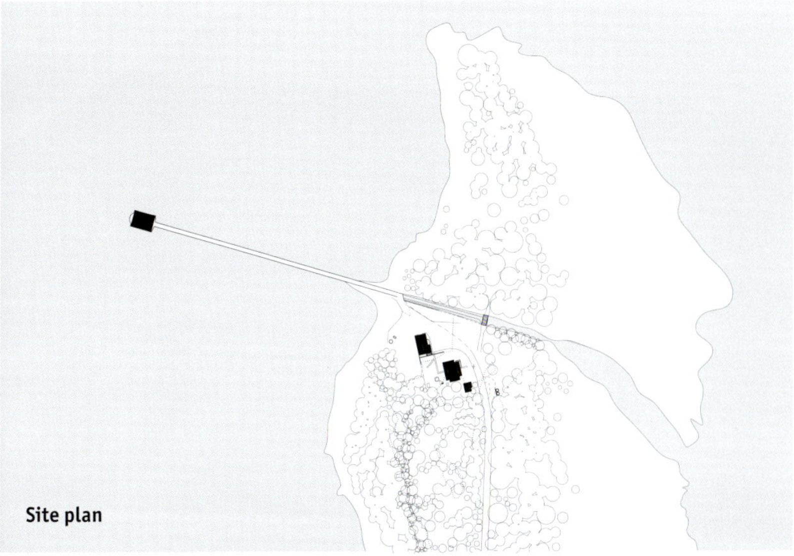

Site plan

Stuart Gibson

Devil's Corner 089 C
1 Sherbourne Rd, Apslawn
Cumulus Studio
2015

Located on the scenic drive along Tasmania's East Coast, the new Devil's Corner Cellar Door and Lookout sits within one of Tasmania's largest vineyards, with a panoramic view over the Freycinet Peninsula. Reopened in 2015, this project for Brown Brothers seeks to amplify the experience of enjoying this iconic view. Originally a small demountable building, the Cellar Door has been extended and expanded, paired with a lookout and complimentary food experiences, providing a backdrop for seasonal events. The Cellar Door and Lookout were designed as a loose collection of timber-clad buildings that, through similar aesthetic and material treatment, form a modern interpretation of traditional farm and rural settlements that gather over time. The Cellar Door and food market have been collected around a courtyard space which gives shelter and respite from the surrounding environment while allowing views through the tasting space to the Hazards beyond and access to open deck spaces. Through the careful placement of a series of timber-clad shipping containers, visitors are invited to visually explore the landscape within and around the vineyard through curated framed views. The lookout element is a critical component of the design, not only in providing a visual signifier for the settlement but also as a way of interpreting the landscape from which the Devil's Corner wines originate. In the same way that an appreciation of wine can be gained through understanding its subtleties and varying 'in-mouth' sensations, there are many ways landscape can be appreciated. The lookout plays with this idea. The three distinct spaces reference different and unique views from the site, firstly the sky, then the horizon, and lastly the tower which winds its way upward providing views to each of the compass points before culminating in an elevated and expansive view of the bay. The dynamic scenic lookout and the associated facilities draw visitors to the new upgraded cellar door for the Devil's Corner wine label. *PA*

Tanja Milbourne

Sarah Zahradnik

Sarah Zahradnik

Melbourne

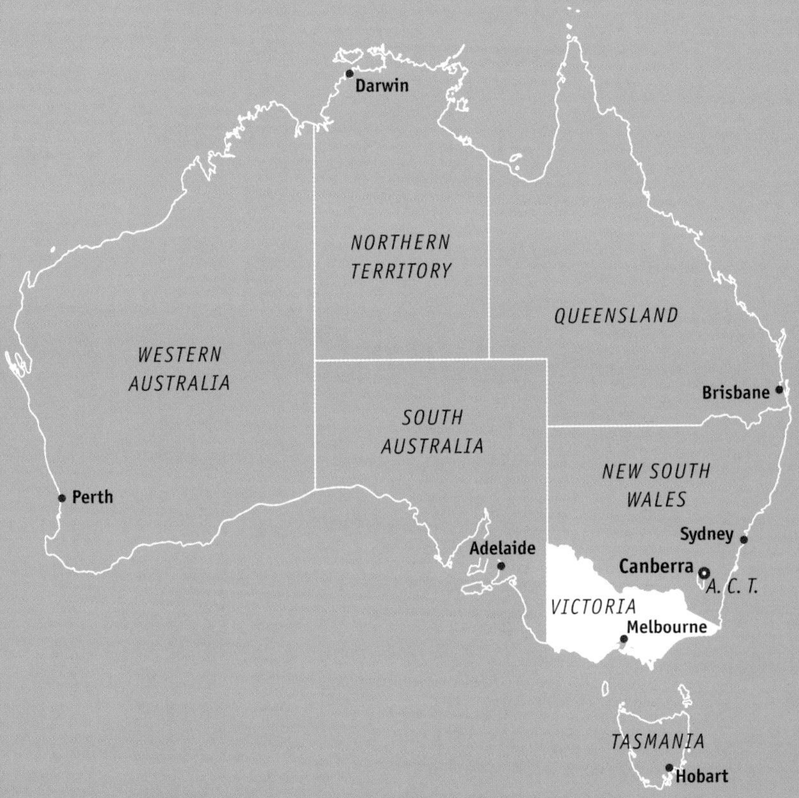
Darwin
NORTHERN TERRITORY
QUEENSLAND
WESTERN AUSTRALIA
Brisbane
SOUTH AUSTRALIA
NEW SOUTH WALES
Perth
Sydney
Adelaide
Canberra
A. C. T.
VICTORIA
Melbourne
TASMANIA
Hobart

D
Melbourne
127
113
125

D

129
111
128
124
093
097
108
107
090
115
114
095
092
103
119
091
099
102
098
101
096
112
100
121
126
110
116
109
105
106
122
104
117
131

Melbourne

Melbourne is nothing short of an international benchmark city. It has been ranked the world's most liveable city in the world seven years in a row by the Economist Intelligence Unit's Global Liveability Index, which assesses living conditions in 140 cities globally. Melbourne lives up to its reputation with its commendable social stability, healthcare, culture, environment, education, and infrastructure. The city's lively and artistic culture demonstrates a certain 'Melbourne' style owing to its art scene, sport and education, bustling laneways, street art, and of course, its enviable coffee culture. The initial inner-city street grid of Melbourne, founded in 1835, was set out by architect and surveyor Robert Russell. The surveyor Robert Hoddle later took over Russell's task and formally defined the city's generous street design, today known as the Hoddle Grid, which has grown to be a metropolis. Melbourne's convict settlement was more modest in size compared to those of other Australian cities such as Sydney and Hobart. As a result, the city's early buildings were ephemeral and unpretentious, with elements of the Georgian style. Early Victorian public buildings in Melbourne were largely built with

Nils Versemann

bluestone, a more readily available material compared to sandstone, which was more commonly used in Sydney and Hobart. The city's growth was driven by the discovery of gold and the 1893 introduction of a cable tram network, which was one of the largest in the world at that time. These milestones resulted in an increase in the city's population and wealth, and Melbourne was in fact Australia's largest city until the twentieth century. In 1916, a building height limit of 40 metres was introduced. This limit was then abolished in the 1950s, which led to the densification of the city centre and explorations of tall-building designs, an example of which is the Eureka Tower (2006), a 297-metre-tall skyscraper. Melbourne's historic architecture offers a blend of architectural styles, including Renaissance Revival, Classical, Italianate, Gothic Revival, and Federation. These days, superb contemporary buildings stand in dialogue with their historic neighbours. A perfect example is the Swanston Street and Flinders Street gateway, with great works of architecture such as the Neo-Gothic style St Paul's Cathedral adjacent to French Renaissance-inspired Flinders Station and the contemporary Federation Square. *SZ*

© David Iliff

Dave Ballell

State Library Victoria 090 D

328 Swanston St
Joseph Reed, Bates, Pebbles & Smart
1856

The heritage-listed State Library Victoria, formerly known as the Melbourne Public Library, is Australia's oldest public library and one of the first free public libraries in the world. The building sits perched on a 67-square-metre site facing the busy Swanston Street. Victorian-era architect Joseph Reed designed the dignified library in the Academic Classical style, although only the main entrance foyer and central Queen's Hall above it remain in their original forms. The library has been redeveloped many times since its completion in 1856. New wings were introduced at the southern end of the building in 1859 and northern end in 1864, which almost doubled the size of the original Queen's Hall. The building's grand stone façade, completed in 1870, features distinct Corinthian columns in its octastyle portico. The Domed Reading Room, which has a diameter of 35 metres, was built in 1913 to a design by architect Norman G. Peebles. The reading room later underwent renovations and was reopened in 2003 with the new name La Trobe Reading Room. This superb octagonal space contains an information centre, reading room, and gallery spaces. A grand marble staircase connects the foyer, the Domed Reading Room, and Queen's Hall. *SZ*

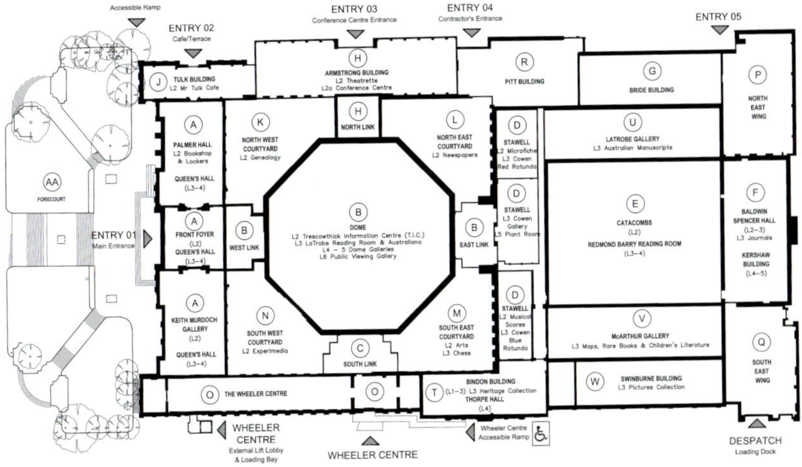

Ground Floor Plan

Overlooking the extravagant Parliament of Victoria building, which faces the intersection of Spring Street and Bourke Street

091 D

iStock (Interbober)

Old Treasury Building

091 D

20 Spring St, East Melbourne
John James Clark
1862

The Old Treasury Building, in the Renaissance Revival style, is one of the most praiseworthy examples of nineteenth century architecture in Australia. It is hard to believe that this elaborate building was designed by 19-year-old architect John James Clark, who was working for the Public Works Department. His high-quality design incorporated the classical architectural orders, the Doric, Ionic, and Corinthian. The elegant exterior is made of readily available materials: brick, sandstone in the façade, and slate in the roof. Construction was completed in 1862, but the decorative interiors, by Alexander Borthwick, weren't completed until 1872. *SZ*

Parliament of Victoria

092 D

Spring Street, East Melbourne
Charles Pasley, Peter Kerr
1858 -

The extravagant Parliament House of Victoria has faced ongoing construction since the mid 19th century. Its grand design can be credited to colonial engineer Charles Pasley, with significant help from architect Peter Kerr, who further developed Pasley's initial design. It took the Legislative Council and Legislative Assembly a mere 10 months to receive the required permit documents to begin construction. In 1856, works began on the Legislative Chambers, in the form of two free-standing, bluestone buildings with impressive classical interior decoration. The Library was built during the second stage of construction, which began in 1858. This eastern wing connected the two

Main façade of the Old Treasury Building, Melbourne. Architectural drawing: ink, pencil on tracing paper and cartridge paper

Sarah Zahradnik

legislative chamber buildings, resulting in a U-shaped floor plan. No further construction was carried out on the building until 1878, when works on the Grand Hall (now known as Queen's Hall) and Vestibule were initiated. These additions aimed to fill the empty spaces between the chambers and library. It wasn't until 1881 that works commenced on the Spring Street frontage. This western façade and colonnade, the most intricate sections of the building, were completed in 1888 after a seven-year construction period. The North Wing, a basement level, was added during the last of the 19th century construction stages beginning in 1893. Further construction continued in 1929, resulting in the North-East wing. In 2016, the contemporary office building was added to the North-East wing's rear. The overall building makes for a remarkable piece of architecture to be admired. *SZ*

Polina Yun

Royal Exhibition Building
9 Nicholson St, Carlton
Joseph Reed
1880

093 D

Sitting proud in the lush Carlton Gardens, the Royal Exhibition Building was completed in 1880 to serve as a grand exhibition space for Melbourne's first International Exhibition in the 19th century. It was Australia's first building to be included on the World Heritage list back in 2004. The magnificent structure was designed by renowned British architect Joseph Reed, who was one of Victoria's most influential architects of the Victorian era, although this particular design was evidently inspired by Gothic Revival styles. It remains functional to this day, predominantly hosting trade shows, fairs, and cultural events. The building's prestigious exterior was influenced by Byzantine, Romanesque, Lombardic, and Italian Renaissance buildings, and particularly by Brunelleschi's cathedral dome in Florence. Cladded in brick, the sandstone façade features four entrance porticoes on each side. The interior has been restored and includes lengthy central naves, large gallery spaces, lofty domes, and decorative artwork. The internal joinery was painted green, and the great dome was painted to represent the sky. The western end of the building houses the Great Hall, covering 12,000 square metres, and includes many non-permanent annexes. The building continues to be used as an exhibition hall to this day. *SZ*

iStock (sasimoto)

Stephen White

Sarah Zahradnik

Rialto Building 094 D

525 Collins St

William Pitt

1885

The enchanting heritage-listed Rialto building is a significant example of the 'Boom Style' building movement of the early 1890s. Victorian architect William Pitt's design was greatly influenced by Venetian Gothic style architecture. It was built in polychromatic red brick with decorative materials including cement, ceramic tiles, and pressed zinc. The original five-storey façade has since been integrated into a glazed atrium for the InterContinental Hotel Rialto and can be appreciated from within. The complex was further developed into a twin-tower office building, which became one of the tallest office buildings in the southern hemisphere upon its completion in 1986. Though it was once merely the frontage of a site with small warehouses, it is now the heart of Collin Street's business district. *SZ*

Richard Giles

D

Princess Theatre

095 D

163 Spring St
William Pitt, Henry White
1886, 1992

In 1886, Architect William Pitt designed the theatre, drawing from the French Second Empire style. Its symmetrical façade is made of rendered brick with a slate roof. Above, three domed pavilions are crested in iron and below a veranda cantilevers over the footpath. Its impressive interior is significant for its circular opening in the ceiling that slides to reveal an operable gabled roof that opens to the sky. New Zealand-born theatre architect, Henry White, remodelled the interior in 1922, adding a lateral vestibule space and redecorating the building in the elegant 'Adam' style. *SZ*

Sarah Zahradnik

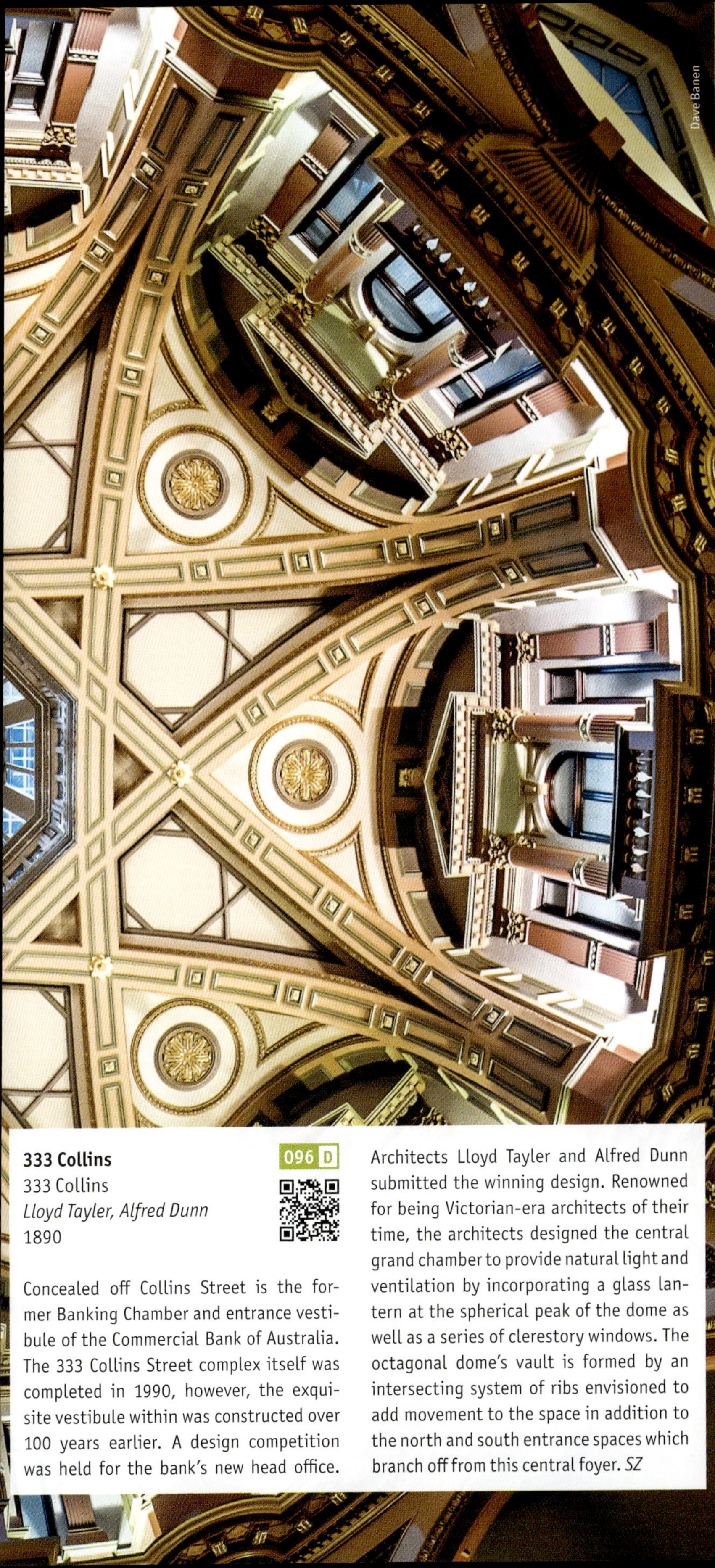

Dave Banen

D

333 Collins
333 Collins
Lloyd Tayler, Alfred Dunn
1890

096 D

Concealed off Collins Street is the former Banking Chamber and entrance vestibule of the Commercial Bank of Australia. The 333 Collins Street complex itself was completed in 1990, however, the exquisite vestibule within was constructed over 100 years earlier. A design competition was held for the bank's new head office. Architects Lloyd Tayler and Alfred Dunn submitted the winning design. Renowned for being Victorian-era architects of their time, the architects designed the central grand chamber to provide natural light and ventilation by incorporating a glass lantern at the spherical peak of the dome as well as a series of clerestory windows. The octagonal dome's vault is formed by an intersecting system of ribs envisioned to add movement to the space in addition to the north and south entrance spaces which branch off from this central foyer. *SZ*

Wikimedia Commons

State library of Victoria

The Melbourne City Baths circa 1914

Melbourne City Baths
420 Swanston St
John James Clark, E. J. Clark
1904

097 D

Located on a unique triangular site off Swanston Street is the City Baths building, one of Melbourne's most distinctive Edwardian Baroque style buildings. Public bathing establishments played a crucial role in late-nineteenth-century Melbourne, as few houses featured private bathing facilities at the time. The first municipal baths building on the site was opened in 1860. However, a design competition for a new building was held in 1903, which was won by the Victorian architect J. J. Clark and his son E. J. Clark. The public baths building was completed in 1904 and provided segregated bathing facilities for men and women. The interior includes two large swimming baths, slipper baths, spray baths, Jewish Mikveh baths, and Turkish baths. The two-storey building is built in the typical Edwardian Baroque style with red brick and cement mouldings and features arched openings and cupola-roofed belvederes. The symmetrical façade, mirror-reflected around the central entry, provides separate access for men and women. The number of clients had significantly reduced by the mid 1950s after the construction of suburban pools. There were attempts to close down and demolish the building, but the decision was eventually made to carry out major restoration works, which took place between 1981 and 1983. The additions include spas, saunas, squash courts, and a state-of-the-art gymnasium. *SZ*

Wikimedia Commons (Flekkh)

Wikimedia Commons (Donaldytong)

Sarah Zahradnik

Forum Theatre
154 Flinders St
John Eberson
1929

098 D

Situated on the corner of Flinders Street and Russel Street is the deteriorating yet awe-inspiring Forum Theatre, formerly the State Theatre, a venue for film, cabaret, comedy, and live music. The architect John Eberson designed the atmospheric theatre with a Mediterranean-style auditorium space which displays a cerulean ceiling, giving the illusion of an evening sky with artificial stars and projected floating clouds. Theatre attendance decreased in the 1960s with the advent of television, which prompted the State Theatre's split into two separate volumes. These were later opened as Forum I, downstairs, and Forum II, upstairs. The building, listed on the Historic Buildings Register, features an astonishing Moorish Revival-style exterior with a copper-domed clock tower and highly ornate decoration. *SZ*

Melbourne Town Hall
099 D

90–130 Swanston St
Reed and Barnes
1870

The Town Hall is one of Melbourne's finest examples of Victorian architecture. It is centrally located, on the corner of Collins Street and Swanston Street, and is occupied by the City of Melbourne's local government. But it also serves as a multi-use space for theatre productions, exhibitions, and school concerts. The original hall was opened in 1854 but demolished not long afterwards. Construction of the present-day town hall commenced in 1867 and was completed three years later in 1870. The architects, Reed and Barnes, won the commission after winning the design competition held for the building. Designed in the French Renaissance style, the town hall has slate mansard roofs, a rusticated bluestone plinth, Corinthian columns, pilasters, and a corner clock tower. Additions were made later, including the façade's grand entrance portico and balcony and an administration building to the north of the town hall. Another competition was held for the site of this administration building, which was erected in 1908. The architects J. J. and E. J. Clark won the commission to design the exterior. Meanwhile, the architects Grainger, Kennedy and Yulle designed the council chamber inside, incorporating abstractions of Australian flora from the Federation era. An unexpected fire in 1925 resulted in various alterations being made to the building. *SZ*

Melbourne Town Hall, circa 1910

Sarah Zahradnik

VICTORIA UNIVERSITY

QUAY WEST

Flinders Street Station

100 D

207–361 Flinders Street
Fawcett and Ashworth
1854, 1909

The marvellous Flinders Street Railway Station is the main source of the hustle and bustle on the corner of Swanston Street and Flinders Street. It was originally opened in 1854 but later reconstructed as a passengers' central station for which a design competition was held in 1899. The winning architects, James Fawcett and HPC Ashworth of Fawcett and Ashworth, named their design 'Green Light'. They drew inspiration from the French Renaissance style, incorporating a prominent green copper dome, a tall clock tower, and arched roofs over the platform. The upper levels were originally designed as a library, gym, and lecture hall, but this design intent changed when the once-dominant arched entrances at Flinders Street was lowered. A fourth storey was added to the main building along with overhead skylights to allow more natural light to enter the space. Remodelling of the beige building was completed in 1909 and the recognised heritage landmark is now the oldest train station in Australia as well as the busiest suburban railway station in the southern hemisphere. Around 1,500 trains pass through the station daily. Its main platform has a length of 708 metres and is believed to be the fourth longest railway platform in the world. *SZ*

iStock (ai_yoshi)

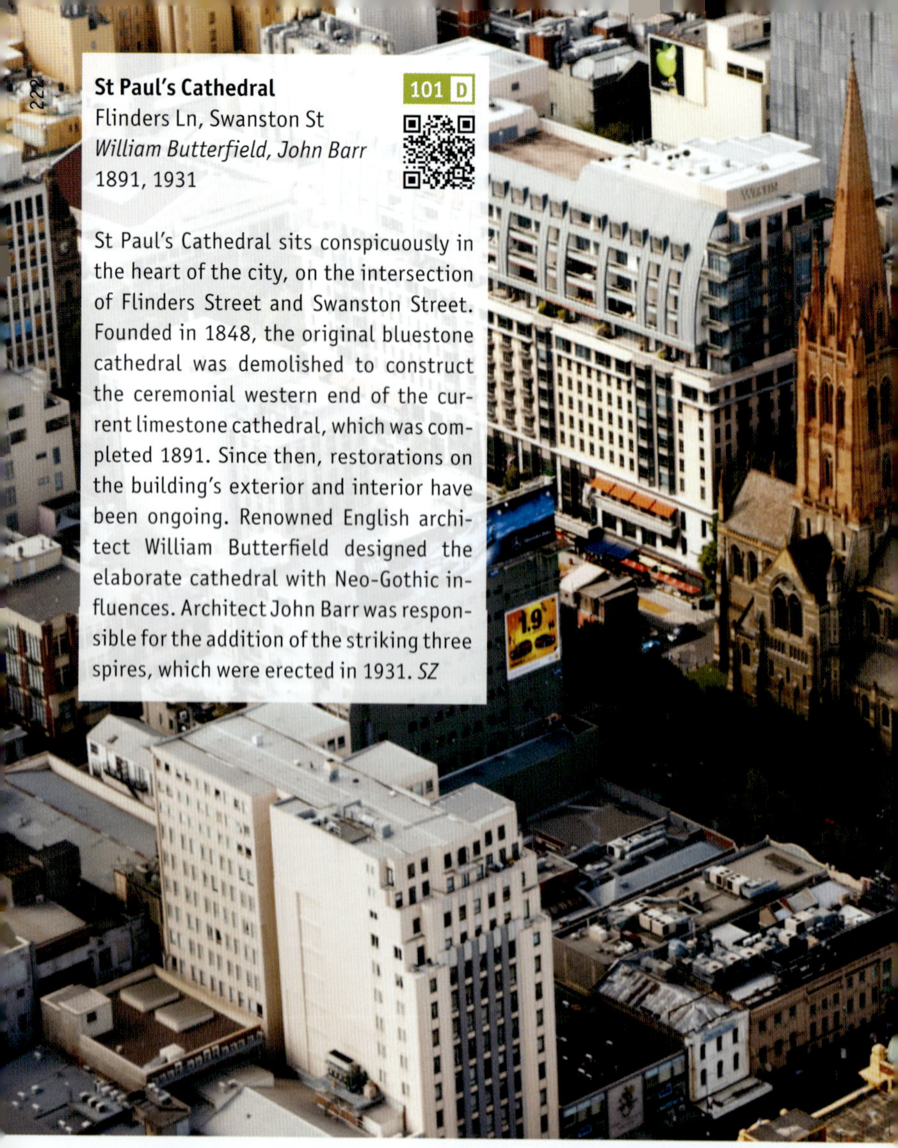

St Paul's Cathedral 101 D
Flinders Ln, Swanston St
William Butterfield, John Barr
1891, 1931

St Paul's Cathedral sits conspicuously in the heart of the city, on the intersection of Flinders Street and Swanston Street. Founded in 1848, the original bluestone cathedral was demolished to construct the ceremonial western end of the current limestone cathedral, which was completed 1891. Since then, restorations on the building's exterior and interior have been ongoing. Renowned English architect William Butterfield designed the elaborate cathedral with Neo-Gothic influences. Architect John Barr was responsible for the addition of the striking three spires, which were erected in 1931. *SZ*

» Manchester Unity Building 102 D
220 Collins St
Marcus R Barlow
1932

The magnificent Manchester Unity Building, completed in 1932, is an architectural masterpiece. It was designed by Marcus Barlow as the new headquarters of the Manchester Unity Independent Order of Odd Fellows, a non-profit friendly society. The 12-storey-tall skyscraper is a great example of the inter-war Gothic Revival and Art Deco styles and catches the eye of passers-by on the busy corner of Collins Street and Swanston Street. Its steel structure is cladded in moulded terracotta tiles supported by buttresses. The verticality is emphasised by narrow columns that step up and reach their peak at 164 metres. The interiors feature rich marble, timber, gold, and copper finishes. The lower levels house retail stores, kiosks, cafés, and commercial offices. The rooftop level includes a small outdoor terrace accessed by an intricately detailed spiral staircase and provides stunning views not only of the tower but also the city. Dental practitioner Dr Kia Pajouhesh purchased the mezzanine level in 2003 and converted the original retail spaces into dental suites. He later bought the upper levels as well as the tower, which had been redeveloped earlier to house luxury apartments. With the help of Robert Mills Architects and Andronas Conservation Architecture, he respectfully restored the building's interiors back to their original state. *SZ*

D

Matt Chan

Cameron Tout

Nick Morieson

« St Patrick's Cathedral

103 D

1 Cathedral Pl, East Melbourne
William Wardell
1858, 1868

St Patrick's Cathedral is the mother church of the Roman Catholic Archdiocese and sits on an east-west axis on a corner site of Eastern Hill. It is the largest cathedral in Australia and a prime example of Gothic Revival architecture. Remnants of the original 1858 cathedral have been incorporated into the south aisle of the current bluestone and sandstone structure completed in 1868. Influenced by the Gothic Revival style, William Wardell designed the cathedral's floor plan in the shape of a cross with a central nave linked to side aisles and two bell towers at its main entrance. The altar was traditionally built at the eastern end to symbolise belief in the resurrection of Christ. *SZ*

Shrine of Remembrance 104 D

Birdwood Avenue
Philip Burgoyne Hudson, James Hastie Wardrop (1934), ARM Architecture (2003)
1934, 2003

The Shrine of Remembrance war memorial sits prominently in the Kings Domain parklands. It was built in 1934 and soon became the city's most important public monument offering a place to remember those who served in the First World War. It is the largest monument of its kind in Australia and annually hosts national ceremonies such as Anzac Day and Remembrance Day. A national design competition was held, which was won by Phillip Hudson and James Wardrop, Australian architects and veterans of the war. This remarkable example of neo-classical architecture with its colonnade at the main entrance was inspired by the Mausoleum at Halicarnassus in Turkey. ARM Architecture and landscape architects Rush\Wright associates later developed the undercroft, incorporating two courtyard spaces to complete the original masterplan which called for axial symmetry. The undercroft provides space for exhibitions, galleries, and educational purposes. Hanging over an amphitheatre in one of the courtyards is an impressive steel-and-cloth poppy-shaped canopy. *SZ*

Daniel Sallai

Holden Centre

105 D

10–30 Olympic Boulevard
Kevin Borland, Peter Mcintyre, John & Phyllis Murphy
1956

The design was selected in a competition held in 1952 for the Olympic Swimming Stadium. The winning design features steel rods that support a V-shaped trussed structure on either side. The building bears close structural resemblance to the nearby Sidney Myer Music Bowl. Completed in 1956, the venue's pool was later filled in after the pool tank ceased to function due to unstable ground conditions. In 1980, the building was transformed into a performance venue by architects Borland Brown. Since 1999, it has been used as a sports centre and is today home to the Collingwood Football Club – the almighty Magpies. *SZ*

Sidney Myer Music Bowl

106 D

Kings Domain Gardens
Yuncken Freeman Ltd., Griffiths and Simpson, Gregory Burgess
1959, 2001

Nestled within the Kings Domain Gardens, the heritage-listed multi-purpose outdoor venue sits within the entertainment precinct in close proximity to the Arts Centre and the National Art Gallery. The venue, named after the Australian entrepreneur Sidney Myer, was opened in 1959. Melbourne architect Barry Patten from Yuncken Freeman, one of Australia's leading architectural firms, designed this open-air amphitheatre, integrating it into the natural slopes of its landscape setting. Its fascinating tent-like canopy is made of aluminium-faced plywood supported by steel cables and masts. Gregory Burgess Architects later extensively redeveloped the original facilities, and the revamped venue was reopened in 2001. *SZ*

⌃ Storey Hall, RMIT University 107 D

336–348 Swanston St
Tappin, Gilbert and Dennehy (1887)
ARM Architecture, Allom Lovell
1887, 1959, 1995

Built in 1887 during a time of social and political protest, the Storey Hall building played an important role as a place of feminist debate and Catholic activism. The colourful green-and-purple entrance, unmissable from Swanston Street, extends to the adjoining Building 22. The design for its entrance was inspired by the amethyst geode crystal, and it has been said that the building's colour palette is a reference to a former feminist organisation's purple, white, and green flag. ARM Architects, graduates of RMIT University, redeveloped the interior to accommodate a 230-seat lecture theatre, seminar rooms, exhibition and conference spaces, a gallery, a café, and commercial catering facilities. *SZ*

» Building 8, RMIT University 108 D

360 Swanston St
Edmond and Corrigan, Demaine
1993

The abstract Building 8 is home to RMIT's library and School of Architecture and Design. The postmodern educational building has won numerous awards since its completion in 1993. Melbourne-based architects Edmond and Corrigan in association with Demaine intended to interrupt the continuity of the city streetscape with bold and detailed fragmented elements. The nine-storey-high façade features a diverse mix of brightly coloured stones and mosaics, exposed services, polychromatic brickwork, and protruding, gold-framed, gothic-style windows. The liveliness of the exterior is carried through into the interior of the rectangular floor plan which has been functionally designed with double- and triple-height ceilings. *SZ*

Sarah Zahradnik

Sarah Zahradnik

≈ National Gallery of Victoria 109 D

180 St Kilda Rd, Southbank
Roy Grounds (1968), Mario Bellini (2003)
1968

The statuesque heritage-listed National Gallery of Victoria (NGV) is Australia's oldest and largest art museum. It was opened in 1968, as part of the first stage of executing the masterplan for the Arts Centre Melbourne. Originally designed by Roy Grounds, it was later redeveloped by Mario Bellini. The building's rectangular form is cladded in bluestone and is topped by upturned eaves. A moat wraps around the entire building at its base. A large arched entrance frames a wall with a water feature intended to serve as a barrier from the chaotic city. The water wall is completely environmentally sustainable, reusing recycled rainwater. The interior features three courtyard spaces with a stained-glass ceiling by artist Leonard French. *SZ*

flickr (Tama Leaver)

Arts Centre Melbourne/ Spire and Hamer Hall

110 D

100 St Kilda Rd
Roy Grounds, John Truscott
1982, 1984

The heritage-listed Arts Centre Melbourne masterplan was designed by Sir Roy Grounds in 1960 and consists of Hamer Hall, a concert hall, and the Theatres Building, under an iconic spire. Both sit close to the Yarra River. Hamer Hall, the Theatres Building, and the National Gallery of Victoria are all connected by a covered porch. The concert hall and theatre building were originally intended to sit below ground level but ended up sitting prominently at street level for structural reasons. Hamer Hall was completed in 1982, and its cylindrical form is made of precast panels with a faceted cave interior serving as the concert hall. The Theatre Building's spire sits above its concrete plinth and is a cultural icon in Melbourne, visible throughout the city and emphasised at night by lighting. Completed in 1984, its open lattice space frame is surrounded by striking gold-coloured webbing at its circular base. The upper section of the spire, originally 115 metres tall, began to deteriorate, resulting in its reconstruction. It now stands even taller, with a height of 162 metres. *SZ*

flickr (Pascal)

Sarah Zahradnik

Sarah Zahradnik

The concrete-cladded fort of Hamer Hall from a distance

Richard Glover

Melbourne Museum 111 D

11 Nicholson St, Carlton

Denton Corker Marshall

1996

Denton Corker Marshall won the international competition to design a new campus for the Museum of Victoria. Now known as 'Melbourne Museum', it is the largest museum in the southern hemisphere and Victoria's most important cultural institution. Located on an extremely sensitive site, adjacent to the World Heritage-listed 1880s Royal Exhibition Building, the response demanded a building that would not overpower its older neighbour, but one that still had a presence in its own right. The brief called for 'a campus of elements', rather than a singular monumental object. As such, all the elements are grouped around the north/south extension of the park and the Royal Exhibition Building. The Forest Gallery, a large lightweight enclosure housing trees, birds and fish, waterfalls, and other elements of a Victorian temperate forest, forms the centre-point of this axis. The distinctive blade roof at the rear of the museum is an architectural response to the dome on the Royal Exhibition Building – a complementary iconic skyline element. The canopy that slopes down towards the centre, another eye-catching element, serves to draw visitors from the streets on either side of the site. The plan groups various architectural elements beneath an enveloping and controlling grid framework. This volumetric framework is significant because it allows the complex to be read as a unified campus of interconnected facilities with distinguishable characters and functions. *PA*

Richard Glover

Richard Glover

Aerial view over Melbourne's Central Business District (CBD) with St Paul's Cathedral to the bottom left and Federation Square in the centre alongside the Yarra River

Wade Tregaskis

Federation Square 112 D

Corner Swanston St & Flinders St

Lab Architecture Studio, Bates Smart

2002

Federation Square is Melbourne's most used public square. It stretches over an area of 38,000 square metres and sits among landmark buildings such as Flinders Street Station and St Paul's Cathedral. This site marks the place that the Kulin confederacy of Aboriginal people have called home for thousands of years. Aboriginal clans occupied the land even after European settlement. Plans to build a new complex on this site began in 1996, with a view to opening the new space in time for the centenary of Australia's Federation in 2001. The aim was to establish a 'civic and cultural' space of identity that would connect the city's edge with the neighbouring Yarra River. An international design competition was held in 1996 for which the winners, a joint venture collaboration between London-based architects Lab Architecture Studio and local firm Bates Smart, were to include cultural and commercial buildings and an open amphitheatre with the capacity to seat up to 15,000 people. The buildings are built from the same sandstone, zinc, and glass materials and feature a tessellated façade design based on triangular glass elements. This space, which has won numerous awards, attracts millions of visitors annually and is not to be missed. *SZ*

flickr (Ted_Travis)

iStock (fotofritz16)

Federation Square with Flinders Street Station and Eureka Tower in the back

John Gollings

Derek Swalwell

«≈ National Australia Bank

113 D

700 Bourke St, Docklands
BVN Architects
2004

The National Australia Bank building sets a benchmark in the design of workplaces. Designed from the inside out, the project is an integrated fit-out with a tailor-made base building. The building embodies the premise that people are a corporation's greatest asset and reflects the company's move towards a more collaborative, people-focused model. The development represents a number of sustainable advances in energy use, materials choice, and internal environments. The striking multi-coloured exterior ensures significant presence in the Docklands precinct. Its horizontal shape is the opposite of the traditional skyscraper, providing flexibility and requiring less energy to build, run, and maintain. The interior reflects a new way of thinking about office layouts. Atria, flooded by natural light, separate the two main building blocks. Large open-floor plates with attached service cores provide flexibility for future change in work patterns and office arrangements. Bridges and stairs enable staff to move between floors, and a range of meeting spaces increase opportunities to interact. *PA*

QV

114 D

Swanston St & Lonsdale St
NH Architecture
2004

QV is an urban village occupying an entire block in the heart of Melbourne. It stitches the city's 19th century urban fabric back into the contemporary central grid with new laneways and spaces becoming part of 'public' Melbourne's collective network of lanes and arcades. The site represents a rethink of shopping as a primary element of urban activity. The prevailing doctrine for major retailers entails a big box, small doors, and no windows, offering only an occasional public gesture. QV resists the certainty of this typology, focusing instead on generating a sense of urban diversity and integration. This usually takes time to accumulate. As such, the project engages with the city fabric and its laneways, generating an urban form which rescales the site from a monolithic city block to a series of buildings separated by public space. Rather than creating an object for the city, it defines a precinct within the city. Layered onto this strategy is a re-evaluation of how multiple programmes can infiltrate the city without the usual commercial sterilisation. *PA*

» Melbourne Central
115 D

La Trobe St & Swanston St
Kisho Kurokawa, Bates Smart (1983–92)
ARM Architecture (2001)
1983, 2001

The revolutionary design of Melbourne Central's retail complex is an amalgamation of the 1890 industrial shot tower and factory with the distinctive cone-shaped dome. This heavily photographed signature dome structure was designed by architect Kisho Kurokawa in collaboration with Bates Smart McCutcheon. ARM Architecture contributed to the redevelopment of the retail complex's functionalism, connecting retail, commercial, and the train station railway through a series of 17 interconnected laneways which allow the public to move in and out as well as through the building with ease. *SZ*

» Eureka Tower
116 D

7 Riverside Quay, Southbank
Fender Katsalidis Architects
2006

The Eureka Tower is Melbourne's tallest skyscraper, stretching high above the city's skyline. Melbourne-based firm Fender Katsalidis Architects designed the 297-metre-high tower, alluding to the Victorian gold rush of 1854 with its name and its distinctive 24-carat-gold-plated glass at the top ten levels. Since its completion, the tower has been most famous for its skydeck, an 'edge experience' created by an extended glass cube that cantilevers almost 300 metres high. It is the highest public observation deck in the southern hemisphere. Throngs of visitors queue up waiting their turn to see the city's panoramic views from this altitude. *SZ*

116 Eureka Tower

101 St Paul's Cathedral
112 Federation Square
John Gollings

Melbourne Grammar School

117 D

355 St Kilda Rd
John Wardle Architects
2007

The Melbourne Grammar School, founded in 1858, is also known as the Nigel Peck Centre for Learning & Leadership. Located very close to the government facilities of Victoria's capital city, it is in the ideal place for a centre dedicated to training talented young minds. The building is at the threshold between the city centre and the historically significant and charming environs of the Royal Botanic Gardens. The project, completed in 2007, was an extension of the school's old Victorian building, and a quick glance at the new building's exterior and placement already gives a sense of the boldness of the new design. The new building complements the old structure, creating a learning campus that shields the existing three-wing facility from the main street. The new building, with its prestigious stairway, library facilities, lecture hall, and seminar rooms, is presented on the street side as a series of conjoined pavilions. A curtain wall shows the new growing out of the old. The juxtaposition is clear, even though the two architectures do not come in direct contact. The annex represents a sophisticated nod to the past. With its sequence of pavilions with giant windows in different shapes, the building manages to give a sense of coherence and change in equal measure. The frosted windows of the library reading rooms feature gossamer-like flower patterns that give the students inside privacy. From the outside, the interior exudes an impressive appearance, while from the inside, the various windows offer views of the historical garden to the rear of the building. The students sit on the street side in the elegant library reading rooms, as if in an oversized showcase window. Passersby on the main street can get a glimpse of the school life taking place inside, while students can learn in an environment that is visually connected to its surroundings. The new building thrives on these reciprocal visual and historical references to the campus: the main library surrounds a huge old elm tree, while a glazed administrative building section serves as a counterpart to the brick-clad library, which, with its book-like layered and polished bricks lends a down-to-earth gravity to the building's openness. *DP*

Peter Hyatt

118 Melbourne Convention Centre

Peter Bennetts

Peter Bennetts

Peter Bennetts

Melbourne Convention Centre

118 D

1 Convention Centre Pl
NH Architecture, Woods Bagot
2009

This Public Private Partnership (PPP) project for the Victorian Government is the first convention centre in the world to be awarded a six-star Green Star environmental rating. NH Architecture, in joint venture with Woods Bagot, aimed to create a public building that belongs to Melbourne, rather than the typical convention-centre stereotype. The triangular design of the new Melbourne Convention Centre gives the cityscape a new feature on the banks of the Yarra River. The distinctive 18-metre-high glass façade gives passers-by a glimpse of the activity within the centre and creates a foyer full of natural light as well as offering views out across the Yarra River to the city beyond. The team also met the challenge of integrating the new centre with the existing Exhibition Centre, while attempting to create a building with its own distinct identity. The two buildings are linked via an enclosed glass walkway, becoming the largest exhibition and convention facility in the southern hemisphere. The roof, with a total area of 20,000 square metres, is a vast, seamless expanse, and its exciting geometry makes for spectacular angles and sweeping planes from any vantage point. *PA*

Peter Bennetts

A willingness to take intellectual risks

Hamish Lyon

Hamish Lyon is Director of Architecture and Design at NH Architecture, where he leads the firm's design thinking and direction. A co-founder of the practice, he is responsible for coordinating the design continuity of the NH studio. He has led several of NH's most significant projects including the ground-breaking QV, Melbourne Convention Centre, Margaret Court Arena, and the masterplan for Melbourne and Olympic Parks. Early in his architectural career, he won the national Robin Boyd Medal, awarded under the chairmanship of pre-eminent Australian architect Glenn Murcutt. He actively engages in the public conversation about architecture through his teaching and writing for design journals.

What differentiates architecture in Australia from international architecture?

Australia is a vast continent with a relatively small but growing population, so there is an ever-growing number opportunities for architects and designers – we're always building. With Australia's geographic remoteness from the powerhouses of Europe and North America and our emerging relationship with Asia, Australian architecture has begun to develop a new and dynamic design culture. Equally, Australian architecture responds to a wide range of climatic conditions, from arid deserts to tropical rainforests and temperate coastlines through to southern exposure to Antarctica. This spectrum of context and place allows architecture in Australia to explore a great variety of design ideas and outcomes.

What role do current architectural trends play in your design approach?

We tend to be wary of short-lived trends. Instead we prefer to directly engage with the life of the city and the re-emerging interest in the public realm. We research how people interact with their surroundings and their emotional responses to place. We are also interested in the latest developments in materials and building techniques. Given the rapid development of digital platforms with the capability to fabricate building elements, such as 3D printing, we are keen to see how design thinking can play a part in this ongoing story.

Where do you find your design inspiration?

From anywhere and everywhere! We look to science, the arts, popular culture, as well as first principles research. We also seek to combine inspiration with constant practice. We need to continually exercise our skills in order to maintain inspiration and quality. At a formal level we're interested in the compositional aspect of geometry. Each project's geometry remains a key to the NH way of thinking as both a design generator and design development technique.

Which Australian buildings do you most admire and why?

I'm drawn to the optimism of the 'golden age' of post-war modernism and the refounding of Australian culture through figures such as Robin Boyd along with a number of his contemporaries. As for unique buildings, I admire Bates Smart McCutcheon's ICI House which was Melbourne's first 19-storey skyscraper (1955) and one of Australia's most significant buildings in the International Style. Similarly, Melbourne's 1956 Olympic Pool was another symbol of international optimism in the 1950s, designed by Kevin Borland, Peter McIntyre, and John and Phyllis Murphy. Finally, Sir Roy Grounds' National Gallery of Victoria (1968) was seminal in announcing Melbourne to the international arts community.

What could the rest of the world learn from Australian architecture?

At its best, Australian architecture leads the world by its willingness to take intellectual and conceptual risks. This is further revealed by our evolving building technologies and project procurement models.

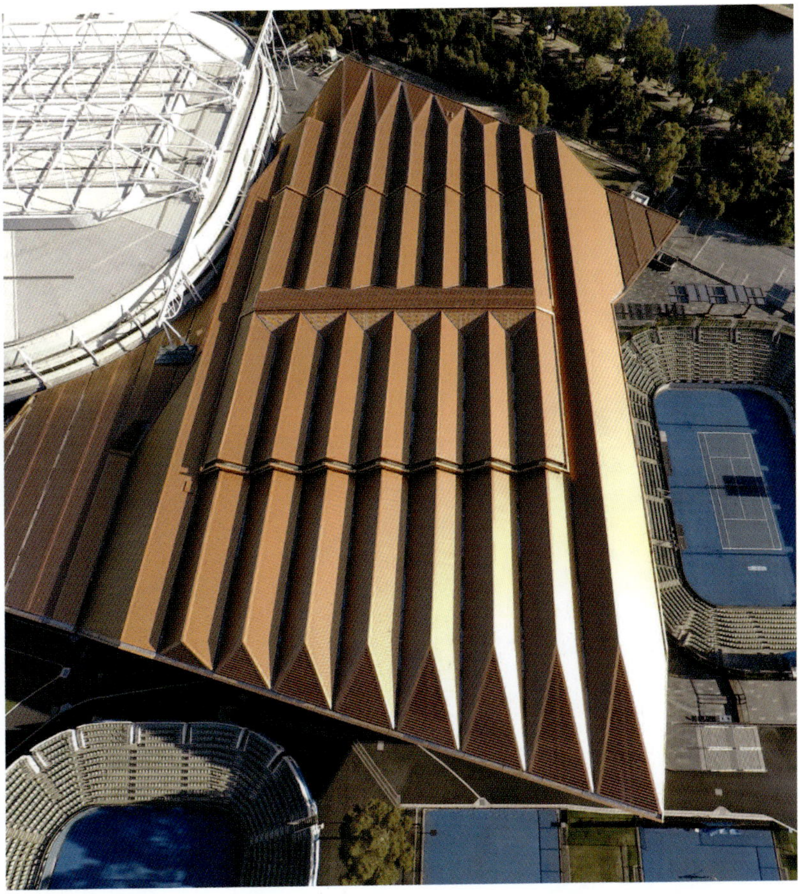

Peter Bennetts

Margaret Court Arena's exquisite, large, copper-penny-coloured roof in all its glory

John Gollings

Myer Bourke Street Redevelopment

119 D

314–336 Bourke St
NH Architecture
2010

In 2007, NH Architecture, with its client Colonial First State Global Asset Management, won the commission to rejuvenate Myer's flagship Bourke Street store. The concept for the redevelopment was driven by bold ideas. The aim was to set new standards in department store design, implement environmentally sustainable initiatives, and create an architectural work that would join the ranks of Melbourne's greatest designs. The most striking emblem of Myer's new face to the city is the faceted golden roof: it defines a new upper-level event space, a destination within a destination. It is a hub of calendar events: launches, shows, exhibitions, and dining. The crystalline form of the pavilion roof has been architecturally sculpted with gold metal and glass to choreograph certain city views from within the space and to bring the cityscape of Melbourne into the heart of the store. The rooftop space is accessed via a dramatic six-level atrium. This inclined and tapering atrium is first visible from the centre of the store's ground floor. The eye is led upwards through a visually and spatially dynamic volume to a large skylight bringing daylight into the depths of the store. The project was also an opportunity to restore the significant heritage components of the original store, including the 1920s Art Deco façade on the Bourke Street Mall, and the famous Mural Hall. The Little Bourke Street façade has been completely rebuilt as a contemporary counterpoint to the southern façade. The distinctive harlequin pattern across the façade is a geometric interpretation of the Art Deco motifs found in the old store. The redevelopment of Myer's city store represents a vision of a contemporary department store for a new generation of Melbournians and ensures it will continue to be a contributor to the life and times of the city. *PA*

Dianna Snape

John Gollings

The Yardmaster's Building

120 D

163-235 Spencer St, Docklands
McBride Charles Ryan
2009

Located in a gravel-surfaced shunting yard in the Melbourne's docklands, this four-storey, multi-purpose building houses the offices of the shunting, signalling, and locomotive controllers, as well as track management and lift and building technology. It had become outdated over the years, and was redeveloped as part of a project that was completed in 2009. Although not accessible to the public, its location makes it widely visible as an elegantly proportioned jewel box contrasting starkly with its no-man's-land surroundings. The building's double-sided concrete shell is covered in geometric incisions resembling paper cuts and a grid of polished flower patterns that creates an attractive façade and drastically reduces its energy consumption. The patterns are inset into the outer layer like polished reliefs. The slabs were made using several processes which had never been carried out before; they make the building hugely attractive, not least because its appearance changes constantly with the weather, and also make it easy to heat. The windows are sealed to keep out dust and smoke, and the simple, almost minimalist interior is designed for easy reconfiguration. *DP*

NATIONAL SPORTS MUSEUM

D

« Melbourne Cricket Ground 121 D

Brunton Ave, Richmond
Populous, Jackson Architecture, Hassell, Cox Architects, Tompkins Shaw and Evans
1854, 2005

The Melbourne Cricket Ground, more commonly referred to as the MCG, sits within Melbourne's Sports and Entertainment Precinct and is one of the largest sporting grounds in the southern hemisphere with a seating capacity of up to 100,000 spectators even though its first grandstand could only accommodate 6000. The stadium has gone through numerous alterations since it was originally opened in 1854. Most recently, around 60 per cent of the stadium was most redeveloped in preparation for the 2006 Commonwealth Games. This introduced three grand atrium entrances and a skeletal structure made of stainless-steel rods which support the glazed façade. *SZ*

≈ AAMI Park 122 D

Olympic Boulevard
Cox Architecture
2010

The groundbreaking design for AAMI Park, also known as Melbourne Rectangular Stadium, won the 2011 National Award for Public Architecture. It is integrated into its surrounding landscape, blurring the line between multi-code sports stadium and public streetscape. Its extravagant roof structure is constructed of lightweight steel with individual bioframe shells in unique positions. The façade is cladded in several triangular panels made of glass, metal, and louvres. This dome-like coverage encases the seating area, allowing for optimal coverage and a seating capacity of up to 30,000 spectators, bringing them closer to the action with uninterrupted views. *SZ*

Lemur Exhibit, Melbourne Zoo

123 D

Elliott Ave, Parkville
OLA Architecture Studio
2013

Lemur Island is a treat for all visitors to the oldest zoo in Australia, the Royal Melbourne Zoological Gardens. It offers a close encounter with the lively animals without the distraction of stanchions or nets. The walk-through enclosure of the ring-tailed lemurs, a subspecies of lemurs – which are only found in Madagascar – makes it possible to come closer than ever before to the little monkeys with the comical ringed tails and striking black and white faces. The adventure begins with a passage through a funnel-shaped tunnel made of rattan wickerwork with an unforgettable main path leading to the island. Visitors at this point only have a vague notion of what awaits them. The main path leads through a lock directly into the ring-tailed lemur habitat with a waterway running through it. A slightly raised wooden walkway meandering through the enclosure begins on the ground and leads in stages to the level on which the so-called tree house is located. Since ring-tailed lemurs are active during the day and spend much time on the ground, visitors have many opportunities to interact with the animals during their walk through the enclosure. Ring-tailed lemurs are highly sociable, living in large matriarchal groups and communicating with the aid of smell, body language, and an entire repertoire of sounds. On cooler days they spend much time sunbathing, assuming a yoga-like sitting posture with their upper bodies upright, legs spread, and arms resting on their upper thighs to expose their stomach to the warm rays of the sun. The tree house rounds off the facility. It is made of rows of 'rattan husks' nestled into each other. Although they all have the same geometric structure, no two look alike. This is a protected space, separated by a lock. Daylight is gently filtered by wickerwork, and the threats posed by modern industrialisation to tropical rainforests are presented in the form of prints and large-format photos along with interesting scientific information about the lemurs. The current mining of coltan, an ore used in the manufacture of mobile phones, poses a major threat to the natural habitat of the more than 100 different lemur species in Madagascar. The Melbourne Zoo is therefore taking part in a mobile phone-recycling programme in order to stem the continued destruction of the rain forest. With Lemur Island, the zoo also aims to give children and youth a look into the real world beyond the digital world available through their phones and computer screens. The form of the outdoor enclosure was inspired by nature, with onion-like tree houses and trumpet-shaped rattan pipes. Two striking structural interventions lend an architectural accent to the tour. The first is the lock-like access from the main path and the second is the exhibition pavilion standing on stilts in the form of a tree house. The tree house opens like a box theatre to the 'stage', offering a protected space with a lookout post. *NM*

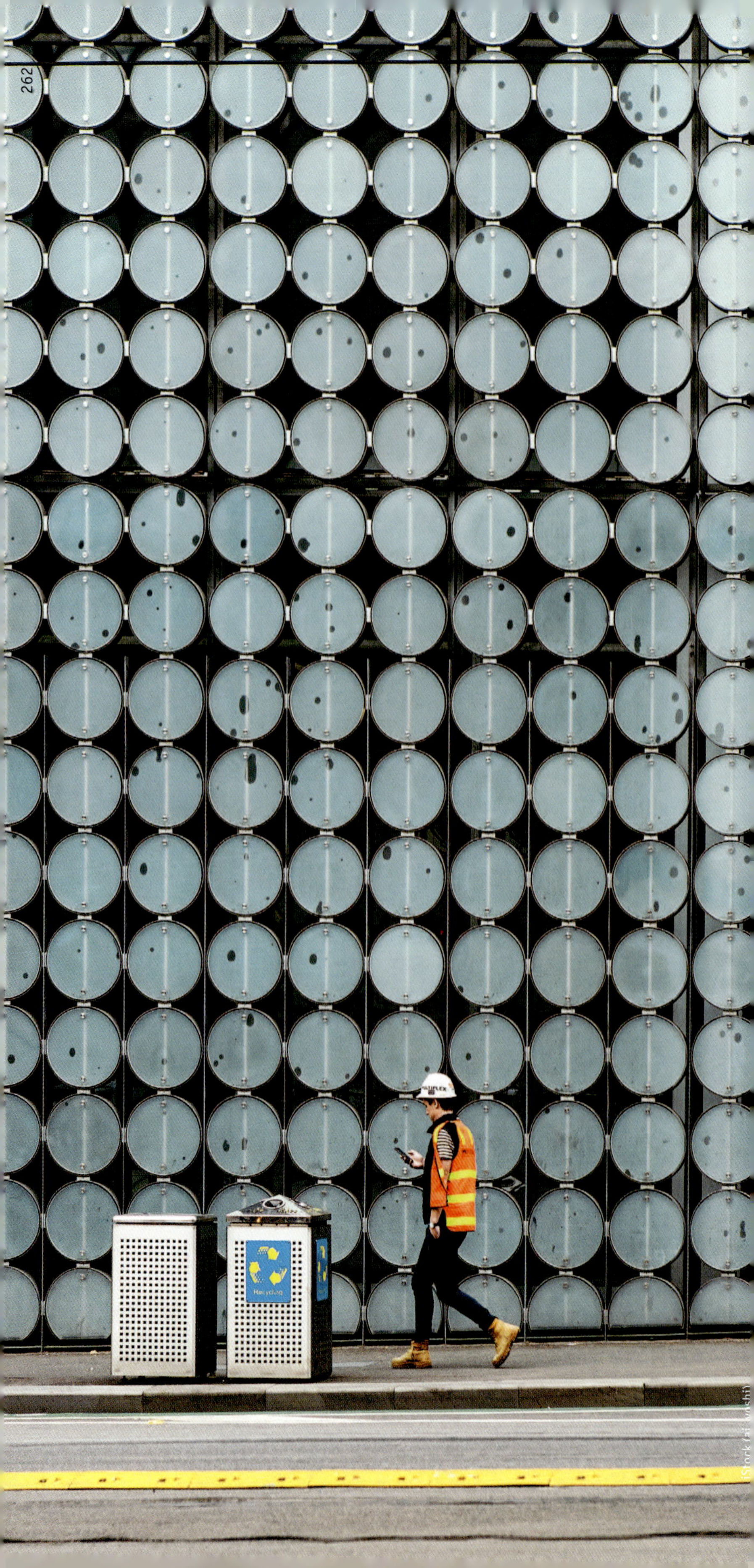

iStock/ai_yoshi

« RMIT Design Hub

124 D

130, Victoria St
Promenade, Docklands
Sean Godsell Architects
2012

Behind the disc-covered façades of the RMIT Design Hub are spaces for interdisciplinary research, workshops, exhibitions, events, and a design archive. The outer skin of the university building is made up of more than 17,000 sandblasted glass discs, each 60 centimetres in diameter, which, as part of an automated system, adjust their angle to shade the interiors from the sun. The façades house environmentally friendly elements: photovoltaic cells are included and replaceable, so there is the potential for upgrades and student experimentation as solar technology evolves. Part of a double-glazed inner skin, air intakes and fine mist sprinklers cool the underfloor air distribution system and improve the air quality indoors, while saving on energy costs. As an essential task for the RMIT Design Hub was to encourage interaction between the post-graduate researchers based there, its interiors are adaptable and teams can modify the open-plan 'warehouses' to meet their needs. The architects made the internal spaces suitable for incidental meetings, and the public areas – such as the exhibition space, café, and design archive – provide other platforms for exchange. *DP*

Dianna Snape

˄ Library at the Dock

125 D

107 Victoria Harbour
Promenade, Docklands
Clare Design, Hayball Architects
2014

The Library at The Dock is a multi-award-winning interactive learning environment combining traditional library collections with a ground-floor café, multipurpose community spaces, a 120-seat performance venue, rehearsal and recording spaces, a gallery, meeting rooms, and quiet study areas inside and out. The building maximises views from Buluk Park through to the water and vice versa through openness and transparency. Its construction on a 75-year-old heritage wharf was possible through the use of cross-laminated timber (CLT), which is 30 per cent lighter than comparable building materials. It was the second building in Australia to use this material and the first building to be awarded a six-star Green Star rating under the public buildings pilot tool from the Green Building Council of Australia. While the wharf forms the building's sub-structure, columns and beams are made from glulam, and upper floors, roof slabs, and structural walls from CLT. Solar roof-panels supply approximately 30 per cent of the building's total operational power. Mechanical operable louvres on all four sides allow the building to be opened to the elements in favourable conditions. *PA*

Margaret Court Arena Redevelopment (Evonne Goolagong Arena)

126 D

Olympic Boulevard
Populous, NH Architecture
2014

Sports architecture has traditionally occupied a territory that drifts between engineering and industrial sheds. The dominant aesthetic is usually composed from steel trusses, generic concourses, and an international language that is repeated elsewhere and everywhere. The ambition for the redevelopment of the existing Margaret Court Arena was to counterpoint to this 'Brutus Maximus' sports style. The aim was to create a civic landmark that belongs to the legacy of Melbourne's public buildings dotted along the Yarra River: the 1956 Olympic Swimming Pool, the Myer Music Bowl, the Victorian Arts Centre, and more recently Federation Square. It was also driven by the desire to ensure the venue maintains the Australian Open's place at the forefront of world tennis and for the arena to host a range of premier concerts and public occasions. The transformed Margaret Court Arena features an additional 1,500 seats, the world's fastest retractable roof, and new enclosed concourse areas that enjoy spectacular outlooks not just to the precinct's tennis courts facilities, but also to the river, parks, and the Melbourne city skyline. Responding to its prominent riveredge location, the transparent outer skin of the building allows the inner timberclad arena to be on show throughout the Melbourne Park precinct. This connection is further reinforced by the large copper-penny-coloured roof that reflects the materiality of the Yarra's existing public buildings: patina copper, black zinc, Kimberley sandstone, concrete, and polished stainless steel. The big roof generates large overhanging canopies that fold down to pedestrian level and affords patrons and visitors respite shade from the extremes of the Australian Open's summer and protection from Melbourne's famous 'four seasons in one day'. The pleated roof is also a response to the global influence of the 'virtual visitors' who access the venue via the image broadcast by the ever-present sky chopper. *PA*

Peter Bennetts

Peter Bennetts

Medibank HQ
720 Bourke St
Hassell
2014

127 D

This building, completed in Melbourne's Docklands in 2014, serves as the headquarters of Medibank, Australia's largest health insurer. The company wished to promote better health for everyone, including its employees, and this aspiration led to the creation of one of the healthiest workplaces in the world. Medibank's people can now select from more than 26 types of work settings, ranging from indoor quiet spaces and collaborative hubs to WIFI-enabled balconies and places to stand and work. Employees who want a more vigorous workout during the day can make use of a multipurpose sports court at ground level. Adjacent to the sports court, an edible garden sits near a demonstration kitchen that Medibank uses to promote healthy eating to both staff, not-for-profit organisations, and the wider community. Within the workplace, plants help relieve stress, improve internal air quality, and transform views from grey to green. With around 10 per cent of the building's exterior covered by native Australian plants, it's a 'living, breathing building'. More than just a building, Medibank Place is a gateway to Melbourne's Docklands precinct. It succeeds in 'giving something back' to its surrounding community by creating a welcoming public precinct at ground level with a timber amphitheatre, cafés, shops, and a public park. *PA*

Earl Carter

Earl Carter

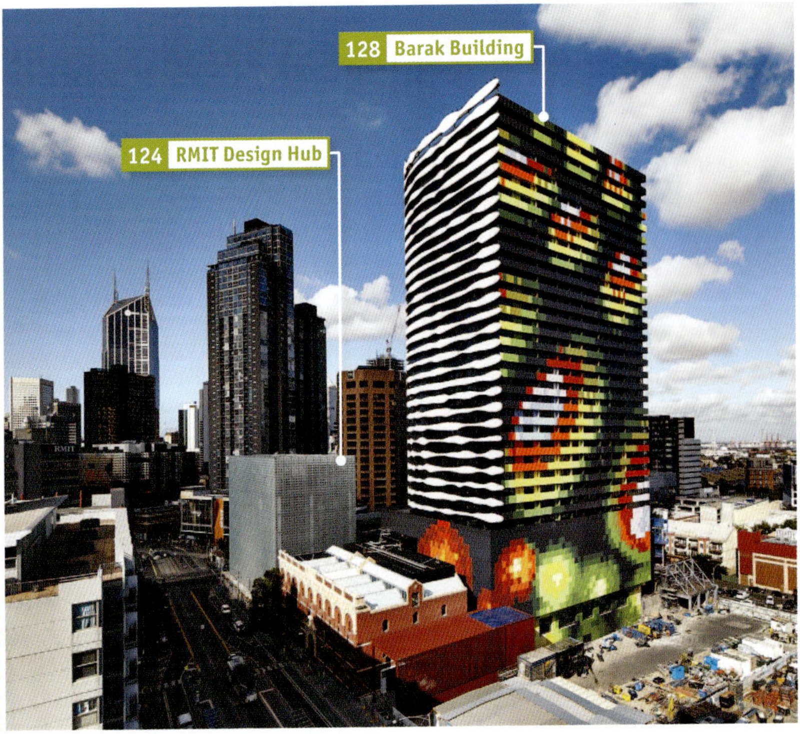

ARM Architecture

John Gollings

Barak Building

128 D

551 Swanston St
ARM Architecture
2015

The 85-metre-high portrait of the last traditional elder of the Wurundjeri Aboriginal community, William Barak, on one façade of this building is created through white panels on black balcony slabs. At 32 stories, and with other bold facades, the building is a prominent feature – and mark of recognition – in Melbourne. *DP*

ARM Architecture

Melbourne School of Design

129 D

Masson Rd, Parkville
John Wardle Architects, NADAAA
2014

This building for the Melbourne School of Design at the University of Melbourne occupies six levels, and the new facility includes a series of studio spaces, a studio hall, an atrium, lecture theatres, a library, exhibition spaces, specialist workshop spaces, and the integration of two significant historical elements, the 1856 Bank of NSW façade and the Japanese Room. A transparent ground plane opens up the building to passers-by and encourages further engagement between the building and the broader campus community. The major themes of the building brief were Built Pedagogy, the Studio, the Academic Environment, and the Living Building. Building systems are exposed, construction layers are pulled apart, and elements like windows and partitions are operable. In exploring Built Pedagogy, the building reveals through its composition, material make-up, experience, and structural and services systems, that built form and matter have the ability to teach and to 'produce knowledge'. The spatial layout of the administrative and faculty offices and the teaching studios is interwoven, bringing the disciplines of architecture, building, urbanism, and landscape architecture into more active contact and collaboration with each other. *PA*

Peter Bennetts

Story-tellers who weave together many strands of inspiration

Stefan Mee

Mee is responsible for leading design at John Wardle Architects. He relishes the rigour of seeing design intent through to completion on all JWA projects. He brings strong conceptual skills together with a passion for the inventive use of materials and architectural systems to achieve new and unconventional outcomes. Mee is an active contributor to the architecture community: he is regularly invited to lecture at RMIT University on design detailing; he is a frequent guest design critic at the University of Melbourne; and he has led a Masters of Architecture Design studio at the University of Melbourne. He is a regular jury member for the AIA (Victorian Chapter) Architecture Awards Program, previously sitting in on juries for Institutional Buildings, Residential Additions, and the Melbourne Prize.

What differentiates architecture in Australia from international architecture?

There are many commonalities between local and international work as we are all increasingly connected. Yet, there are specifics about place that create differences. The country is large and there are identifiable schools of thought that differ between our cities depending on the influences of history, climate, geography, and architectural discourse. This leads to a creative eclecticism when considering the country as a whole, rather than a consistent national flavour. Our many landscapes – coastal, bushland, agrarian, outback – are individual worlds with their own contexts of colour, vegetation, and topography to work within. The light in Australia has a particular directness and creates high contrasts between light and shadow. It requires inventive ideas to modify and soften as it travels to the interior. Much of our work is in the cities along the coast. In the urban realm generally, there is a willingness to experiment. This might be with materials, narrative, or programmatic use. This makes for a vibrant local architectural culture.

Construction is underway for the Learning and Teaching Building, Monash University (Right)

What role do current architectural trends play in your design approach?
We tend not to focus on trends and instead have developed a number of themes that we explore over a significant period of practice. For example, this might include the way we like to tease out programmatic uses to create what we describe as an explanatory building. These thematic strands can sometimes be placed in a longer lineage of architectural culture. Our interest in material and craft, for example, is part of a conversation amongst architects that has been ongoing since the discipline was established. We also bring the influence of new technologies to bear with new digital modelling techniques and off-site fabrication to expand the possibilities of craft. This then ties back to a global interest in experimenting with these new mediums.

John Wardle Architects

Where do you find your design inspiration?
Our design inspiration comes from our clients, the site, and the world around us. We are story-tellers who enjoy weaving together many strands of inspiration into a building. We make references to diverse sources, from art, architecture, and history, that spark design conversations. As we are a collaborative practice, different people involved in the design process will bring their own experiences to the conversation. John Wardle often speaks of his admiration for the work of expert tradespeople who inspire him to design almost specifically to exploit their skills.

Which Australian buildings do you most admire and why?
Admirable Australian buildings such as the works of Robin Boyd and Roy Grounds contributed to a culture of experimentation that persists today amongst Melbourne's architects. The Walsh Street House by Boyd is a gem, with its courtyard typology and draped catenary roof structure. The original NGV designed by Grounds riffed on the courtyard model at the scale of the civic institution to great effect. Our pavilion for the NGV 'I Dips Me Lid' was a homage to the optimism of the 1960s embodied in structures like the Sidney Myer Music Bowl, by Yuncken Freeman, completed in 1959. Our structure supported hundreds of digitally cut, folded, and riveted polycarbonate shapes that form a shade canopy of riotous colour.

What could the rest of the world learn from Australian architecture?
We recently completed the new Melbourne School of Design for the University of Melbourne, a project that was designed collaboratively with NADAAA, a Boston-based practice. Unusually, all aspects of the project were designed together without demarcating separate areas of responsibility. We felt that this approach was particularly appropriate for a design school, in that both design practices were constantly reviewing, critiquing, and learning with and from each other. Perhaps this example demonstrates the benefits of being open to a global discourse and maintaining a constant curiosity.

John Gollings

John Gollings

Arts West

130 D

148 Royal Parade,
University of Melbourne, Parkville
Architectus, ARM Architecture
2016

The Arts West redevelopment for the University of Melbourne is the new home of the Bachelor of the Arts and is located on the main university spine known as Professors Walk, within the 'Arts Precinct' opposite the heritage-listed Old Arts building. The new building embeds the concept of object-based learning, showcasing the university's extensive and prized artefacts collection and encouraging students to engage, in a physical sense, with these objects and artefacts as part of the on-campus learning process. Architectus joined forces with ARM Architecture to design and deliver the project which extends over seven levels of two interconnected buildings – one repurposed and the other a new build. *PA*

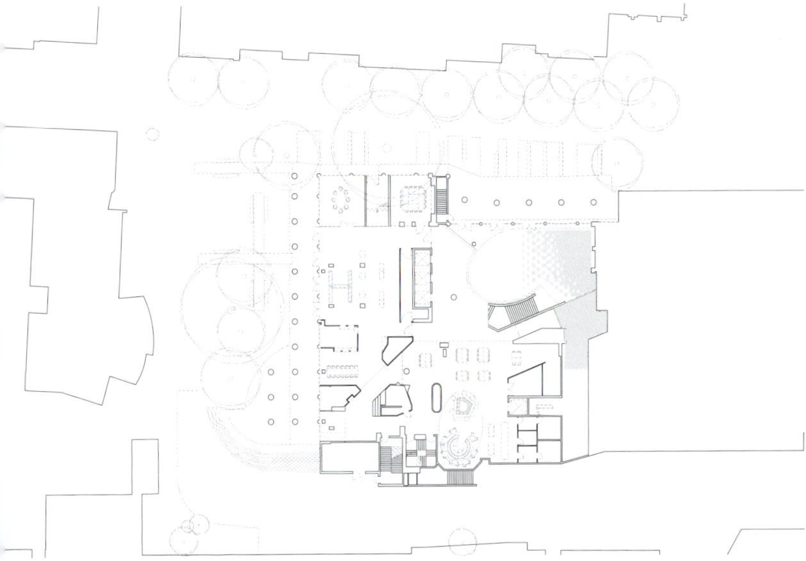

Site Plan

Bunjil Place 131 D
2 Patrick NE Dr, Narre Warren
FJMT
2017

The City of Casey is one of the fastest growing regions in Australia. However, it is not well served by civic and community facilities, with the immediate area being dominated by retail. It is therefore important that there is a greater variety of uses. The region needs a communal, cultural, and civic heart that can represent the values of the community and instil a new sense of place, pride, and ownership in the residents. The architects' vision seeks to create authenticity and 'place' for Narre Warren and the City of Casey. This is of prime importance given the loss of identity that resulted from the development of the region's semi-rural residential towns into a major growth corridor and the rapid expansion of new housing developments that has been taking place. The architects' approach reinforces the history and diversity of the area and is intended to keep alive the stories that have shaped the community, which continues to grow and evolve. They found inspiration in two stories in particular: 'The Meeting of Many Paths' and 'Bunjil the Eagle', which appear in Australian Aboriginal mythology. Both are central themes of the culture of the Boon Wurrung people of the Kulin Nation, the traditional owners and inhabitants of the land. The architects' design recognises the importance of the Princes Highway and Magid Drive entry: the building's considered formal geometry fans out from this intersection, creating radial axes and alignments of building forms that relate to the neighbouring Arc Building, the entry to the shopping centre, and the alignment of the street. Overlaid upon this arrangement is an informal meandering and organic organisation that create curving ground-plane connections between the various project components and surroundings. They define both internal and external usages, while creating a fluid expression and a sense of arrival at a place with the 'meeting of many paths'. *PA*

Adelaide

Darwin
NORTHERN TERRITORY
QUEENSLAND
WESTERN AUSTRALIA
Brisbane
SOUTH AUSTRALIA
NEW SOUTH WALES
Perth
Sydney
Adelaide
Canberra
A. C. T.
VICTORIA
Melbourne
TASMANIA
Hobart

E
Adelaide
138
151

139
150
153
146
140
147
141
145
144
132
135
137
136
142
134
133
nearmap

Adelaide

istock (Andrey Moisseyev)

Regarded as Australia's second most liveable city, Adelaide is filled with a rich mix of architecture in its characteristic precincts. Although British settlement in the city of Adelaide only began in 1836, the city's roots date back to some 30,000 years earlier, when Indigenous people first occupied the land. Adelaide's organised city grid design with its generous parklands and town squares was later established by surveyors William Light and George Strickland Kingston. Kingston went on to design some of Adelaide's earliest buildings, such as the Government House and the Adelaide Gaol. Adelaide became wealthier through its substantial farming and mining, which lured further foreign settlers to reside on the land. By the 1860s, Adelaide consisted of a sea of low-rise buildings with a considerable amount of churches due to the various religions of inhabitants. Buildings grew taller and new churches continued to emerge, with superb additions such as the late 19th century Gothic Revival style St Peter's Cathedral. The educational precinct of North Terrace began to develop, and its first building was the SA Institute Building. The University of Adelaide, including Bonython Hall and the State Library of SA, came shortly

View from the River Torrens onto Adelaide's entertainment precinct containing the Adelaide Festival Centre, Adelaide Casino and Adelaide Convention Centre

after. It's an eye opener to learn that the city's trademark Riverbank view, which consists primarily of the Adelaide Convention Centre and Festival Centre, was only realised less than 50 years ago. This space has since continued to grow into an entertainment precinct with redevelopments of the Adelaide Convention Centre and the Adelaide Oval. The 2016 addition of the riverbank bridge plays its role in connecting these two attractions. Further down on the other end of North Terrace lie the highly innovative SAHMRI medical research facility and the new Royal Adelaide Hospital site, which liven up this outer north-western edge of the city and define the research and medical precinct. Although often reputed as off-beat in comparison to its neighbouring larger cities, Melbourne and Sydney, this undisturbed city comes to life during its festival season, which peaks in February and March. Popular festivals include the annual Adelaide Fringe Festival (the world's second-largest arts festival), and the Clipsal 500 Adelaide (a four-day supercar event). The architecture of Adelaide continues to grow, with contributions from nationally applauded architects such as the firms Woods Bagot as well as Hassell. *SZ*

Government House and North Adelaide from North Terrace, 1930s

iStock (moisseyev)

Government House 132 E

North Terrace & King William Rd
Edward O'Brien, George Strickland Kingston; English and Brown
1840, 1855

Adelaide's Government House is Australia's oldest permanent Government House building, having been completed in 1840. English architect Edward O'Brien produced the primary set of plans, but the design was further developed by George Strickland Kingston, assistant to the Surveyor-General William Light. This lavish masonry building has been in the making since the erection of the eastern Regency Wing. Major additions began in 1855 after the state's wealth increased following the discovery of copper. These additions were carried out by contractors, English & Brown, who were responsible for the extensions on the western side of the building, including the Small Drawing Room, the Main Entrance Hall, the Adelaide Room, the Ballroom, the Large Dining Room, and several bedrooms. The late 19th century brought about further development, with the east-west building being demolished and replaced by a two-storey successor. A Conservatory (now the Library) was built in 1872, followed by the Billiard Room, the Private Secretary's Office, the Porter's Hall, and Strong Room in 1878. Renovations continued into the beginning of the twentieth century. *SZ*

iStock (moisseyev)

General Post Office

133 E

141 King William Street
Edmund Wright, Edward Woods
1872

The design of Adelaide's General Office was created by local architects Edmund Wright and Edward Woods, winners of the 1866 design competition for the building. The monumental Italianate style building was typical for post offices in Australia at the time. It was built from brick and stone and completed in 1872. It was the most expensive building to be constructed at that time by the South Australian government. Its corner clock tower, named Victoria Tower and erected in 1876, stands 48 metres tall and was reputed to be the tallest building in Adelaide until the twentieth century. The interior is made up of a grand two-storey postal hall with a half-domed roof and clerestory lighting. *SZ*

» Adelaide Town Hall

134 E

128 King William Street
Edmund Wright
1866

The admired town hall building was considered to be the 'largest municipal building south of the equator' at the time of its completion in 1866. Designed by Edmund Wright,former mayor of the city, the classical building features a striking 44-metre-tall regal clock tower in its centre, named the Albert Tower after Queen Victoria's late husband Prince Albert. Both the interior and exterior of this remarkable freestone building display ornamental Corinthian columns. A large pipe organ, built by William Hill & Sons, is presented within the main auditorium space. This iconic venue space, since its opening, has served as a public entertainment space and has hosted concerts, civic receptions, public gatherings, and meetings. *SZ*

iStock (fotofritz16)

SA Institute Building

135 E

North Terrace & Kintore Ave
Edward Angus Hamilton
1860

The historic South Australian Institute Building is one of Adelaide's most important buildings and the oldest cultural building on North Terrace. Colonial architect Edward Angus Hamilton designed the freestanding building in the Victorian Renaissance style. Since its completion in 1860, the cultural centre has served as a library, art gallery, museum, meeting place, office space, adult education space, administration headquarters, and information centre. It has been the home of the School of Design, the Royal Society, the Royal Geographical Society, and the South Australian Society for the Arts and is now part of the State Library of South Australia. *SZ*

Freemasons Hall

136 E

254-60 North Terrace
John Quinton Bruce, William. H. Harral
1927

Freemasons Hall, also known as the Adelaide Masonic Centre, was completed in 1927 and sits on the main street of North Terrace. It serves as the headquarters of the Grand Lodge of the Freemasons organisation of South Australia and the Northern Territory. The architects designed the State Heritage-listed centre, incorporating common South Australian architectural styles of the late 1920s period. Evidence of classical influences are evident in the ornate detailing on the six-storey façade. Four columns line the building's main entrance to the interior, which houses an office, meeting and reception spaces, the Great Hall, a museum, and library. *SZ*

South Australia's History Festival

State Records of SA

Parliament House in 1905

« Old Parliament House 137 E

North Terrace

William Bennett Hays, Edward Angus Hamilton, Edward John Woods

1843

Located on the corner of North Terrace and King William Road, the site of the Old Parliament House is a place of political significance. Initially built to serve as a Legislative Council Chamber in 1843, its original design has undergone many renovations and is now an amalgamation of architectural styles, incorporating elements designed by colonial architects William Bennett Hays, Edward Angus Hamilton, and Edward John Woods. The building that stands today is used by the parliament and consists mainly of offices and committee rooms. Colossal pillars frame the perimeter of the façade, clad in limestone, marble, and granite. *SZ*

≈ Hindmarsh Incinerator 138 E

Coglin Street, Hindmarsh

Walter Burley Griffin, Breuer Eric Nicholls

1936

The Hindmarsh Incinerator sits within a quiet residential neighbourhood. It was completed in 1936 to the design of internationally recognised architects Walter Burley Griffin and Breuer Eric Nicholls. The first of many incinerators built across Australia at the time, it is an example of early architectural modernism in South Australia with its fearless use of cubic, textured brick and strong vertical gestures. It remains in its original state to this day and serves as a facility for incinerating household waste for the Reverberatory Incinerator and Engineering Company (RIECo). Waste is deposited from above to a furnace and is then emptied into a collection bin situated lower down. *SZ*

St Peter's Cathedral

139 E

27 King William Rd
William Butterfield, Edward John Woods
1877, 1911

Situated on the outskirts of the city, just beyond the borders of the bustling North Adelaide suburb, St Peter's Cathedral is an unmissable landmark. This remarkable piece of Gothic Revival architecture was the first of many buildings by English architect William Butterfield. Construction began in 1869 and the cathedral was eventually opened in 1877, although it wasn't until 1911 that the entire cathedral was fully completed. The western exterior of the building bears resemblance to French Gothic styles commonly seen in international cathedrals such as the famous Notre Dame, with its impeccable detailing of the sculptures, clock towers, arched gateways, and central rose window. *SZ*

≈ Elder Park Rotunda

140 E

King William Rd
Macfarlane's Saracen Foundry
1882, 2015

The landmark Elder Park Rotunda overlooks the River Torrens at the gateway to Adelaide's CBD and was established in an attempt to rejuvenate the river area and its surroundings. It was donated to the city council by Sir Thomas Elder, a wealthy businessman and philanthropist who was based in Scotland at that time. Elder arranged for the rotunda to be manufactured at the Macfarlane's Saracen Foundry in Glasgow. The octagonal structure arrived in Adelaide in 1882 made of decorative cast iron with a zinc roof. It is painted in bronze, grey, and blue and sits raised on a granite platform of steps making it visible from afar. The plinth leaves room for underground space that is used when events and presentations are hosted. *SZ*

E

South Australian State Library Redevelopment

141 E

North Terrace & Kintore Ave

Robert Thomas, Woods & McMinn, MGT Architects

1884, 2003

MGT Architects were commissioned in 1998 to redevelop the State Library of South Australia in central Adelaide. The site consists of an ensemble of two historic buildings – the Institute Building and Mortlock Wing, from the 1860s and 1880s respectively – as well as the Spence Wing dating from the 1960s. The architects refurbished the library with a sensitivity to the heritage significance of the nineteenth century buildings and more extensively remodelled the Spence Wing. In so doing, they established a contemporary public institution with improved public access to collections and support facilities as well as new places for public gatherings and exhibitions. Visitors can enter the three buildings via a new 15-metre-high glazed foyer, which links all three buildings for the first time. Filled with natural light during the day, the foyer becomes a lantern in the evening, lighting up the library's interior. The advanced construction technologies and materials used during the refurbishment, and the transparency of the new foyer, contrast with the architectural character of the established buildings. The arrangement of the wall and roof elements in the new building extensively incorporates natural light, animating the formerly introspective environment. Existing external building materials were repaired or refurbished for long-term performance, and in some cases replaced with new materials sympathetic to the historical context. *PA*

John Gollings

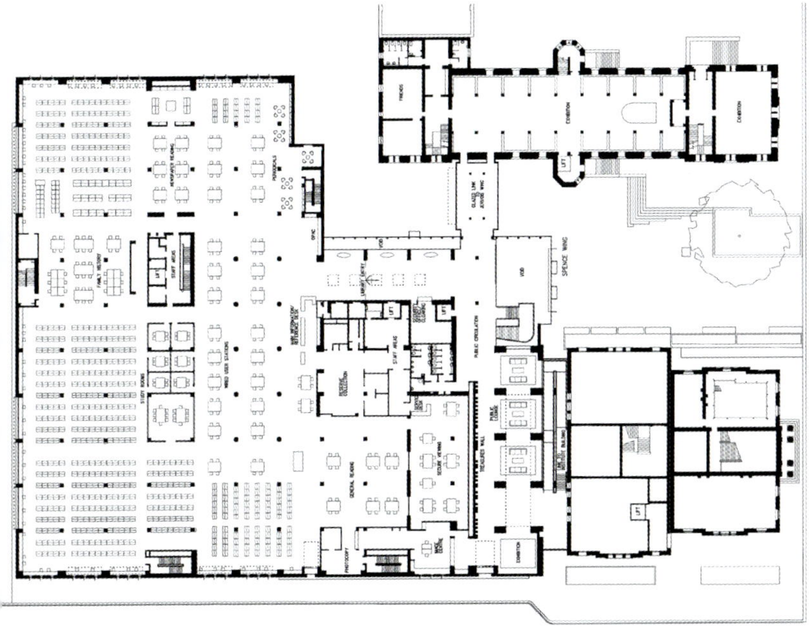

Upper Floor Plan

BEEHIVE
CORNER

Beehive Corner

142 E

Hindley St, King William St
George Klewitz Soward, Thomas English
1897

The Beehive Corner building, with its rare Gothic Revival style, has marked the corner of Rundle Mall and King William Street since its completion in 1897. The site's first building was established in 1849 and was occupied by a drapery shop known as the 'Beehive'. Architects George Klewitz Soward and Thomas English drew inspiration from this name while developing their elaborately adorned design of the building that stands today. The building features a characteristic golden bee at the top of a beehive-shaped corner turret. *SZ*

Carclew House

143 E

11 Jeffcott St, North Adelaide
John Quinton Bruce
1897

Located in a tranquil setting at the summit of Montefiore Hill is the Federation style Carclew House. The building's site changed ownership numerous times prior to its handover to the successful businessman Hugh Robert Dixson in 1862. The architect John Quinton Bruce designed the North Adelaide mansion with several spacious rooms and three balconies on the second storey. It was completed in 1897 and later sold to Sir Langdon Bonython, who named the building Carclew House. Today the building serves as a multipurpose youth arts centre. *SZ*

E

Sarah Zahradnik

flickr (07in0H)

E

Bonython Hall
University of Adelaide
Walter Hervey Bagot
1936

144 E

The medieval style Bonython Hall, otherwise known as the Great Hall, fronts the busy North Terrace, undoubtedly adding a distinct character to the street's frontage. It stands segregated from the surrounding buildings that belong to the University of Adelaide campus and serves as the university's main ceremonial hall and venue for hosting public events. The hall is named after Sir John Langdon Bonython, owner of the *Advertiser* newspaper, whose generous donation led to the beginning of the hall's construction in 1933 and thankfully provided employment to almost 600 people during the Great Depression. Architect Walter Hervey Bagot, from the firm Woods Bagot, created a grand gothic design, bringing to life Bonython's vision for the hall to resemble historic English universities. The heritage-listed building was completed in 1936 and is built from steel, reinforced concrete, and textured limestone with a slate roof. The interior and exterior joinery is made of timber oak. The windows are set back within arches to provide sun protection during the harsh South Australian summers. *SZ*

iStock (alicat)

E

Adelaide Festival Centre
King William St
John Morphett
1973

145 E

The Adelaide Festival Centre was Australia's first performing arts complex to be constructed and remains a national arts icon for Adelaide to this day. It was opened in 1973, three months prior to the completion of the famous Sydney Opera House. The multi-functional venue was designed by architect John Morphett and consists of three geometric volumes which are made of folded white planes. The centre's floor plan sits at a 45 degree angle to the city's grid structure and is enveloped by a vast open plaza. The plaza features an art installation by German environmental artist Otto Herbert Hajek. The centre includes a number of theatre and concert hall spaces – such as the Festival Theatre, seating close to 2,000 – as well as an outdoor amphitheatre. *SZ*

Bicentennial Conservatory 146 E
Botanic Gardens
Raffen Maron Architects
1989

Open to the public and nestled in the serene landscape of the Botanic Gardens sits an admirable example of late modern architecture – the award-winning Adelaide Bicentennial Conservatory. The conservatory was built to celebrate Australia's 1988 bicentenary, hence its name. Designed by Guy Maron, of Raffen Maron Architects, its contemporary form follows its function. It features the optimal height for hosting its ecosystem of lowland tropical rainforest plants and canopy of high-reaching trees. Many of the plants found inside are endangered or at risk of being endangered in their natural environments. It was essential that the building be protected from the harsh climate of the South Australian summer. As such, it was given a glazed exterior with a surface area of 2,434 square metres. This glass envelope plays a crucial role in maintaining a constant climatic condition. The curvilinear structure – 100 metres long, 47 metres wide, and 27 metres high – is the largest single spanning conservatory in the southern hemisphere and also the youngest listed building on the South Australian Heritage Register. *SZ*

Sarah Zahradnik

National Wine Centre

147 E

Hackney Rd & Botanic Rd
Cox Grieve Architects
2001

The National Wine Centre, occupying an area of 6,000 square metres, sits on the corner of one of Adelaide's busiest intersections. The centre's steering company commissioned the Adelaide-based firm Cox Grieve Architects to design a building that would serve as the flagship of the country's wine industry, a cultural and educational centre, and a tourist attraction. The architects drew on the heritage elements of the site as well as the landscape surroundings of First Creek. In particular, they created a northern forecourt with a radial geometry, incorporating the row of jacarandas that border the Botanic Gardens. A ramp leads visitors to the main entrance. The ramp is lined by a rammed-earth wall on one side, and on the other side by a curved arch with steel columns and horizontal slats connecting to a semi-covered canopy. The materials used inside feature a variety of surface textures and include stone, timber, steel, and rammed earth, which can all be typically found in a vineyard. The interior contains both public and intimate spaces for exhibitions, functions, offices, and educational purposes. *SZ*

146 Bicentennial Conservatory

147 National Wine Centre
nearmap

Kaurna Building

148 E

Hindley St, City West Campus,
University of South Australia
John Wardle Architects, Hassell
2005

The Kaurna Building is part of the second stage of the University of South Australia's (UniSA) City West Campus development and is home to the Louis Laybourne-Smith School of Architecture and Design and the South Australian School of Art. This four-storey building creates a face for the university on Hindley Street. Irregularly finned precast panels hovering over a transparent undercut create a detailed texture along the length of this street. The existing campus buildings, completed in 1996, possess a strong uniformity. Compared to these 'absolute' buildings that are contained within strictly defined envelopes, the new works defy their site boundaries with exuberant undercuts and overhangs. UniSA expressed an aspiration for the architecture to create a counterpoint to the existing campus buildings, and to express their commitment to connecting with the city and revitalising this precinct. The Kaurna Building offers legibility by providing a transparent building skin to Hindley Street. This 'explanatory' building reveals the activity it houses and its functional relationships; it is an exposition of its academic programme. This presentation to the public realm is symbolic of a shift to a more open, transparent, and engaging institution. An art gallery to the southern end of the building showcases the work of students, graduates, staff, and visiting designers and artists. The first floor provides office space for the staff from the schools of art and architecture. The second floor accommodates teaching and office space, while the top floor houses teaching studios for architecture, interior, and industrial design disciplines. The planning of the building encourages interplay between budding artists, designers, and architects, between staff and students, and between the schools and the community. The challenge of creating architecture that houses the study of architecture was resolved by elaborating the building's construction. Rather than offering students a symbolic representation of assembly, the craft of assembly is on display. The construction process is legible, demonstrating the creative potential of economical and robust fabrication techniques. The unique properties of precast and in-situ concrete are emphasised and juxtaposed throughout the building. The super-white precast panels exploit the precision and high level of finish achievable with this technology, as well as the serial nature of a panellised façade. The in-situ concrete is left grey, and made to cantilever, incline, and distort. *PA*

Sam Noonan

Hawke Building

149 E

55 North Terrace
John Wardle Architects (Design Architects), Hassell Architects
2007

The Hawke Building incorporates a political archive, seminar rooms, and conference spaces, including a 400-seat lecture theatre, the university's corporate headquarters, and the Anne and Gordon Samstag Museum of Art. The Hawke Building is a significant landmark within the clearly defined city edge delineated by Adelaide's formal boulevard North Terrace. Articulated and lustrous, the North Terrace façade is in counterpoint to the sober mass of existing adjoining buildings. Off-white precast concrete panels are designed to weather gracefully, signifying the persistence of the institution over time. Inset copper panels will slowly change colour as oxidisation occurs, with the green residue ultimately making its way down the concrete face. The Bradley Forum was conceived as a symbolic meeting place for the university. It features a large cut-away drum-shaped upper-level gathering space. This is given architectural prominence in the overall architectural schema and evokes notions of Australian political culture and identity. Open to view from outside, the seminar room becomes the alchemist's crucible – inside is the experiment: a free and fearless argument. The Hawke Library is the home of the former prime minister Bob Hawke's political archive. The library provides supported workspaces for visiting scholars in a space that cantilevers dramatically from the south side of the building. The Kerry Packer Civic Gallery runs the full length of the building, the gallery connects the public entry at North Terrace at one end, through the Auditorium, to the heart of the campus at the other end. This arrangement of physical space is matched by an aspiration to promote discussion of contemporary social issues in a context poised between academia and the public realm. The Anne and Gordon Samstag Museum of Art responds to a long-standing need for a second art gallery of scale in Adelaide. Arranged over two levels, the exhibition spaces are visually linked through and across a large double-height space. A single large gallery is located at ground level, and a medium and small gallery at the second level. The material palette includes high-quality exposed-concrete surfaces contrasted with the soft tones of recycled iron bark timber flooring and smooth white hanging walls. Interior details incorporate fibreglass, carbon fibre, stone, and leather. *PA*

Zoo Entrance Precinct and Giant Panda Forest

150 E

Frome Rd

Hassell Architects

2009

Hassell Architects designed two elements of Australia's Adelaide Zoo: its Entrance Precinct and its Giant Panda Forest, home to the southern hemisphere's only giant panda zoo exhibit. The Adelaide Zoo Entrance Precinct was the result of an ambitious project that incorporated architectural, cultural, and organisational strategies. The central considerations driving the design were conservation, environment, education, and research. The new entrance was built to coincide with the arrival of Wang Wang and Funi, the giant pandas expected to significantly increase the number of visitors to the zoo. The Entrance Precinct includes ticketing, retail, conference, and administration facilities as well as public areas inside and outside the zoo. The main building features a purpose-designed 'green roof', which offers shelter for wildlife and extensive walls of living native plants. This means the building serves as a horticultural park and research centre as well as an exceptional zoo facility. A series of interlinked forecourts unfold over 2,000 square metres, creating a natural transition and physical connection between the zoo and surrounding roads, parklands, and waterways. Once inside the zoo, visitors journeying through the Giant Panda Forest will find themselves immersed in a landscape resembling the Chinese Highlands. The exhibit aims to follow best practices in animal management, with a state-of-the-art holding facility, water features, chilled rocks, and mature trees. The exhibit conveys an understanding of both the natural habitat of the giant pandas and the research and conservation efforts associated with the Wolong Sanctuary, the original home of Wang Wang and Funi.

The Adelaide Zoo Entrance Precinct includes a number of sustainability measures made possible through close collaboration between the government, the Adelaide Zoo horticultural experts, and the multi-disciplinary design team. Unique 'living walls' were designed in such a way that they would not lead to a net loss of habitat. These walls showcase plant species that are indigenous

to the Adelaide Plains and demonstrate the zoo's place as a significant horticultural and zoological park. The Entrance Precinct building's green roof is the first of its type in Australia to shelter wildlife and enable biodiversity intensification. The living environment will evolve in accordance with the normal life cycle of plant species, which will change the character of the Entrance Precinct over time. Ongoing research, testing, and prototyping to encourage native species to inhabit the precinct will further stimulate change and evolution. Water management is a major environmental issue in Australia, which is why the Adelaide Zoo Entrance Precinct project includes water-conserving features. Concrete tanks below the forecourt hold 160,000 litres of rainwater, captured from the roof above the conference spaces, and from the Santos Conservation Centre. Runoff from the forecourt is first filtered through biofiltration garden beds to remove contaminants. Biofiltration garden beds, also known as 'rain gardens', are low depressions planted with native plants which capture rainwater runoff from paved surfaces, naturally filtering the rainwater before it is stored in the underground tank. The biofiltration garden bed uses a combination of sand and gravel layers and the plant's root systems to filter the water as it soaks down through the soil. It is then collected by an underground pipe and directed to the underground tank. The Adelaide Zoo Entrance Precinct project will serve as a platform for ongoing collaborative research between Hassell Architects and the university. Specifically, it will support and promote urban ecology by allowing the exploration of alternative models in stormwater management, in addition to improving solar power generation efficiency. *PA*

South Australian Health and Medical Research Institute

151 E

North Terrace
Woods Bagot
2013

Woods Bagot was engaged by the South Australian Government to design and deliver the South Australian Health and Medical Research Institute (SAHMRI). Nine research modules house up to 675 researchers, fostering innovation and improvements in community health services. The innovative façade design encloses approximately 30,000 square metres of space in an iconic and sculptural form in the heart of Adelaide's new medical and health precinct west of the city. The built form of the SAHMRI acknowledges its sense of place within the green belt of the Adelaide parklands, seamlessly interacting with its surroundings, including Adelaide's public transport, cycling, and walking networks. The architecture is raised off the ground, creating an open ground plane in an integrated landscape, opening the building to the public as well as users and allowing for greater porosity through the site. Its forecourt, adjacent to the new hospital, encourages interaction between staff, visitors, and the general public. The SAHMRI's sculptural, iconic form is characterised by a striking transparent façade that unifies the organic diamond-shaped plan while showcasing the two atria inside the building. Inspired by the skin of a pine cone, the building's unique triangulated diagrid façade responds to its environment like a living organism. Both functional and aesthetic in nature, the façade is designed to improve access to daylight, reduce heat and glare, and maintain vision for a healthy internal environment. The interior palette is designed to breathe light and life into the working environment. A restrained selection of materials acknowledges the play of light created by the building skin and allows it to transform the spaces over the course of the day. Injections of colour are introduced though permanent walls and flexible furniture pieces that will be moved over time to suit

Peter E Barnes

the users' needs. Intensive environmental analysis dictated the building's form, allowing it to achieve its best solar orientation. Internal floor plate functions are arranged to allow maximum daylight in east-facing write-up spaces while the enclosed solid lab support spaces located on the west provide protection from the harsh western sun. The project's commitment to ecologically sustainable development (ESD) includes the passive design of the floor plates that respond to the internal programme and provides maximum daylight where needed. *PA*

Peter Clarke

151 E

Riverbank Bridge
River Torrens
Tonkin Zulaikha Greer
2014

152 E

In collaboration with landscape architects Taylor Cullity Lethlean, TZG won the competition for this monumental public infrastructure in 2012. The project was the first part of the implementation of the Riverbank Masterplan, which aims to connect and enliven the city's waterfront parkland. The eight-metre-wide bridge links the redeveloped Adelaide Oval to the city, spanning nearly 75 metres over the River Torrens through the Parklands. The elegant curve of the bridge was designed with maximum lightness and simplicity. Its faceted profile, cladded in white glass, reflects the water and greenery and is supported by angled V columns. To the south, there are expanded facilities for the Festival Centre; to the north, there is a new informal amphitheatre and a plaza linking to the Oval's redeveloped forecourt. At the end of the bridge, a dramatic belvedere hovers above the river, where a new water wall will aerate and cleanse the lake. *PA*

View over the Riverbank Bridge with the Adelaide Oval in the background

iStock (ymgerman)

Adelaide Oval Redevelopment 153 E

War Memorial Dr, North Adelaide
John Pickering, Henry Sparks (1871), Cox Architecture, Walter Brooke and Hames Sharley, HASSEL (2014)
1871, 2014

Situated on the outskirts of the city centre, the Adelaide Oval is a multi-purpose stadium and gem of Adelaide's sport and entertainment precinct. It has hosted football and cricket events since colonial times. Originally constructed in 1871, its seating capacity increased from 34,000 to 50,000 thanks to its most recent redevelopment, completed in 2014. This was a collaborative effort between COX Architects, Walter Brooke, and Hames Sharley, who retained the historic elements of the stadium such as the scoreboard, fig trees, and breath-taking views of the site. The stadium consists of three separate and unique pavilions positioned around the northern mound. Each responds to its own context, internal programme, and function during events on the pitch. The firm Hassell contributed to the stadium's development, designing the new western grandstand. *SZ*

151 SAHMRI

E

139 St Peter's Cathedral
153 Adelaide Oval Redevelopment
140 Elder Park Rotunda
152 Riverbank Bridge
145 Adelaide Festival Centre

JEFFREY
SMART
BUILDING

Jeffrey Smart Building

154 E

243 Hindley St , City West Campus,
University of South Australia
John Wardle Architects,
Philips Pilkington Architects
2014

Wrapping around a central courtyard, the Jeffrey Smart Building incorporates a diverse spectrum of teaching and learning spaces. A central courtyard, with its open-air cinema screen, green public area, and an established tree, works to reinforce the urban character of the campus. The community of learning, brimming with student activity, animates all levels of this building. The interior concepts of the Jeffrey Smart Building were developed to provide experiences for students beyond traditional library activities yet support functional needs relating to teaching and learning. The building is a learning and social hub, where casual and informal interactions are as relevant as formal ones. Named after an Australian artist of international repute, the Jeffrey Smart Building is the fifth building designed by John Wardle Architects at the University of South Australia, this time in collaboration with Phillips Pilkington Architects. This building strengthens the university's relationship with the city and its surroundings. At the outset of the project, the University of South Australia outlined an ambitious brief for an iconic learning centre incorporating a full range of library services, active teaching and learning spaces, and student services at a strategic location within the City West campus. The building comprises eight floors and 12,480 square metres of gross floor area and has achieved a five-star Green Star Education (v1) rating. The tall and expansive ground-floor spaces are enclosed behind a transparent façade that can be made more or less permeable to the Peter Hoj Courtyard, depending on outside weather conditions. The façade is richly detailed and scaled by the various seating and sill elements around the perimeter. The main entry into the building is marked by a portal clad in sheet steel. The detail of an occupied edge behind a self-shading façade is repeated vertically to create signs of inhabitation to the street. A sequence of forms along the length of the Hindley Street frontage reinforces the dynamism within. The transparency at the ground floor is offset by the solidity of the off-white precast panels in the floors above. The panels are configured in a rational and repetitive arrangement that is suited to efficient production. A single repeated pattern recalls the spine of a book and results in a pillowed texture across the surface of the façade. The façade is self shaded with a combination of horizontal sun shades as well as deep, angled, concrete fins that span from floor to floor. Amongst other functions, the ground floor comprises lively social learning spaces, and a gallery with a tiered seating platform and large screen. *PA*

Adelaide Convention Centre (Redevelopment)

155 E

North Terrace
Woods Bagot, Larry Oltmanns, V3 Architects
1987, 2015

The original Adelaide Convention Centre was completed in 1987 and more recently redeveloped in 2015 by internationally renowned architecture firm Woods Bagot in collaboration with V3 Architects. This impressive redevelopment is situated on the corner of North Terrace, Montefiore Road, and Festival Drive and has amplified the famous River Torrens setting. With a seating capacity of 3,000, the centre serves as a single venue or three divided sections which connect to the existing buildings, incorporating interconnected meeting rooms, plenary halls, and facilities for hosting functions. The façade design was inspired by regional geological forms and colours of the vibrant South Australian outback. The customised cladding of the augmented exterior is supported by a galvanised-steel rain screen with a custom-folded profile. *SZ*

E

flickr (Woods Bagot)

Treetop Studio 156 E
Kingston Park*
Max Pritchard
2013

Rather than undertake a difficult addition to an iconic, heritage-listed, 25-year-old, elevated, steel-and-glass house, architect Max Pritchard chose to build a separate structure for his own studio. This garden structure is a two-level circular tower wrapped in golden plywood sheeting, with hardwood battens covering sheet joints and expressing the timber frame structure of vertical wall studs and radiating roof beams. The interior was developed in conjunction with the structural system and external appearance such that all are integrated, with bookshelves and windows all positioned and detailed to follow the pattern developed from the roof and wall structure. Hardwood battens define matching plywood segments of the ceiling and floor. The sharpness created by this patterning is repeated in the detailing of the bespoke circular table. The slope of the land allows access to the studio via a timber-decked bridge, with a curved timber-decked path leading to the house. There is no artificial heating or cooling. Vertical banks of louvres provide ample cross ventilation in the coastal environment in summer, with the flat 'lid' roof providing shade. Working on the principle that designers should be able to build their creations, Pritchard undertook all construction himself, also designing and building the circular table. *PA*

* Private Residence not open for public

Sam Noonan

Interview

Transparent architecture that intrudes minimally on a vast landscape

Max Pritchard

Max Pritchard Gunner Architects is a design-focused practice established by Max Pritchard in 1986. Andrew Gunner and Tess Pritchard joined Pritchard as Directors in 2015. Together they aim to offer unique designs tailored to clients' requirements, site, and the local climate. The firm has designed hundreds of individual houses and received international recognition for tourism projects including Southern Ocean Lodge on Kangaroo Island and Seppeltsfield Winery in the Barossa Valley. The practice has received more than 40 awards and commendations from the Australian Institute of Architects.

What differentiates architecture in Australia from international architecture?
Residential architecture in Australia is perhaps not so constrained by tradition and can thus respond more positively to changes in climate and lifestyle.

What role do current architectural trends play in your design approach?
I would like to think that my architecture is not fashionable. An advantage to being a mature practitioner is that one can look back on early work and assess whether it was timeless or fashionable. I would hope timeless.

Rolling hills, deep valleys, and distant views dictated the form of this striking rural house of contrasts.

Southern Ocean Lodge is being described as Australia's first 'Super Lodge': introducing Kangaroo Island to international visitors to appreciate the abundance of rare wildlife and stunning scenic beauty.

Where do you find your design inspiration?

Clients are my biggest inspiration, followed by their site and the climate. I hope to bring a fresh, new attitude to each project, rather than developing personal themes. Clients' passion for design is often coupled with their research ability, and they become valuable, informed design partners, particularly on issues of sustainability.

Which Australian buildings do you most admire and why?

Generally the work of Glen Murcutt with its lightness, sculptural qualities, and climate responsiveness has been an inspiration to many architects, including myself. Before Murcutt, in the 1950s, there were many unique experimental houses in Australia which offered new, vibrant, optimistic alternatives to European tradition. This spirit has to an extent survived.

What could the rest of the world learn from Australian architecture?

Australians have a robust, irreverent character, relatively free from pretention. This is reflected to an extent in an open, transparent architecture which often seems a minimal intrusion on a vast landscape.

Robertson House, Fleurieu Peninsular, South Australia

Perth

Darwin
NORTHERN TERRITORY
QUEENSLAND
WESTERN AUSTRALIA
Brisbane
SOUTH AUSTRALIA
NEW SOUTH WALES
Perth
Sydney
Adelaide
Canberra
A. C. T.
VICTORIA
Melbourne
TASMANIA
Hobart

F
Perth
177
182
16

173
179
180
76
164
162
167
159
175
169
161
174
160
158
166
163
170
157
172
165
178
181

F

Perth

Bird's-eye view over Perth's winding Swan River

The capital city of Western Australia, Perth, is surrounded by the lush natural settings of the Swan River and the stunning Kings Park, which is the largest inner-city park in the southern hemisphere, covering more than 400 hectares. The land had been occupied by the indigenous Noongar people for some 40,000 years before the city was founded by Captain James Stirling in 1829. As there was no financial assistance and limited labour skills at that time, the city's urban development took place much more slowly than in other Australian cities. It wasn't until the 1850s, when convicts began to arrive, that construction began to take off. With the influx of convicts, many public buildings were completed, the most notable of which was the Perth Town Hall. The discovery of gold in the late 19th century led to a further increase in population, and the city slowly transformed from a colonial landscape into a vibrant Victorian town. Perth continued to expand and eventually had one of the highest rates of car ownership per capita in the world. In 1955, Gordon Stephenson and Alistair Hepburn introduced the 'Plan for the Metropolitan Region', a plan for the metropolitan area of Perth and Fremantle. This plan included

F

a transport network, which was intended to minimise the city's dependence on vehicles. Perth's population grew even larger after the 1960s mining boom, and the city acquired an expanding skyline to match its growing wealth. By the 20th century, Perth had an established city centre with a linear strip of tall buildings running from the east to the west of the city and surrounded by low-rise buildings. The city comprises what are called 'activity centres' – such as Perth, East Perth, West Perth, and Northbridge – which have the highest commercial and employment activity in the metropolitan area. Major state institutions including government, cultural, and public organisations can also be found in these activity centres. What are called 'district centres' surround the activity centres. The precinct of Cathedral Square, which can be viewed as the city's historic centre, contains three interconnected heritage buildings, known as the State Buildings (former government buildings) which have been transformed and redeveloped into invigorating pedestrian links and dining and retail hubs. The musical Bell Tower and eccentric Perth Arena are some modern additions to this thriving cosmopolitan city. *SZ*

» Government House

157 F

St Georges Terrace
Henry William Reveley (1834), Edmund Henderson (1863)
1834–1863

In 1834, England-born civil engineer Henry William Reveley began to prepare drawings for the first Government House on behalf of James Stirling, who had been granted temporary ownership of the Officers' Barracks. After Stirling's departure for England in 1839, four successive governors resided in the well-proportioned Georgian building between 1839 and 1855. Several complaints were made about the unsuitable living conditions of the house. In response, the Legislative Council passed an ordinance in 1858 to fund the construction of the Government House (1863) that stands today. Lieutenant Colonel Edmond Henderson designed the new Government House with Jacobean and Gothic influences. The exterior's exquisitely detailed stonework and bonded brickwork incorporate the square windows and are accentuated by the gabled roof with its capped turrets above as well as the Gothic arcading at the ground level. The interior accommodates several rooms for public and official entertainment including an entry hall, morning room, drawing room, music room, dining room, executive council room, and a small boardroom. *SZ*

» St George's Cathedral

158 F

38 St Georges Terrace
Edmund Thomas Blacket
1888

St George's Cathedral is a commendable exemplar of the English Victorian Gothic Revival style. In 1879, English architect Edmund Thomas Blacket was invited to design Perth's new cathedral. Construction was completed in 1888, after the death of the architect. Blacket was

particularly renowned for his church architecture. The building is made from local and imported materials such as brick, stone, timber, marble, and stained glass. The timber for the hammerbeam roof truss was laid in the Swan River for two years so that it would become soft enough to be carved. In 1902, bells were fixed within the tower as a memorial to Queen Victoria. In 1923, the original Chapel House was replaced with the Soldiers' Memorial Chapel, which was added in memory of Western Australian soldiers who had died during the First World War. *SZ*

David Mallett

» The Cloisters

159 F

200 St Georges Terrace
Richard Roach Jewell
1858

A landmark frontage to St Georges Terrace, the Cloisters building is one of Perth's few remaining convict-built colonial structures from the mid 19th century. Completed in 1858, the brick building was home to the Perth Church of England Collegiate School, the first secondary school in Western Australia, which attracted sons of wealthy families. Convict architect Richard Roach Jewell designed the lavish Tudor style building for Bishop Mathew Blagden Hale, who had a close association with the building. Jewell found inspiration for his design in great works of British architecture such as Hampton Court Palace. By the mid 20th century the building had gone from being used for secondary education to serving as a school for girls, private residences, boarding house, theological college, and hostel for the University of Western Australia. It was in 1904 that the building was first referred to as the Cloisters. Plans to develop the building arose as an alternative to the Anglican church's proposal to demolish the building. Today the building accommodates commercial offices and has been incorporated into a plaza and shopping arcade on the office tower behind it. A statue of Bishop Hale stands outside the front door. *SZ*

State Buildings

160 F

54 Barrack Street
George Poole
1874

The State Buildings, which consist of three interconnected heritage buildings – the Central Government Offices and Old Treasury Building – have housed predominately government offices since they were completed in 1874. Architect Richard Roach Jewell originally gave these government buildings a simplistic design, which colonial architect George Temple Poole was later commissioned to redevelop and expand. His grand design linked the various wings of these major buildings, drawing on elements of the French Second Empire style. Since then, they have undergone careful redevelopment to become a hospitality and retail complex that includes the luxury COMO The Treasury Hotel. They are located in the historic Cathedral Square, the heart of Perth. The entrance lobby, Postal Hall, forms the midpoint of the complex. *SZ*

COMO The Treasury Hotel

« Perth Town Hall

161 F

Hay St, Barrack St
Richard Roach Jewell
1870

The Perth Town Hall has marked the corner of Perth's Hay Street and Barrack Street since its completion in 1870. British architect Richard Roach Jewell designed the exquisite medieval style hall with Victorian Gothic Revival influences. Jewell was known for his public buildings in Perth in the 19th century. This particular building consists of brick and wooden shingles, stained glass windows, a cantilevered Juliet balcony, Gothic arches, and decorative heritage elements. It includes an undercroft, a clock tower, three smaller towers, and a gabled roof. *SZ*

≈ Wesley Uniting Church

162 F

75 William St
Richard Roach Jewell
1870

Wesley Uniting Church, which sits on the corner of William Street and Hay Street, was opened to the public in 1870. It was designed by Richard Roach Jewell, the same architect responsible for the Perth Town Hall and many of Perth's important public buildings. The colonial church was designed in the Gothic Revival style. Its brick façade features long vertical windows and wall buttresses. The pitched roof is made of clay with gabled parapets and a capped metal spire. On the inside, buttresses separate the nave wall into five bays. *SZ*

iStock (demerzel21)

Michal Lewi

His Majesty's Theatre

163 F

825 Hay St
William G. Wolfe
1904

His Majesty's Theatre is Australia's only functioning Edwardian Baroque style theatre. With a seating capacity of 2,500 people, it was the largest Australian theatre when it was opened in 1904. American architect William G. Wolfe designed the ornately decorated reinforced-concrete building inspired by international nineteenth century theatres. The interior features a stunning marble staircase and a dome roof, which was originally designed to slide open to improve natural ventilation in the auditorium. However, the domed roof was permanently sealed during the extensive restoration works that took place after the Western Australian government purchased the building in 1977. The theatre hosts large-scale musical and theatrical events amongst others and is home to the West Australian Ballet and West Australian Opera. *SZ*

≈ Perth Mint

164 F

310 Hay St, East Perth
George Temple-Poole
1899

The colonial Perth Mint building is located in East Perth and was designed by British architect George Temple-Poole during what was the greatest gold rush in Australia's history. The heritage-listed building was completed in 1899 and is one of the oldest operational mints worldwide that still operates from its original location. The Perth Mint not only specialises in minting precious metals, it also exhibits historic images and artefacts as well as multimedia and interactive displays through which visitors can learn about the history of gold in Western Australia. The fine Victorian building features a limestone façade with a grand central entrance and a colonnade on each side. It displays Italianate style elements, seen for example in the low pitched roof with overhanging eaves, arched windows, and long balconies. *SZ*

flickr (David Stanley)

Supreme Court Building 165 F
28 Barrack St, Perth
John Harry Grainger
1903

The Supreme Court of Western Australia is the highest state court in the state of Western Australia. Its first court house was built in 1837 and is believed to be the oldest public building still standing in Perth. This heritage-listed building currently serves as the Francis Burt Law Education Centre. The Supreme Court relocated many times before the decision was made to build a new court building on Barrack Street between what are now the Stirling Gardens and Supreme Court Gardens. The building was opened in 1903 and is located adjacent to the Old Court House building. Its historical significance stems from its Federation Academic Classical-style design by John Harry Grainger, chief architect of the Public Works Department of Western Australia. This architectural style was common for major public buildings of the period. The design of the two-storey brick building called for the use of local materials, which resulted in a mix of Donnybrook stone, Meckering granite, and jarrah wood. However, it wasn't possible to quarry sufficient quantities of the Donnybrook stone, which meant stucco and cement were used instead. Similarly, galvanised iron was used instead of slate for the roof, and a white paint finish was used for the main foyer space, which was originally intended to reflect the coloured patterns of the stained-glass domes above. *SZ*

Michal Lewi

» St. Andrew's Uniting Church 166 F

St. Georges Terrace
James Hine
1907

The heritage-listed St Andrew's Church is Western Australia's first Presbyterian church to be constructed. England-born architect James Hine designed the bold red-brick building with a contemporary take on the Gothic style. The church contains a nave, wide transepts, and three towers, one of which is topped with a large metal spire. An organ was added in 1924, positioned at the eastern transept. The St. Georges Terrace site of the church has been sold to Singapore-owned Global Premium Hotels with plans to construct a hotel. However, the church's heritage elements will be retained. *SZ*

» General Post Office 167 F

Forrest Place
John Smith Murdoch, Hillson Beasley
1923

Perth's General Post Office is situated in the city's main civic space and is a key central building of the Forrest Place precinct. It was the largest building in Perth at the time of its completion in 1923. Architects John Smith Murdoch and Hillson Beasley designed the monumental building in the Beaux-Arts style with symmetrical and sculptural qualities evident in both the exterior and interior of the building. The seven-storey building is built from local materials and is rendered in granite at its lower front walls, piers, and steps. The upper walls, columns, and corner pavilions are rendered in freestone. The enormous scale of the exterior is emphasised by giant-order Corinthian columns. *SZ*

State War Memorial 168 F

68 Fraser Ave, Kings Park

J. Talbot Hobbs

1929

Disconnected from the busy city centre within the Kings Park setting, the State War Memorial cenotaph is situated at the centre point of the popular viewing edge which offers some of the best views over the City of Perth and Swan River. The memorial itself attracts over 40,000 visitors for every Anzac Day Dawn Service ceremony. It was designed by the architect and soldier General Sir J Talbot Hobbs and was completed in 1929 to commemorate those who lost their lives during the two world wars. The 18-metre-high granite structure sits on a raised platform, which features an inscription on the front with the words 'lest we forget'. Two Australian flags hang on masts on both sides of the monument. One of the four faces features a large cross in its centre. Bronze plaques are fixed to the outside walls of the undercroft, listing more than 4,000 soldiers who died during the Second World War. Meanwhile, the internal walls of the undercroft list on marble tablets the names of over 7,000 soldiers who lost their lives during the First World War. *SZ*

London Court

169 F

647 Hay St
Bernard Evans, Oldham, Boas and Ednie-Brown
1937

London Court is a popular open-air shopping arcade and enduring tourist attraction in Perth's central business district. It was designed for the notorious financier and scam artist, Claude de Bernales. British architect Bernard Evans and local architectural practice Oldham, Boas and Ednie-Brown were commissioned to design the Tudor style shopping arcade. Gabled roofs cover 53 shops, a basement inn (now a board games retailer), 55 offices, and 24 residential apartments. Its main entrances off St Georges Terrace and Hay Street are lined with wrought-iron gates and include semi-timbered walls that feature gargoyles, masks, shields, and crests. Sitting above the entrance at each street is an animated clock with a figure that moves in and out to the sound of chimes every 15 minutes. The clock at St Georges Terrace has a figure of St George slaying a dragon and the clock at Hay Street has four circling knights. The opening of the arcade in 1937 was a spectacular affair, celebrated with a three-day 'Olde English Fayre'. Volunteers dressed up in Elizabethan costumes, and the entertainment included performances of scenes from Shakespeare's *Twelfth Night*, madrigals, and folk songs. *SZ*

» Council House

170 F

27-29 St Georges Terrace
Howlett and Bailey
1963

The landmark Council House is located on Perth's main business street, St Georges Terrace. It was completed in 1963, after the city had hosted the 1962 British Empire and Commonwealth Games. The building's heritage value was heavily debated in the late 1990s, with some critics even calling for its demolition. But the building was retained, and it received the 2015 Enduring Architecture Award from the Australian Institute of Architects. Howlett & Bailey Architects designed this admirable example of post-war modernist civic architecture, with refined yet minimal detailing. After its completion, the 13-storey glass façade became a much-imitated model throughout the state, with its coherent and uninterrupted floor-to-ceiling glazing. The floor levels are demarcated by distinctive T-shaped sunshades that protrude from the glazed surface as part of a regular pattern repeated throughout the entire façade. *SZ*

iStock (64031576 2)

Uwe Zahradnik

≈ Mount Eliza Apartments 171 F

71 Mount St
Krantz & Sheldon
1964

One of Perth's most iconic buildings, the Mount Eliza Apartments tower is affectionately referred to as the 'thermos flask' due to its finned, rocket-like form. The residential complex sits high above its Mount Street location between Kings Park and the Swan River and can be seen from afar. It has been a landmark building of the neighbourhood since its completion in 1964. The modernist tower was designed by Krantz and Sheldon Architects, a father-and-son practice that specialised in designing flats, from low-rise apartments to luxury medium- and high-rise apartments in the mid twentieth century. Their designs were known for their rigorous detailing, spatial planning, and strong emphasis on urban living. The tower's circular floor plan is designed around a central service core which includes two interlocking circular stairways and allows for 180-degree views. The 16-storey building accommodates single apartments on each of the top five levels and two apartments on its lower levels. It was one of Perth's first apartment buildings to have only one or two apartments per floor. *SZ*

» Perth Concert Hall 172 F

5 St Georges Terrace
Howlett and Bailey Architects
1973

Viewed from the southern end, the building rests on a podium containing three levels of covered parking space. The northern end is raised slightly above a large courtyard that links the building to St Georges Terrace. This off-form concrete building, constructed by the firm SABEMO in 1973, was based on what were at the time highly innovative design and construction principles, with large free spans and a structural grid. It is an important example of mid-century brutalist architecture and is known for its exceptional acoustic qualities, which are recognised as being the best in the southern hemisphere. The year-round venue is the primary performance venue of the West Australian Symphony Orchestra. *SZ*

» Marsala House 173 F

38 Sycamore Rise, Dianella
Iwan Iwanoff
1976

Bulgarian-born architect Iwan Iwanoff is known for his creative use of concrete blocks, his attention to detail, and his belief in architecture as art. He established his practice, Studio of Iwanoff, in Perth in 1963, and from then until his death in 1986, his small office produced innovative buildings, including many domestic works. One such building is Marsala House in the suburb of Dianella. The hilltop home, which was originally the residence of builder Sergio Marsala and his wife Tina, who wanted to make a design statement with their home, establishes its uniqueness through the concrete blocks that make up its every element: from the asymmetric window layout to the rainwater channels and grand stairway to the front entrance. The Marsalas helped shape the interiors: they sourced furnishings and artworks from their travels, and requested an illuminated disco floor after a trip to Las Vegas. New owners purchased the house in 2005, and, together with Donaldson and Warn Architects, restored it to its former glory. The 1970s interiors have earned the home its nickname: Disco House. *DP*

Heritage Council

Sheffield Property Group

≈ Allendale Square

174 F

77 St Georges Terrace
Cameron Chisholm & Nicol
1976

A grand example of modern architecture, the Allendale Square development is an amalgamation of commercial, residential, and religious buildings. The complex comprises a 32-storey office tower with an underground shopping complex, a chapel, and residential accommodation. The 132-metre-high tower's square floor plan is set at a 45-degree angle to St Georges Terrace. Its faceted façade redirects views through its folded planes that frame the windows. Eastern and western planes are clad in anodised aluminium, while the religious chapel's exterior has distinctive sculptured masonry forms. The underground shopping complex is connected to the city via pedestrian accessways. The vertical perimeter of columns combined with the central service core made it possible to use column-free floorplates. *SZ*

≈ Central Park

175 F

152-158 St Georges Terrace
Forbes and Fitzhardinge
1992

Central Park is a 51-storey tower situated in the heart of Perth's central business district. It has two prominent frontages: one onto St Georges Terrace, Perth's primary business strip, and the other onto Hay Street, Perth's main shopping precinct. It is the tallest office building in the city, with a height of 249 metres from the ground to the tip of its spire. The architectural firm Forbes and Fitzhardinge designed the high-rise tower, considering the surrounding urban space and streetscape. The building accommodates approximately 66,200 square metres of office and retail space. The design allows much daylight to stream into the lobby, thanks to the tower's façade materials, which comprise polished granite and double glazing. Construction was completed in 1992. The building is considered a key component of Perth's skyline. *SZ*

QV1
250 St Georges Terrace
Harry Seidler & Associates
1991

176 F

The impressive 43-storey QV1 tower sits within the Parliamentary Precinct in West Perth, offering incredible panoramic views over the Swan River. At its time of completion in 1991, it was the largest single building in the city. The tower was designed with a humanistic approach by Harry Seidler, who is known for his modernist multi-storey office developments, among others. A large portion of the site was initially open to the public and consisted of a landscaped two-level urban plaza – an 'oasis' of waterfalls, palm trees, and a meandering pool – established as a retreat in the midst of the commercial racket. However, this space was recently heavily altered by other designers. The façade features angled vertical blades for sun shading, double-glazed glass walls, high garden terraces, and a 50-square-metre suspended glazed canopy above the entrance. Sitting at the forecourt of the southern entrance is a beautiful sculpture designed by American artist Charles O. Perry. The load-bearing structure is based on a concrete core and perimeter columns at the upper levels, which enable wide spans of clear space inside to house offices. *SZ*

John Gollings

Chancellery & Business School 177 F

100 Joondalup Dr, Joondalup
FJMT, HASSELL
2003

Edith Cowan University launched the 'Campus West' project in 2000 in order to establish a new main campus in Joondalup. It held a design competition, specifying in the brief a wish for a new identity for the university as well as a clear and formal relationship to the City of Joondalup. The Campus West site sits at the head of a masterplan, developed by Cox Howlett and Bailey Woodland, which incorporates existing buildings from the former College of Advanced Education (CAE). A pedestrian mall runs through the low-scale buildings to the City of Joondalup to the north. The design for the Campus West precinct assembles the three primary components of the brief – the Chancellery, the Business School, and the University Lawn – in a considered relationship along the campus axis and opens the campus to Joondalup. The folded ground plane of the podium and Business School and the rising structure of the Chancellery give form to the university's desire to embrace the place and landscape of Joondalup and present an iconic and contemporary identity to the community. The programme, comprising public interface functions, administration offices, executive offices and facilities, teaching spaces, and parking, was interpreted to provide accommodation of high amenity, functionality, and security. Vertical circulation is arranged with a generosity of dimension and light to encourage movement and exchange. The conceptual strategies sought to elevate the new buildings beyond their programmatic requirements to perform a greater civic role. The Chancellery building was arranged as two parts on two sides of the university mall with a jarrah screen offering a welcoming gesture to the City of Joondalup. The stepped façade of the Business School provides places for formal and informal gatherings. The Chancellery provides a dramatic backdrop for events held in the ceremonial open space. These design features demonstrate how the buildings have been configured to contribute to the civic quality of the campus and the metropolitan hub. *PA*

nearmap

Uwe Zahradnik

John Gollings

F

Interview

Evolution from a sense of being on the periphery

FJMT is a multi-disciplinary design studio with a particular commitment to enhancing the public domain. The studio culture revolves around project-based collaboration. It is an organic environment, made from interlocking and overlapping collaborative groups.

Richard Francis-Jones, Design director, *Francis-Jones Morehen Thorp (FJMT)*

What differentiates architecture in Australia from international architecture?
Australian architecture has evolved from a sense of being on the periphery, of being at a distance from the centre of culture. However, this has some advantages, as it is often the periphery where the most innovative and interesting work takes place. This distance has allowed an authentic exploration of place, culture, and climate to develop, while at the same time producing a longing to be connected, and a sense of insecurity. This peripheral sense gives a cultural independence but also a desperate longing to be part of the centre. It is a blessing and a curse.

What role do current architectural trends play in your design approach?
Architecture is by its nature slow and lasting, while the speed of fashion and beguiling interest is quick and passing. So there is a tension between architecture and trends, and caution is needed. In our work, we want to embrace the great potential of developments in material and systems technologies while avoiding the flux of popular image consumption that our screens encourage.

Where do you find your design inspiration?
The key sources of inspiration are the purpose of the project and the place of the project. By purpose I don't really mean the brief but the deeper aspiration and the cultural implications that lie behind the brief. The place of the project is more than merely a site; it is the history and memory imprinted on the site, it's interconnection with a larger built or natural landscape. The inspiration for our architecture is this duality; it is human purpose woven into a place.

What could the rest of the world learn from Australian architecture?
Australian architecture is evolving from a struggle between globalisation and localisation. It is seeking to find a way to become more authentically of this place and yet also be part of the evolution of global architectural culture. It is a difficult line to tread and I think there is something to learn from both our failures and our successes.

John Gollings

A museum below clouds and historic brickwork: Newcastle Museum, New South Wales (2011)

John Gollings

A gentle layered curve to the lake and landscape: Ben Chifley Building, Canberra (2015)

John Gollings

A new civic cultural hub: Port of Sale, Wellington Shire, Victoria (2017)

Design proposal for The Star Ritz-Carlton Hotel, Sydney (2017)

« Swan Bells Tower

178 F

Barrack Square, Riverside Dr
Hames Sharley
1988

The Swan Bells Tower, perhaps the world's largest musical instrument, was designed by the firm Hames Sharley. The 82.5-metre-high tower contains eighteen bells, twelve of which were originally in the Church of St Martin-in-the-Fields on Trafalgar Square, London, and six of which were custom cast. The tower's concrete structure houses six levels, containing a belfry, ringing room, sound chamber, lift shaft, spiral staircase, and public viewing dock. The architects used a steel lattice cladded with glass panels for the full-height curtain wall and spire, making them translucent, and capped off the spire with a futuristic finned upper spire. The sail-like façade elements are cladded in copper, in reference to the state's mining industry. *SZ*

Central Institute of Technology

179 F

William St & Aberdeen St
Lyons
2011

Architectural practice Lyons, in association with T&Z, won a competition in 2006 to design the new Central Institute of Technology building. One of the key concepts of this project was for the new building to connect the existing buildings on Aberdeen Street with their 1970s counterparts across the street, thereby creating a larger urban space. The idea was to create a 'social heart' as a connecting device between the structures on opposing sides of the street. This space became a focus for the campus but also a major entrance foyer to the learning commons and other educational spaces within the building. The social-heart foyer in effect triples the size of the implied urban space and connects the old building and the new building together. The social heart is half inside and half outside, and the two zones are visually interconnected, as they are mediated by a large transparent glazed façade wall running diagonal to the street grid. The building has a very large floor-plate size, so the central sky-lit atrium brings natural light deep into the library and learning environment. Rooms are organised around the atrium with large windows looking into the space. The curved north side of the building is formed by the constraint of the adjacent underground road tunnel. Public entrances connect the building to its surroundings on its four corners. *PA*

F

Perth Arena 180 F

700 Wellington St
ARM Architecture, Cameron Chisholm Nicol Architects
2012

The geometrically abstract Perth Arena has served as Western Australia's prime multi-functional venue since its completion in 2012. ARM Architecture collaborated with Cameron Chisholm Nicol to design the arena, drawing inspiration from the Eternity jigsaw puzzle, which consists of 209 irregularly shaped pieces that fit into a twelve-sided board. The architects selected a number of these puzzle pieces to shape the exterior's angular form, which is also echoed throughout the interior spaces. The selected pieces were chosen to resemble characteristic Western Australian icons. The external blue canopy was designed in such a way that its form mirrors the outline of the building when viewed from a certain point on the ground. This point is marked by a recessed triangular tile at ground level. A large section of the exterior façade is coated in International Klein Blue, a bold colour originally mixed by the French artist Yves Klein. The flexible arena has a seating capacity of up to 15,000 spectators, an operable roof, VIP boxes, and five multi-purpose event rooms that offer views onto the main arena and the surrounding city. *SZ*

Wikimedia Commons (Samuel Wiki)

flickr (Lori Schokman, Purple Lorikeet)

Peter Bennetts

Orangutan Enclosure

181 F

20 Labouchere Rd, South Perth
Iredale Pedersen Hook Architects
2014

Perth Zoo was opened in 1898 with the purpose of showing the Australian public many unknown species from faraway Europe. Today the zoo is dedicated to an entirely different purpose. It is organised geographically, with each area dedicated to a specific region: Asia, Africa, America, and Australia. Animals from continental Europe are no longer kept at the zoo. The zoo's current focus is on keeping and breeding domestic animals, such as the many species of kangaroos, koalas, dingos, and emus found in Australia. Winters on the west coast of the country are relatively mild, which means Perth Zoo can, for the most part, do without weatherproof animal buildings. Moreover, luxurious swathes of tropical flowers and palms flourish quite happily without greenhouses. The zoo does not keep Arctic and Antarctic animals. When the zoo first opened, orangutans were among the few animals shown in the zoo. Since then, Perth Zoo has become a global leader in the captive breeding of Sumatran orangutans: 26 of the red-haired great apes have been born in Perth since 1970. There are far more Borneo orangutans living in the wild (with a population of 55,000) than Sumatran orangutans (with a population of 7,500), which are in grave danger of extinction. The great apes are highly intelligent and spend most of their time in trees. Their new enclosure in Perth has a futuristic steel-frame structure, which has nothing in common with enclosures at other zoos that make great efforts to reconstruct the natural living space of the animals as faithfully as possible. The 'steel trees' in Perth rise up to a height of 14 metres in the air, tied together with many adjustable ropes that facilitate the swinging from tree to tree typical for the species. The shorter steel masts anchor the ropes and sway with a similar motion as do real small trees. The platforms on the large steel masts are equipped with drinking-water stations and shady roofs made of recycled eucalyptus wood. These platforms serve as lookouts and sleeping places. The only longer-term relations among orangutans are between females and their offspring. As a rule, orangutans operate alone within fixed territories, and it is difficult to facilitate this territorial behaviour in captivity. Different opportunities for activity are located throughout the entire enclosure in order to provide the animals with intellectual stimulation and offer them some diversion as they search for food. Marmalade-filled tubes encourage the intelligent animals to fashion little tools from sticks in order to get at their meals. The animals can also playfully spray each other with water at the many watering holes. All elements of the zoo have been modelled after nature. However, the design process for the climbing towers in the Perth Zoo began by dispensing with any attempts to imitate nature. The steel trees, which have a high load-bearing capacity, have a highly abstracted form. But they nonetheless reflect the characteristics that the animals would find in forest trees without appearing artificial or cheap. Structural engineers created the trees, and the swinging ropes have deliberately been placed at eye level. *NM*

Peter Bennetts

F

Ngoolark Student Services Building

182 F

Edith Cowan University, Joondalup
JCY Architects and Urban Designers
2015

'Ngoolark' is the word the Noongar peoples use for the endangered white-tailed black cockatoo, also known as Carnaby's Cockatoo. It is also the name of Edith Cowan University's new Student Services Building B34 on its Joondalup Campus in Perth. This building is a new, vast, and sculptural place which connects numerous buildings and 'paths' through the university that had been left disconnected during ECU's rapid growth in recent years. The site is located at the confluence of a number of important campus pedestrian paths, between the new library, also designed by JCY Architects and Urban Designers, and an existing lecture theatre building. This site is a residual piece of land that was previously more of an obstacle than a connector between the buildings and also formed a barrier to the ECU's primary administrative buildings (B1 and B2) as well as the rest of the campus. The sloping terrain on the site, which was previously a hindrance, was integrated into the design with great success. Ngoolark comprises a vast forum and market level, a podium level, and a six-storey building at its core. It has two primary ground levels which together link the library, the B1 and B2 buildings, the lecture theatre, and the existing buildings to the east, with all primary pedestrian links on the east, west, north, and south. The whole complex acts as a web with a vertical spine created by a lofty atrium located within the eastern portion of the building itself. Internal levels are interconnected via a set of 'hanging' timber stairs and walkways located on each level and overlooking the atrium. The central building, comprising five levels with a major rooftop plant level, has been designed as a simple, flexible, and sustainable high-quality office building with large floor plans, excellent exposure to northern and southern light, and exceptional views. Structurally it is based on a large column grid with smaller areas

to house vertical service shafts. There are escape stairwells and other amenities, located primarily on the west with a secondary staircase to the east. This base building provides exceptional office spaces and sophisticated workplace environments on all levels with fresh open plans, collaborative work areas, and social spaces placed both internally as well as opening out to the atrium spaces to the east. The building is currently fitted out primarily for use as an office building, but it has been designed such that it can later be converted to house classrooms and teaching spaces to meet changing requirements as the university evolves.

Embedded within the fabric of the interior and exterior of the building are a number of motifs which were developed and brought to life through consultation with Kurongkurl Katitjin, the ECU's Centre for Indigenous Australian Education and Research, as well as with the local Noongar community. These motifs include the golden, folded, perforated aluminium veil which is wrapped around the three upper levels of the building; the ceramic frit on the glazed façade; and the bespoke carpet design throughout the building. The design for the golden aluminium veil stems from a desire to create a skin based on the shimmering scales of a butterfly wing. The gold anodised colouring was selected for its ability to glimmer and change its colour as the light changes at different times of the day, during different times of the year, and depending on each panel's location and orientation. The panels were designed to form a skin that remains continuous but was folded and modulated as it was put in place around the building. This golden fabric was then stretched and rolled to the east to become the floating sculptural roof above the café structure. The perforated patterns punched into each of the panels are derived from the curved and overlapping patterns on the chest feathers of the Carnaby's Cockatoo. These are represented as solid and void in the gold aluminium sunshade, creating a rich patina externally and a wonderful shadow and silhouette on the inside, reflecting and bouncing light, colour, and shade in a myriad of patterns around and throughout the building. *PA*

Rob Ramsay

Darwin and Surroundings

G

Darwin
NORTHERN TERRITORY
QUEENSLAND
WESTERN AUSTRALIA
Brisbane
SOUTH AUSTRALIA
NEW SOUTH WALES
Perth
Sydney
Adelaide
Canberra
A. C. T.
VICTORIA
Melbourne
TASMANIA
Hobart

G Darwin

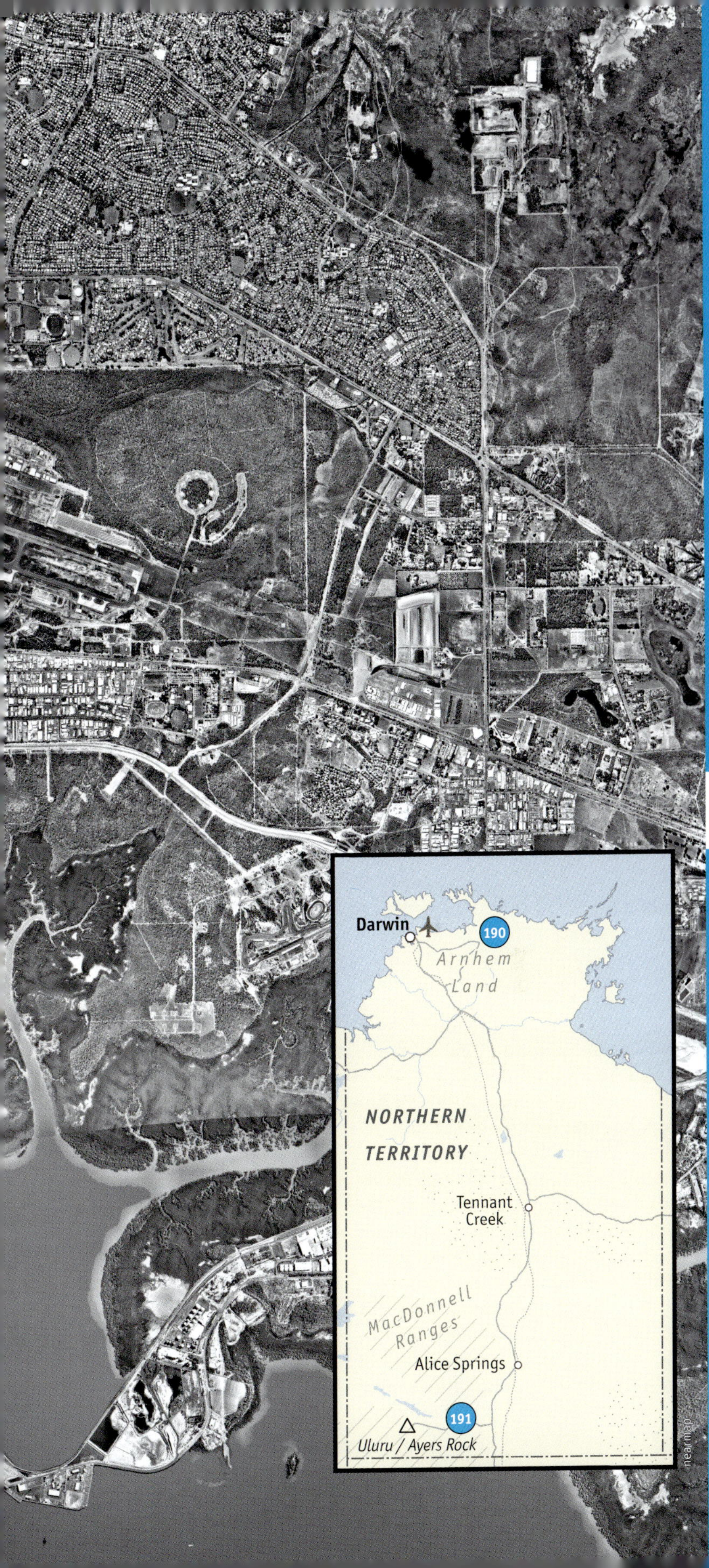
Darwin
190
Arnhem
Land
NORTHERN
TERRITORY
Tennant
Creek
MacDonnell
Ranges
Alice Springs
191
Uluru / Ayers Rock
nearmap

Darwin and Surroundings

Scenic view onto the waterfront by the Darwin Fisherman's Wharf area

The city of Darwin lies in Australia's outback Northern Territory and remains actively occupied by its traditional owners, the Larrakia people. Although Darwin was formally founded in 1869, the first inhabitants of the land were Indigenous Australians. The British settlement was initially named Palmerston, and it wasn't until 1911 that the city's name was changed to Darwin after the evolutionary biologist Charles Darwin. The city is the hub of Australia's mining and horticulture industries, offshore oil and gas production, and pastoralism. With a population of less than 150,000, it is the least populated of Australia's state capitals, and the city's workforce consists primarily of government employees. Darwin's growth accelerated substantially after the discovery of gold at Pine Creek in 1871. The city lies very close to Southeast Asian countries and is known as Australia's gateway to Southeast Asia. This proximity has not only influenced business but also the architectural styles in this thriving city. Early buildings were simple constructions with simple designs, and the hot and humid climate made for uncomfortable living conditions. Building modifications emerged later: verandas were added to buildings, for

iStock (John Carnemolla)

example, to provide sun protection and relief from the hot climate. Readily available materials such as timber and bark were heavily used in construction. Asian settlers introduced the use of bamboo as a building material, which provided better ventilation. The late 19th century brought about a change in building styles and earlier materials were replaced with corrugated iron and local stones. Darwin was heavily bombed by the Japanese during the Second World War, which resulted in the destruction of many of the city's first buildings. The city, prone to cyclones, has undergone major reconstruction numerous times. The strongest cyclone to date was Cyclone Tracy in 1974, which destroyed over 70 per cent of Darwin's homes. With time, the city was rebuilt into what is now the most modern capital in the nation. Materials such as masonry and concrete became predominant as they offered better resistance against cyclones. Yet these materials led to poor ventilation in interior spaces, which increased demand for air conditioning. Troppo is one of the Northern Territory's most celebrated architectural firms and has tested this design approach to tropical conditions with its design for the Bowali Vistor Centre and DHA Prototype Housing. *SZ*

Design for the Hot-Humid Tropics

David Bridgman

The climate and its effect on health and comfort have been a preoccupation of architects from at least the time of the Roman Architect Vitruvius. In his *Ten Books on Architecture*, Vitruvius pointed out the virtues of appropriate orientation, shading, and placement of windows for light. Closer to home, Robert Haddon's 1908 book *Australian Architecture*, and JW Drysdale's 1947 classic *Designing Houses for Australian Climates* provided advice specific to Australian conditions. It would be no exaggeration to say that since Europeans settled in the humid tropics, the design of buildings and their relation to climate have been of interest to both architects and residents alike. By the middle of the twentieth century, appropriate design for the tropics had become a government concern, with Australia becoming one of many countries to establish research organisations intent on investigating design and construction methods. The energy crisis of the 1970s led to a flurry of research into energy efficiency through passive design and in more recent years emphasis has once again been placed on ecologically sustainable development and on designing in response to the climatic conditions of a region. However, this is not to argue the case for environmental determinism in architecture. As history demonstrates, climate and environmental considerations have always been adapted to the dominant architectural language of the time, and this with varying degrees of success. Furthermore, early settlers were notoriously ambivalent towards the climate, and their clothing, diet, and behaviour responded more to traditions from home than to the region. This was certainly the case in the tropical regions of the Northern Territory colloquially known as the 'Top End'. This area has a wet-dry climate that, as the term suggests, consists of two distinct seasons: a cool, dry, winter (dry season) and a hot, wet summer (wet season). The dry season is characterised by cool evenings and mornings, warm days, low humidity, and little or no rainfall. The wet season is characterised by high day temperatures and fairly high night temperatures, high humidity, high levels of solar radiation, high rainfall, and regular monsoon activity. The sky is often cloudy, resulting in high levels of glare, and there is a risk of tropical cyclones in coastal regions. These are general climatic conditions, however, and each location has a microclimate influenced by a number of factors including topography, vegetation, patterns of prevailing winds and rainfall, proximity to the coast, and existing buildings. How then should an architect respond to these climatic conditions? In purely climatic terms the ideal habitable space for the

flickr (Geoff Whalan)

humid tropics is the area beneath a shady tree, open to the breezes and protected from the heat of the sun. Any departure from this is a compromise in terms of climatic performance. There are, of course, many good reasons not to live under a shady tree and a development from this is a raised platform with a covering roof supported on columns. The construction of walls that delimit space, the provision of services that necessitate closure, and the desire for privacy and security all involve some form of compromise in terms of the climatic performance of a building. From the discussion we can identify three broad principles for design in a humid climate: the need to maximise shading, maximise ventilation, and minimise heat gain. In practice, however, these simple principles are not universally applied in the design of buildings. A review of many of the early civic and commercial buildings in the Northern Territory reveals design influences from colonial models more appropriate to temperate climates. This can be seen in the use of heavy stone walls with high thermal mass, minimal roof overhangs providing little shade to the walls, and small windows providing little ventilation to the interiors. With little concession to the climate, these buildings attempt to provide a refuge from an alien landscape. The Palmerston Town Hall, completed in 1883 to a design

G

NT Archives Service, Darwin City Council

English, Scottish and Australasian Bank, circa 1880, Northern Territory

Commercial Bank of Australia, 1887, Northern Territory

Town Hall, 1887, Palmerston, Port Darwin, Northern Territory

by John George Knight, is one example of this approach where heavy stone walls separate the internal and external environments. Despite written accounts detailing Knight's understanding of climate issues and his acceptance of the importance of ventilation in the tropics, when he designed the Town Hall it was the symbolic role of the building that was clearly more important. The Town Hall was a solid, imposing building signifying the presence and permanence of settlement in the Northern Territory. The Town & Country Bank (1884) was built to a design based on a protected core and a surrounding colonnade. Trading as the Commercial Bank of Australia from 1887, the 'stone bank', as it was called, was clearly influenced by colonial experience in India. The heavy stone colonnade running along two sides of the building provided protection to the stone walls of the bank building while offering a refuge from torrential rain and a shaded walkway along Darwin's main commercial street. Its mass and form, however, is the very antithesis of the traditional lightweight tropical building. Other buildings, such as the English, Scottish & Australasian Bank, however, demonstrate a design approach that would become more common in the tropics. The bank was constructed in 1873, and although details are scarce, it was most probably a portable iron building sent from Adelaide with the verandas added in 1882. Colloquially known as the 'tin-bank', it was constructed of lightweight metal cladding that responded quickly to changes in temperature, and the surrounding veranda acted as a buffer to shade the walls of the building while providing a protected outdoor space for customers. Screens, slats, and vines were used to provide additional shade from the early morning and afternoon sun. This Anglo-Indian typology, of a protected central core of rooms and open encircling verandas, would appear throughout the tropics and in rural Australia from the beginning of settlement and remains a common residential typology today. By the early twentieth century, buildings emerged that were more appropriate for the climate. These were often made of local materials such as woven bamboo, thought to have been introduced by Asian immigrants drawing on traditions and skills from their homelands. The caretaker's cottage, constructed in the early decades of the twentieth century, illustrates this approach with large shutters to promote ventilation and woven bamboo walls that were quick, easy, and cheap to construct from material readily available on site. By the 1930s architects settling in Australia introduced a building typology common in British colonies in Malaysia and Singapore to the Northern Territory. These tropical houses were ideal for the climate and consisted of little more than open verandas with permeable walls to promote ventilation, large roof overhangs, and shutters to provide shade to walls and openings. While a building incorporating some or all of the above characteristics can be comfortable for most of the year, the air temperature inside fully ventilated buildings, no matter how well designed they are, will not be less than the air temperature outside. While the outdoor air temperature in coastal regions is seldom far above comfort level, in other regions and for some periods of the year, internal conditions can be unpleasant and some form of mechanical cooling is usually necessary. The simplest means of modifying internal conditions is to increase the circulation of air within a room through the use of ceiling or pedestal fans while the more traditional but less efficient colonial device was the large punkah. However, in extreme conditions mechanical air-conditioning may be the only means of ensuring comfortable indoor temperatures. While purists may object to the use of air-conditioning on philosophical grounds, a humid afternoon in late November is capable of making converts of even the most resolute. Although the use of mechanical air-conditioning in the hot-humid tropics cannot be rejected, it must not be considered a substitute for a passive design approach. One of the challenges facing architects today is to provide owners with the option of either using air-conditioning or of opening the building to enjoy the outdoor spaces.

NT Archives Service, Darwin City Council

Tropical House, 1939, Northern Territory

≈ Administrator's Offices

183 G

14 Esplanade, Darwin
John George Knight
1884

The Darwin esplanade site of what is today the Administrator's Offices formerly contained the city's police station and courthouse. The Royal Australian Navy used it as their main headquarters during the 1940s. Former cell blocks have since been reconfigured to serve as mechanical plant rooms. Designed by British architect John Knight, the buildings were constructed with locally sourced lime stone and feature gable roofs and wide bordering verandas to reduce the tropical heat. *SZ*

Wesleyan Methodist Church

184 G

George Brown Botanic Gardens
David Bridgman (2001)
1897, 2001

The first Wesleyan Methodist Church, a timber-framed building dating from 1873, was badly damaged by a tropical cyclone in January 1897. The congregation sought a replacement church that would be better able to resist future cyclones. They commissioned a steel-frame building from the Adelaide-based Simpson Company, a metalworking firm established in 1852 by the English born and trained tinsmith Alfred Simpson. The church was prefabricated in Adelaide

The Wesleyan Church and adjacent parsonage, late 19th century

with steel imported from Scottish mills, erected in the company carpark, and then dismantled. Each element was then numbered and shipped to Darwin where it was erected on an inner-city site. The church underwent significant changes over time with timber-framed transepts added in the 1940s to cater to an increased wartime congregation. In later years the church was used as a store for the Methodist Inland Mission and was, for a time, a motorcycle repair shop. The building was left derelict for many years and in danger of being lost when a decision was taken by the government to relocate the building from the city centre to the George Brown Botanic Gardens. It was subsequently reconstructed back to its original form and a new structural frame was added to brace the building against cyclonic winds. This nationally important prefabricated steel church is characterised by a light web of T-section and flat-bar steel frames that support the metal wall cladding. Veranda columns feature a sophisticated head casting slotted to accommodate the roof framing which may well have been fabricated in Australia by local artisans. The framing is extremely lightweight and is held down by chains extending from the eaves at the hips to concrete anchor blocks buried in the ground. Darwin's oldest church is now a popular café. *PA*

flickr (rjcox)

≈ Government House

185 G

29 Esplanade, Darwin
John George Knight
1871

The heritage-listed Government House is also generally known as the 'House of Seven Gables' for its ridged roofs. Completed in 1871, it is the oldest European building in the Northern Territory. The house is the official residence of the Administrator of the Northern Territory. Its prime location overlooks the stunning harbour and is surrounded by a thicket of tropical greenery. The building is made from local stone, and a bark-roofed veranda wraps around its exterior. British architect John George Knight was involved in the extensive renovation works which took place in 1879. It was one of the few buildings to survive Cyclone Tracy and the bombing raids during the Second World War. *SZ*

Geoff Whalan

Supreme Court

186 G

State Square, Darwin

Peter Doig, Ron Findlay, Roger Linklater

1991

Established in 1911, the Supreme Court of the Northern Territory has changed its place of residence more than once. It was originally located at the Administrative Offices site until 1942, when, as a wartime security measure, it was relocated to Alice Springs. It wasn't until 1991 that the court's 14,000-square-metre site in the State Square was opened. The building's tropical design intentionally bears resemblance to the neighbouring Parliament House and is adapted to Darwin's tropical climatic conditions. The building's masonry walls, colonnades, and verandas provide an ample amount of sun protection. Inside are courtrooms, judges' chambers, a library, a sheriff's office, the Supreme Court Registry, administrative offices, and a public coffee lounge. Polished granite has been used for the flooring of the stairway, foyer spaces, and the front veranda. Australian timbers are used throughout the interior. *SZ*

Darwin Visitor Information Centre

187 G

6 Bennett St

1967

Ken Hodge

Located on the corner of Bennett Street and Smith Street is what used to be Darwin's Reserve Bank, which opened in 1967 and closed in 1997. Since 2007, the building has been known as Darwin's Visitor Information Centre and is used as a tourist centre at a prime location, considering its close proximity to the Darwin Waterfront and the Convention Centre. The building itself is recognised as a noteable example of the late 20th century Stripped Classicism style and is listed on the Northern Territory Heritage Register. *SZ*

Parliament House

188 G

State Square, Darwin
Meldrum Burrows and Partners
1994

Situated on Darwin's State Square, the Parliament House was part of the 1988 government precinct project, which included the development of the Supreme Court. In 1990, the old Legislative Assembly building was demolished to make way for the current day Parliament House, completed in 1994. Architectural firm Meldrum Burrows designed the building, which features Asian influences and is capable of withstanding extreme weather conditions, including cyclones. There is a certain lightness in the façade, with its white colonnades that support the thin roof. The wide overhang of the roof and the setback windows along with decorative screening all play a part in diffusing direct sunlight. Interior spaces are built from mostly Tasmanian timbers, pink marble, and black, brown, and white granite. The 550-square-metre main hall hosts up to 1000 people for parliament receptions and exhibitions. *SZ*

Christ Church Cathedral

189 G

2 Smith St, Darwin City
Wilkins, Klemm and Morrison
1977

Only the western-end wall and porch remain of the original Christ Church Cathedral. The rest of the building was completed destroyed when Cyclone Tracy hit on Christmas Day, 1974. Architectural firm Wilkins, Klemm and Morrison designed the new church building, which was opened in 1977. Inside, adjacent to the altar, a contemporary stained-glass window has been inserted into the harbour wall. This window, depicting fishing nets and rising waves, is a memorial to Cyclone Tracy and was designed by Darwin artist George Chaloupka and funded by the Gollin Kyokuyo Trust. Gollin Kyokuyo was a Darwin-based joint fishing venture that had unfortunately lost some of its sailors, fishermen, and trawlers when Cyclone Tracy hit. *SZ*

G

View from the billabong looking down an open link to the administration offices

Bowali Visitor Centre

190 G

Kakadu National Park
Glenn Murcutt, Troppo Architects
1993

The Bowali Visitor Centre is an award-winning landscape-interpretation centre designed by Glen Murcutt in association with the practice Troppo Architects. The building sits nestled within the Kakadu National Park's dramatic bushland setting. Its architecture responds to the surrounding site and climate conditions as well as the local indigenous community. Its design incorporates local materials, sourced in part with the efforts of the Traditional Owners. Walls are built from rammed earth, corrugated metal, glazing, and timber battens. The complex's long, linear form sits on a north-east and south-west axis and is raised off the ground. The visitor centre, public display, presentation, as well as craft and library spaces are centrally located under the metal roof and are linked by a long external pathway along the north-eastern side to the southern end's administration offices. *SZ*

Patrick Bingham-Hall

Patrick Bingham-Hall

Kata Tjuta Cultural Centre

191 G

Uluru Rd, Uluru
Gregory Burgess Architects
1995

The Kata Tjuta Cultural Centre was completed in 1995, against the backdrop of Uluru, a large sandstone rock formation that is sacred to Anagu, the Aboriginal people of Central Australia. It was the wish of Anangu that the building design express their working together 'as one' with the Rangers of the Australian Nature Conservation Agency in the joint management of the Uluru-Kata Tjuta National Park. This unique integration of indigenous knowledge and wisdom about nature and land management with western science has proved highly successful. The building celebrates the spirit of Anangu culture: it maintains an animated relationship with its powerful site, extensively uses sustainable materials, consumes low energy, and responds sympathetically to both people and environment. The building is situated about a kilometre to the south of Uluru, just off but visible from the main road. To the approaching visitor, the building appears as a mysterious undulating presence of skin, sinew, and shadow, emerging and disappearing. Red sand, bloodwood, and copper are transformed and animated. Anangu spoke of the two serpentine buildings as representing the snakes Liru and Kuniya, watching each other warily across the site of a battleground. The buildings arc about a dead desert oak in a natural clearing facing the southern face of Uluru, on which the Tjukurpa (traditional law) of Liru and Kuniya are inscribed. The sequence of spaces and materials throughout the building is modulated by contrast: of scale, of light and deep shadow, of openness and opacity, of movement and stillness, of weight and lightness. Through this rhythmic play, an elusive resonance develops between the building, the culture, the landscape, and the visitor, and the Anangu presence is sensed. Metaphorically, the building elaborates the underlying serpentine Tjukurpa with its writhing plan, sliding sinewy roofs, skeletal ridges, and various smaller details throughout. *PA*

John Gollings

DHA Prototype Housing 192 G
Muirhead*
Troppo Architects
2016

The firm Troppo Architects was commissioned by Defence Housing Australia (DHA) to design new accommodation for defence personnel in the suburb of Muirhead. The result, Tropology, introduces a new paradigm of housing in Darwin. The building draws on the rich history of climatically responsive design for the tropics and is instantly recognisable as belonging in the Top End. Current technologies were combined with long-standing design principles to create homes that cater to the requirements of a modern family looking to revel in the Darwin lifestyle. The project brief demanded a contemporary housing prototype that could change perceptions of small-lot housing. The compact, efficient footprint still achieves a sense of spaciousness through open, single-loaded planning and the integration of outdoor living spaces. The site plan accounts for

the storage requirements of transient residents working as defence personnel but also facilitates extracurricular activities popular in the Top End. It consists of multipurpose semi-outdoor and outdoor spaces: to host children's wet-season birthday parties, to park the trailer or tinny, and to grow bananas and pawpaws. Hard-wearing, low-maintenance materials withstand regular tenancy changes and reduce whole-life costs for DHA. Australian hardwood is specified throughout for structural, framing, screening, and shading uses, softening and balancing the feel of the spaces. Two-storey, long-and-thin plans allow for a cross breeze to enter every room. Ground-level living spaces connect with the garden and street. Upper-level sleeping spaces offer views of Buffalo Creek, drawing evening breezes from nearby Casuarina Beach. The tropical garden and green roof provide shade and protection and can also be used to produce food. *PA*

* Private residence not open for public

Rozak House

193 G

Lake Bennett*
Troppo Architects
2002

The self-sufficient Rozak House is a remarkable example of a self-sustaining building that doesn't require large amounts of supplied energy. The architects implemented typical tropical design principles, using large amounts of lightweight and heat-reflective materials and ensuring ample cross ventilation and shading of walls and openings. The building collects its own power through solar voltaic cells stored on site and converts this power for use in the house. It collects and stores water in rainwater tanks on the roof. A solar hot-water system heats the water. The open living experience of this elevated building can be experienced by all guests who come to spend a night or two here. *SZ*

* Private residence not open for public

Darwin Convention Centre
10 Stokes Hill Rd, Darwin City
HASSELL
2008

194 G

Designed by the practice HASSELL, the Darwin Convention Centre is an iconic public building that sits surrounded by the stunning Darwin Waterfront precinct. Since it was opened in 2008 it has earned a reputation as a world-class venue, with its modern design and outstanding multipurpose and flexible event spaces. The centre is large enough to host conventions of 1,200 delegates but is also small enough to offer intimate event experiences. The venue is 22,900 square metres in size and includes an adaptable auditorium space with a seating capacity of 1,200 visitors which can also be divided into two separate spaces. Four column-free halls are also included which can be used as exhibition, banquet, or theatre spaces. Spectacular harbour views can be experienced from various locations within the building. *SZ*

flickr (Geoff Whalan)

G

Darwin Waterfront

195 G

19 Kitchener Dr, Darwin City
HASSELL
2009

The vision for the Darwin Waterfront development was to transform the city's former port into a world-class, mixed-use, urban community, attracting local residents, business travellers, and tourists. The masterplan by HASSELL builds on Darwin's strong cultural heritage, incorporating and interpreting the site's historic headland landforms, re-establishing natural vegetation, and acknowledging indigenous associations and past uses. It extends the street pattern of the city, bringing it to the water's edge like 'fingers' in the harbour. The development was designed as a series of staged precincts with each providing a defined identity. This first precinct, Stage 1, focused on the development of the public domain, with extensive new public parklands, a wave lagoon, and swimming beach, as well as key public buildings, including the Darwin Convention Centre. The newly created connection to the harbour includes an active beach, defined by patrolled paddling pools and a contained sand beach for year-round swimming. The Territory's first outdoor wave lagoon provides a year-round facility for active water play. The swimming beach, wave lagoon, and surrounding parklands are the public heart of the Darwin Waterfront. It is the space people descend to from the city and congregate in for beachside activities and cultural events – it is Darwin's new destination. The retention and integration of specific heritage items and a sympathetic relationship to the escarpment were significant factors influencing the layout of the site. Soft and hard landscaping throughout the precinct reflects the heritage of the site. One can see the widespread use of native tropical species and plants that have significant cultural meaning. The incorporation of public art and a heritage trail interpreting the past uses and associations of the area are all evident at Darwin Waterfront today. *PA*

Tropical Veranda

196 G

5 Stirling Place, Larrakeyah
David Bridgman Architects
2006

Tropical houses built after the Second World War exemplified the ideals of the modern movement. They were constructed throughout inner-city Darwin in their hundreds by the Commonwealth Government from the early 1950s. These houses, providing workers' accommodation for government employees and responding to a period of austerity as much as a design philosophy, were provided with outdoor veranda areas that were often very small or limited and in some cases little more than landings at the top of stairs. A growing desire to move out of the confined space of the house saw a resurgence in veranda construction on these early buildings as they passed from government into private ownership. The 2006 project on 5 Stirling Place resulted in a large veranda being added to a tropical house. Perched high above the ground, it provides a spectacular entertainment and recreational area for the owners. Independent of the main house, the veranda is accessed by a long, ceremonial covered walkway that terminates in a lookout providing spectacular views down the escarpment to Kahlin Oval, Cullen Bay, and the broad expanse of Darwin Harbour beyond. While the setting sun can bathe the veranda in rich colours, the veranda is for the most part there to provide refuge from the heat of the tropical days. Timber battens act to screen the veranda, providing protection from the sun while allowing the cooling afternoon sea breeze to penetrate and add to the pleasure of the space. More recently, the owners demolished their old house to make way for a new tropical residence off the veranda, successfully integrating the two elements through the use of form and colour. *PA*

Bullocky Point Education Precinct

197 G

10 Atkins Drive, Darwin
David Bridgman Architects
2016

An exemplar of contemporary architecture, excellence in site planning, and respect for context, the Bullocky Point Education Precinct is a purpose-designed building forming the new administration centre for Darwin High School, one of the first NT Government independent public schools, and an innovative home for the Northern Territory School of Distance Education, a secondary distance education facility. Steeped in history and part of the traditional lands of the local Larrakia people, the site was formerly a meatworks established by William Lord Vestey and his brother Sir Edmund Vestey in 1917. It became the home for Darwin High School in 1963. Little remains of the former meatworks other than a section of the large concrete water tank that was converted into a gymnasium and dance/drama auditorium for the school in 1987. Located immediately adjacent to the heritage-listed water tank, the design language of the Bullocky Point Education Precinct pays homage to the form, scale, and materiality of this striking and important historic element through the use of an industrial vernacular of steel and concrete. The large overhanging roof, deep shadows, strong vertical elements such as the multi-faceted columns that resolve into delicate branches supporting the roof, and the layering of form on all the façades characterise this striking building. Landscaping, still in embryonic form, will grow in time to further enhance the school and its setting. The shared needs of Darwin High School and the School of Distance Education are addressed through the creation of separate identities within the educational environment. Spatial planning is functional and the complex inter-relationship between the two schools resolved in a delightful manner through the use of colour, texture, and a broad range of materials including several green walls featuring tropical plants. Winner of the Australian Institute of Architects' top Northern Territory Architectural award in 2017 and described by the jury as 'most assuredly a work of the Northern Territory', the Bullocky Point Education Precinct was designed by a team led by MODE Studio Director and Principal Architect, Dr David Bridgman, with Stefney Schultz, Kelly Ingrames, Lucy Baker, and Jovette Tan. *PA*

The particularities of place

David Bridgman

David Bridgman is an architect and architectural historian specialising in the field of heritage conservation. He holds degrees in architecture, history, sociology, and music. David has completed a range of specialist architectural and heritage conservation projects throughout the Northern Territory and has undertaken significant research into the built environment of the northern tropics. He is an authority on the architect BCG Burnett. His PhD examined government housing provided for senior public servants in Darwin during the immediate pre-Second World War period with emphasis on the various influences coming from colonial architecture in India and the Southeast Asian region. His design skills have been recognised by several awards and he is committed to environmental sustainability and energy-efficient design principles. He is a Fellow of the Australian Institute of Architects, a Member of the International Council on Monuments and Sites (ICOMOS), a member of the National Trust of Australia, and a member of the Society of Architectural Historians of Australia and New Zealand (SAHANZ).

What differentiates architecture in Australia from international architecture?

Australia is a vast country with a relatively small but broadly multi-cultural population and significant climatic differences between the tropical north and the more temperate south. Australian architects have drawn and continue to draw inspiration from international architecture. However, we tend to form architecture into a response that reflects both the regional and cultural diversity that is a characteristic of Australia.

What role do current architectural trends play in your design approach?

To the extent that regionalism is a continuing architectural trend, current trends play a key role in my design approach. However, it is an approach that draws on the particular characteristics of a place, rather than simply form for form's sake.

Where do you find your design inspiration?

My architectural design inspiration is drawn from the local climate, history, place, and the social and cultural context in which we build.

David Bridgman

Tropical Veranda. Independent of the main house, the veranda is accessed by a long, ceremonial, covered walkway that terminates in a lookout providing spectacular views down the escarpment to Kahlin Oval, Cullen Bay, and the broad expanse of Darwin Harbour beyond.

Which Australian buildings do you most admire and why?

The Sydney Opera House by Jorn Utzon simply for the way it addresses the Sydney Harbour. Early tropical houses such as the series of government residences that make up the Myilly Point Heritage Precinct in Darwin designed by the architects WT Haslam and BCG Burnett because they demonstrate a response to climate, place, and social and cultural context. Lighthouses and lighthouse keepers' cottages because of their isolation and beauty in what are usually pristine settings.

What could the rest of the world learn from Australian Architecture?

While Australian architecture can be approached from an international perspective, it is the particularities of place and the response to those particularities that give Australian architecture its distinctive quality. Australian identity is reflected in the broad range of building types located across the country. Looking at Australian architecture is seeing how architecture interacts with climate, history, place, and the broader social and cultural context.

David Bridgman

The conservation architect was involved in the reconstruction of the Weslyan Methodist Church.

Brisbane and Surroundings

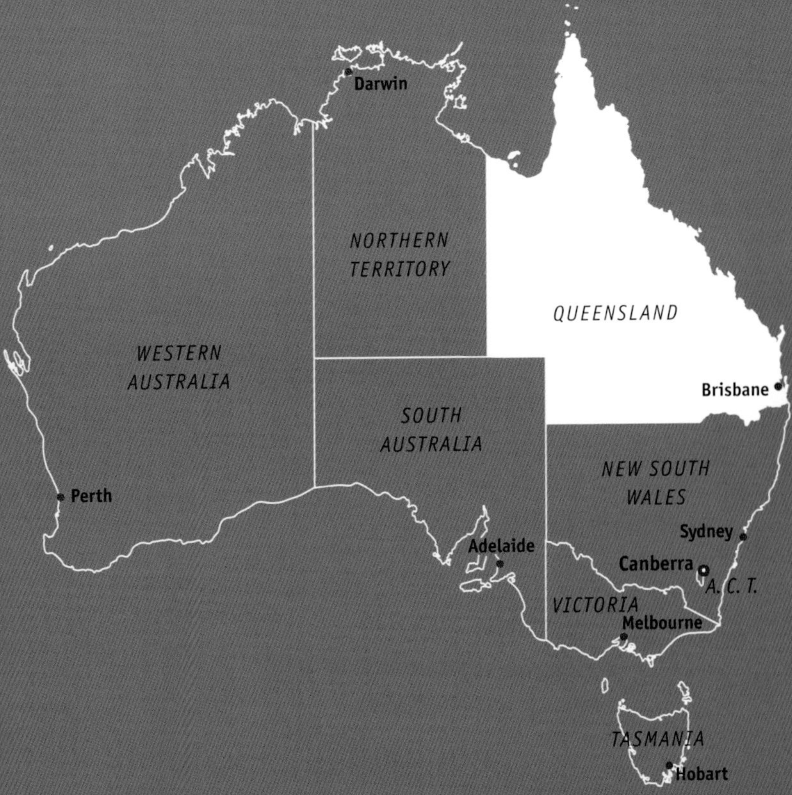
Darwin
NORTHERN TERRITORY
QUEENSLAND
WESTERN AUSTRALIA
Brisbane
SOUTH AUSTRALIA
NEW SOUTH WALES
Perth
Sydney
Adelaide
Canberra
A. C. T.
VICTORIA
Melbourne
TASMANIA
Hobart

8 Brisbane

203
213
209
227
198
211
205
221
210
222
216
220
207
208
200
201
202
199
226
212
214
224
225

Torres Strait
Gulf of Carpentaria
Cape York Peninsula
Coral Sea
Great Barrier Reef
Pacific Ocean
Cairns
228
Townsville
Bowen
204
Mount Isa
Mackay
Great Dividing
Rockhampton
Gladstone
217
218
QUEENSLAND
Bundaberg
Maryborough
Gladstone
Sunshine Coast
Sturt Stony Desert
223
Toowoomba
219
Brisbane
Gold Coast

Brisbane and Surroundings

Residing in the sunny state of Queensland, Brisbane offers 12 months of sun-filled days throughout the year. Queensland is Australia's second largest state, of which Brisbane occupies some 1,140 square kilometres, making it the largest of Australia's six capital cities and the third largest in the world. The unique winding Brisbane River which runs through the city was named after the Governor of New South Wales, Thomas Brisbane, in 1823. Although founded in 1824, Brisbane only became a free settlement in 1842. The first Europeans to inhabit the land established a convict jail in the town of Redcliffe. However, this jail was short-lived and was quickly moved to the city of Brisbane where the natural landscape with the winding river was considered to provide a better barrier against escape. The majority of Brisbane's first buildings were designed by military engineers. Of these, the Commissariat Store (1829) is one of only two that remain. The city had established itself long before the state of Queensland became a self-governing colony in 1859. Construction of the government house began shortly after and was completed in 1860. Queensland's warmer and more humid climate has greatly

Aerial view over Brisbane's central business district and winding Brisbane River

impacted the architectural character of the state, with adequate shading and ventilation becoming necessities for comfortable living. This climatic design approach was realised from the late 19th century to the mid 20th century and led to a typical Queensland architectural style marked by the heavy use of timber materials. Domestic timber houses were known as Queenslander houses and are still being constructed to this day. The noticeable two-storey structure typically included a lightweight timber single-storey section that sat elevated on an empty understorey raised by long vertical timber stumps. Designs were predominately square in shape with hipped corrugated iron roofs and one or more verandas at each side. They often included louvred windows, veranda blinds, wall and ceiling vents, and roof ventilators designed to mediate the high temperatures, humidity, and rainfall of the sub-tropical climate. Brisbane's population has grown rapidly over the years, even after the war and in spite of the slight downturn caused by the 1893 economic depression and floods. Today, it is staked as the nation's third largest city and continues to be one of the fastest-growing capital cities in the country. *SZ*

⇞ Custom House

198 H

399 Queen St, Brisbane
Charles McLay
1889

The Brisbane Customs House is one of Queensland's finest examples of the Victorian Free Classical style featuring grand colonnades, a portico, and a large dome. The current Customs House was built as a replacement for an older one, a moderate red brick building. The much grander, later incarnation was designed by colonial architect Charles McLay. A two-storey façade fronts Queen Street while three storeys can be seen on the river's edge. The interior contains an elegant public space, known as the Long Room, which is crowned by a copper dome. Nowadays, this space is used for cultural, community, and business functions while the rest of the building accommodates university activities. *SZ*

Old Government House

199 H

2B George St, Brisbane
Charles Tiffin
1862

Neighbouring the Botanic Gardens in central Brisbane sits the historically significant Old Government House which became the city's colonial hub upon its completion in 1862. The building's elevated location led to its prominence during colonial times, as visitors and immigrants arriving by ship could easily see it. The building's palace-like appearance stood out, contrasting with the surrounding wooden huts, and represented the prosperous opportunities in store for newcomers to the city. It was Brisbane's first public building to be listed on the heritage register in 1978 and also the first of many domestic buildings designed by colonial architect Charles Tiffin, who was well regarded for his Victorian-era

flickr (Lance)

public buildings in Australia. Tiffin gave the building a grand Greek Revival style design, but modified some of the conventional stylistic elements to better suit the local climate. The house was used as the private residence and official state office of Queensland's governors for almost fifty years. The colony's first governor to reside in the house was Governor Bowen. After 1910 it became the University of Queensland's initial building. From 1972 until 2002, it served as the headquarters of the National Trust of Queensland. Thereafter, the Queensland University of Technology obtained custody of the property, which was extensively restored before being reopened to the public as a historic house museum in 2009. The museum includes a multimedia centre, a private venue space, and a gallery which houses the works of respected Australian artist William Robinson. *SZ*

flickr (Olivier Navenne)

≚ St. Mary's Catholic Church

200 H

20 Merivale St, South Brisbane
George Simkin, John Ibler; Cavanagh and Cavanagh Architects
1893; 1929

State Library of Queensland

The heritage-listed St Mary's Roman Catholic Church stands nobly on Merivale Street in the South Bank cultural precinct. The original church building was first opened for service in the mid 1860s, but as Brisbane's population grew, it became clear the building needed to be expanded. The new church was completed in 1893 and was also used as a school. The architects Simkin and Ibler designed the church with Italian Romanesque and Renaissance influences. The sanctuary, vestry, and sacristy were later designed by Cavanagh and Cavanagh Architects and completed in 1929. The building is rendered with reinforced concrete and brick and features a large rose window above the main entrance. The interior is composed of terrazzo floors, marble lined walls, a domed plaster ceiling, and stained-glass windows. *SZ*

flickr (Philip Bouchard)

≙ The Mansions

201 H

70 George Street,Brisbane
George Addison
1889

The Mansions were designed in the 'Queen Anne' style by English architect George Addison of the firm Oakden, Addison and Kent. Completed in 1889, the buildings consist of six three-storey terrace houses built in red brick that are well-suited to the tropical climate of the region. Large arcaded balconies line the façade, and limestone cat sculptures sit at the top corners of the buildings. The Mansions were built as investment properties for Boyd Dunlop Morehead, William Pattison, and John Stevenson, three prominent politicians of Queensland at the time. In 1891, the medical officer Dr Lilian Violet Cooper set up her medical practice in the Mansions. Today the buildings house commercial offices and a restaurant. *SZ*

Sarah Zahradnik

⌃ Parliament House

202 H

2A George St, Brisbane City
Charles Tiffin
1868-1889

The grand 19th century Parliament House is one of Queensland's most recognised landmarks. The legislative building is situated on the corner of George and Alice Streets, overlooking the lush Botanic Gardens. Construction of the building took 25 years, from 1864 to 1889. The European financial crisis at that time caused severe financial problems in Brisbane, which in turn delayed the construction process. John Petrie, the first Mayor of Brisbane, became involved in the project, which led to more steady construction progress from 1867 onwards. English architect Charles Tiffin won the design competition held in 1893 to design the parliament building. The building's square floor plan was designed around a central courtyard space that would be occupied by public offices and the parliament house. The ground level of the three-storey building houses offices and reception rooms whilst the upper levels accommodate the legislative chambers. The exterior's solid colonnades were originally topped with a zinc roof which was later rebuilt in copper in the 1980s. Locally sourced timber finishes characterise the striking interior. *SZ*

Queensland State

Old Queensland Museum

203 H

480 Gregory Terrace, Bowen Hills
George Henry Male Addison
1891

Formerly known as the Exhibition Building, the Old Queensland Museum has gone from being the main venue for concerts in Brisbane to its current use as a museum. Australian architect George Henry Male Addison won the competition to design the former Exhibition Building. He further developed his winning design to include a T-shaped floor plan which accommodated an exhibition hall, a concert hall, and a basement dining room. Its façade consists of glazed brick, a corrugated iron roof, and two large towers. Completed in 1891, the building is amongst the most respected public structures built during the 1880s economic boom. It was listed on the Queensland Heritage Register in 1992. *SZ*

Australian Bank of Commerce 204 H
86 Mosman St, Charters Towers
FDG Stanley
1891

The former Australian Bank of Commerce building is among Queensland's finest neo-classical buildings from the late 19th century. Built as the Australian Joint Stock Bank, it was completed in 1891 and resides in Charters Towers, which was at the time Queensland's second-largest city. The masonry building was designed by colonial architect FDG Stanley in the Classical Revival style. Built in rendered brick with a corrugated iron roof, the former bank building is now better known as the World Theatre. Its interior provides an entry foyer, gallery, and offices for the modern theatre and cinema complex, which was added to the rear of the building with a connecting roof and courtyard area. *SZ*

Queensland National Bank » 205 H
308 Queen St, Brisbane
FDG Stanley
1885

The heritage-listed former Queensland National Bank building was completed in 1885. It is a fine example of Italian Renaissance Revival architecture and a symbol of the state's economic growth brought about by the 1880s building boom. The commercial building is said to be the most influential building designed by the architect FDG Stanley. Its three-storey structure is primarily made of sandstone and features large limestone columns with Palladian style detailing. The main entrance's archways are framed by grouped pilasters while the upper level's central bay sits recessed behind balconies. The grand interiors include the formal dining room, the boardroom, and the banking chamber with its glazed roof. *SZ*

flickr (demsbin)

Kangaroo Point residence, 1904

H

Lamb House

206 H

9 Leopard St, Kangaroo Point
Alexander Brown Wilson
1902

Lamb House is an admirable 'Queen Anne' style mansion. It is an enduring example of the grand residential works by the Scottish-born Brisbane architect Alexander Brown Wilson and is arguably his best work. Sitting on top of the Kangaroo Point cliffs, the observation tower of the two-storey residence is a sublime viewing platform over the city and its river. Construction of this divine Federation-period residential building was completed in 1902. Predominately made of brick and timber, its multi-gabled roof is clad in terracotta tiles whilst the entrance portico displays ornate cement mouldings. The building is surrounded by a decorative masonry fence and iron gates at the entrance. *SZ*

Treasury Building
21 Queen St, Brisbane
John James Clark, Allom Lovell Marquis-Kyle
1928, 1995

207 H

The Treasury Building is an admirable example of Italian Renaissance Revival architecture and a symbol of state pride and achievement. It was formerly used as a government building and is listed on the state heritage register. The building was erected in three stages and was under construction between 1886 and 1928. The four-storey building occupies an entire city block, surrounded by Queen Street, George Street, Elizabeth Street, and William Street, but it officially fronts Queen Street. Upon its opening in 1889, it was predominately used as a government base. Colonial architect John James Clark won the design competition held to design the building and was in fact the architect behind many of the major public buildings in Victoria, Queensland, and Western Australia. However, the principal architect on site was Thomas Pye, who was also responsible for documenting the construction process. The building is constructed with Queensland sandstone and features symmetrical arcades from which pavilions jut out at the corners. After being leased to Jupiters Limited in the 1990s, both the Land Administration Building and Treasury Building were converted into a luxury five-star hotel and casino, Treasury Hotel. The practice Allom Lovell Marquis-Kyle was responsible for the extensive renovation works which took place during this time. The building was opened to the public in 1995 as the Treasury Hotel. *SZ*

Treasury Building from William Street in 1904

flickr (Michael)

Land Administration Building **208 H**

142 George St, Brisbane
Thomas Pye, Allom Lovell Marquis-Kyle
1905

The Land Administration Building is the first and finest Edwardian Baroque building to have been built in Queensland during the time of economic recovery in the early 20th century. It was opened in 1905 and accommodated both the Lands and Survey Departments and the offices of the Premier and Executive Council. The Queensland Art Gallery also occupied a portion of the building from 1905 to 1930. The four-storey building is bound by George Street, Stephens Lane, William Street, and Queens Gardens and is located in close proximity to the Treasury Building. It sits on a two-storey granite-faced plinth, and its base is supported by a colonnade of giant order ionic columns terminated by pavilions at the corners of the façade. Thomas Pye designed the civic building, which was one of his major works, with agricultural and mining themes visible in the detailed carvings of the façade carved by New South Wales sculptor WP MacIntosh. Locally sourced Queensland materials such as granite, brown freestone, timber, and stained glass were used in the building's construction. Along with the Treasury Building, the Land Administration Building was later converted into a luxury five-star hotel and casino, the Treasury Hotel and Casino, to a redesign by Allom Lovell Marquis-Kyle. This was believed to be the state's largest heritage conservation project to date. *SZ*

St John's Cathedral
373 Ann St, Brisbane
John Loughborough Pearson
1906, 2009

209 H

The impressive St John's Cathedral is a rare example of Gothic Revival architecture in Queensland. It was designed in the French Gothic style by English architect John Loughborough Pearson, who was nationally known for his expertise in Gothic Revival architecture. Its floor plan is in the shape of the traditional Latin cross. The nave has an aisle on each side, each of which is lined with sandstone columns and arches. These provide support for Australia's only stone-ribbed vaulted ceiling, which has a height of 18 metres. The high altar was designed by Frank Pearson, John Pearson's son, in the Byzantine style and features red-brown and grey-green marble slabs, each framed by a strip of decorative gold and multi-coloured mosaics. Frank Pearson carried out the remaining design work after his father passed away in 1897. The exterior is built of local porphyry and features terracotta shingle roofing. Construction began in 1899 and took place in three stages. The first stage (1910) completed the sanctuary, side chapels, transepts, and one bay. The second stage (1968), supervised by the practice Conrad & Gargett, completed two bays of the nave and side aisles, towers, and the Ann Street frontage. Further work commenced in 1989 and continued until 2009. During this time the nave was extended and the two western towers and central tower were erected. *SZ*

Su-Hwan Pyo

H

King George Square

Brisbane City Hall

210 H

64 Adelaide St
Hall and Prentice, Bruce Dellit, Peter Kaad, Emil Sodersten, Noel Wilson
1928

The heritage-listed City Hall has been a cultural landmark and a symbol of civic pride since it opened in 1928. It has served as the city's main space for social gatherings and community meetings in times both good and bad, which has led to its unofficial title as the 'People's Place'. Architectural firm Hall and Prentice began designing the public building in 1917. They are believed to have drawn inspiration from the classical style, which was common for public buildings built between the 1920s and 1930s. At the time of its completion, it was the tallest building in Brisbane and the second largest building to be constructed in Australia, the first being the Sydney Harbour Bridge. To this day the city hall remains one of Australia's most expensive buildings. Enormous Corinthian columns line the main entrance of the sandstone building, adding weight to the building and making it a dominant presence over King George Square. An even taller central clock tower rises up 92 metres from ground level. Internally, a great circular auditorium space is enclosed by a large copper dome. The domed roof is the largest in Australia with a diameter of 31 metres. It is supported on a brick base, which allows the interior space to be column free. Offices and venue spaces surround this auditorium and a grand marble staircase leads to the levels above. The interior consists of local oak timbers and three types of marble: white, black, and brown. *SZ*

Bozidar Jokanovic

210 H

iStock (DerekJWalker)

« Anzac Square War Memorial 211 H

285 Ann St, Brisbane City
Buchanan and Cowper
1930

The Anzac Square War Memorial sits elevated on Anzac Square. A set of stairs lead up to it from the parklands below. Brisbane's war memorial, like the ones in most other capital cities in Australia, pays tribute to those who fought and lost their lives in times of war. It was dedicated in 1930 and has since been used as an assembly space, particularly for the annual Anzac Day remembrance service on April 25. Sydney-based architectural practice Buchanan and Cowper designed the public monument in the Greek Classic Revival style. The sandstone-clad structure, 10 metres in diameter, comprises a circular colonnade with 18 columns of the Doric order and granite steps. Around the internal top coping are the names relating to the battles in which the Australian military was heavily involved in: Anzac, Cocos Islands, Romani, Jerusalem, Damascus, Pozieres, Bullecourt, Messines, Ypres, Amiens, Villers-Bretonneaux, Mont St Quentin, Hindenburg Line. The Eternal Flame of Remembrance, set in a bronze urn, sits in the centre of the freestanding space. Beneath the memorial and directly accessed from Aanzac square is a pedestrian tunnel which contains a crypt and memorabilia from the Second World War. *SZ*

flickr (Wilson Loo Kok Wee)

H

Great Court 212 H

University of Qld, St Lucia
Hennessy, Hennessy & Co
1939

The heritage-listed University of Queensland's St Lucia campus was designed by state government architects Hennessy, Hennessy & Co who drew inspiration from European quadrangles for their design of the Great Court. Construction of this admirable building began in 1937 and continued for over forty years. The first building of the site was completed in 1939 and was later named the Forgan Smith Building. The ground floor of the Great Court is surrounded by colonnades with carvings on the walls and columns. These carvings include depictions of historical scenes, figures of flora and fauna, and statues of famous scholars and writers. *SZ*

flickr (Ryan Wick)

Centenary Pool Complex 213 H
400 Gregory Terrace, Brisbane
James Birrell
1959

The Centenary Pool complex was Brisbane City Council's principal contribution to the 1959 centenary celebrations of Brisbane's proclamation as a city. James Birrell designed the complex such that it would fit into the slope of the hill overlooking Victoria Park, minimising the need for excavation. The post-war International Style complex loosely takes the form of a rhombus and comprises a swimming pool (measuring 50 m by 18 m), a stepped concrete grandstand (with a capacity of 1,200 spectators), a diving pool, a wading pool, a bath house, and a restaurant. The spatial quality of the complex is characterised by free, rounded forms: the long curve of the bath house, the smoothly crumpled outline of the restaurant, the circular pool, and the indents and rounded corners of the perimeter of the complex itself. The complex was built primarily in concrete, steel, brick, and glass, and is often said to evoke the plastic curves that typify the works of Oscar Niemeyer. *DP*

≫ J. D. Story Administration Building 214 H

Carmody Road, Saint Lucia
James Birrell
1964

This was a progressive building in the way concrete was used and labour deployed during the construction process. For Queensland in 1964 it was a pioneering venture with prefabricated wall and floor elements. The extensive, curving, glass curtain walls, though quite unsuitable for Queensland's climate, also marked a technological step forward. *DP*

≪ Queensland School Building System 215 H

Various addresses
Codd Hopgood Pty Ltd
1975

This building system was developed in 1974 to provide classrooms for Queensland's primary schools. The vertical structure was incorporated into the wall panels, which were delivered fully clad, reducing on-site assembly time. Glass and metal louvred panels allowed ample ventilation, and cantilevered roof overhangs offered generous shading. *DP*

John Gollings

Queensland Art Gallery, Gallery of Modern Art 216 H

Stanley Place, South Brisbane

Robin Gibson & Partners (1982), Kerry and Lindsay Clare of Architectus (2006)

1982, 2006

The Gallery of Modern Art (GOMA) opened in 2006 as the second building of the Queensland Art Gallery (QAG). The new addition is an open, inviting, generous, and democratic 'urban pavilion' that enriches the cultural life of Brisbane. The gallery responds to the curve of the Brisbane River and the grid of the city, serving as the gateway to the cultural precinct. The architects saw the GOMA project as a unique opportunity to create a building that would be impressive and monumental but also direct, open, and fresh – international yet familiar, and responsive to the local conditions in southeast Queensland. The rest of the precinct is characterised by buildings arranged parallel to the Brisbane River. Meanwhile, the new gallery is placed perpendicular to the river. This strong gesture led to several urbanistic effects. It created a public plaza fronting Stanley Street, allowed the new gallery to form a stronger relationship to the 1970s Queensland Art Gallery, created a sheltered outdoor public space near the river, and formed an enlarged public park at Kurilpa Point. The gallery as a pavilion connects with the physical environment of the cultural precinct – with the public square, river, park, pedestrians, and

street patterns. This concept allowed the building to avoid the insularity that often characterises art galleries. The interior extends outwards, becoming a street that forms a clearly ordered, circulating pattern. Visitors are encouraged to move to the centre of the building, where they can orient themselves and gain a sense of the overall floor plan before making a commitment to any direction. There are 15 main gallery spaces and flexible areas that can house additional exhibitions. These spaces each have their own character and function and differ in scale, materiality, and use of light, becoming flexible frameworks for the respective artist and artworks. The technical systems ensure that the art gallery meets the necessary indoor climate requirements. They control the temperature and humidity, provide artificial and natural light, control air pollution, and optimise energy consumption. The building's design responds to the artists' and curators' need for flexibility. The walls are movable; there are generous openings to display big works; and there are optional systems for more flexible lighting configurations. The Asia Pacific Triennial of Contemporary Art (APT), a ground-breaking contemporary art series at the GOMA, demonstrates the gallery's commitment to cultural relationships. The new gallery consciously cites and incorporates this outward-looking approach through its internal 'street', 'public living rooms', and 'public verandas' that open out to the surrounding landscape and city beyond. *PA*

Australian Stockman's Hall of Fame

217 H

Landsborough Hwy, Longreach
Feiko Bouman
1988

The Australian Stockman's Hall of Fame Building is Australia's premier outback heritage centre. Outback artist Hugh Sawrey envisioned a 'tribute to the heroes of remote Australia'. After a significant amount of fund-raising and the help of similar visionaries, his dream came to life. In 1980 an Australia-wide design competition was held, co-ordinated by the Royal Australian Institute of Architects and sponsored by Consolidated Press and the Queensland Government. Sydney architect Feiko Bouman won the national competition with his monumental design which drew inspiration from the Australian outback with its resemblance to silos and water tanks. The centre was opened in 1988, in the rural town of Longreach in central western Queensland. The structure is made from timber, stone, and corrugated iron. The interior comprises 2,500 square metres which house five themed galleries that display the history of Australia's greatest and bravest explorers, stock workers, pastoralists, and indigenous people. Since opening, the centre has attracted over one million visitors. *SZ*

Sarah Stewart

Globe Hotel

218 H

149 Oak St, Barcaldine
m3architecture, Brian Hooper
2009

This project transforms an iconic outback Queensland pub into a cultural and tourism hub. The building contains an information centre, history room, and a commercial tenancy, and sets out the shell for an art gallery. The pub, which was built in 1910, closed down a number of years ago and was purchased by the Barcaldine Regional Council in 2011. The council's vision was for a distinctive contemporary statement on a prominent corner in the main street. m3architecture, in association with Brian Hooper, focused on a series of new layered experiences. The project is a respectful, contemporary version of the single-skin built form and allows the town to both retain, and build on, its history. *SZ*

Micro Health Laboratory 219 H
University of Queensland, Gatton
m3architecture
2001

The Micro Health Laboratory building served as somewhat of a case study of the potential of the brick as a material, and the connotations of brick veneer. Brick veneer is a counter-intuitive construction system where the lightweight holds up the heavyweight. The stoic external appearance of many brick buildings belies the reality of a non-load-bearing 110 mm thick leaf pinned off a lightweight wall. The poetic potential of the term 'leaf' and 'veneer' is seldom explored. A leaf suggests thinness and delicacy. A veneer has connotations of a fine, celebrated outer layer. The architects eroded the veneer of the brick itself, to expose its seldom seen, rich clay innards. Two brick types with two cut types result in a range of textural qualities, the cuts made with a hammer and bolster. The inside of the building is abstracted from the outside world, so as to control the outflow of contaminants. *PA*

Jon Linkins

Shantanu Starick.

State Library of Queensland 220 H

Stanley Pl, South Brisbane
Robin Gibson (1988), BVN, Peddle Thorp
1988, 2006

The original State Library building was designed by Robin Gibson and completed in 1988. This structure was the last building to be finished of the Queensland Cultural Centre precinct in South Bank which includes the Queensland Performing Arts Centre and Queensland Museum. A design competition was held in 2001 to redevelop the existing building for which architectural practices BVN and Peddle Thorpe were the winners. Their redesign is based around a five-storey-high central atrium which separates the old and new portions of the building. This public space is open at all hours and leads to other spaces, consisting of an indigenous knowledge centre, a reception space, auditoriums, exhibition spaces, reading rooms, and decks which extend onto the river. These additions doubled the building's size. The Edge, a digital culture centre, is a new facility by m3architecture and Deicke Richards Architects and is located in an adjacent building to the south. Their design includes mirrored soffits and blade walls added to bay windows that are perched out over the river walk, providing a connection to the surrounding city. The extensive use of shaded clear glass in existing and reconfigured openings (as opposed to the original tinted glass) draws the landscape and the river into the building. The interior features are tough, tactile, and multi-purposed. *SZ*

Jon Linkins

The Edge, a new digital facility by m3architecture and Deicke Richards Architects

Pragmatic, intriguing, and culturally connected to place

Michael Christensen, Ben Vielle, Michael Banney and Michael Lavery
Directors
m3architecture

m3architecture is an Australian architectural firm that was founded in 1997. The practice, using each project's pragmatic requirements as a base, is interested in designing the unexpected – something that makes the work extraordinary. The majority of m3architecture's work is for public and educational organisations. The practice has won numerous national and international awards and has been featured in a wide range of publications and exhibitions. Notably, the practice has been included in the Venice Biennale on four separate occasions.

What differentiates architecture in Australia from international architecture?
Australia has numerous regional quirks and varied climatic conditions. We have a particular cultural history, particular ways of accessing materials, and particular ways of constructing our buildings. For us what differentiates the work, in any location, are the ideas that surround it.

What role do current architectural trends play in your design approach?
Our projects are driven by ideas and are embedded in pragmatic considerations. As such, we avoid 'trends' regarding form, style, or finishes. We are interested, however, in the trend towards innovation, particularly innovations in typology or climatic response to projects.

Where do you find your design inspiration?
Each project is surrounded by numerous conditions – these can be social, historic, or cultural for example. These conditions lead us to interesting ideas that underpin our designs. Often, it is a combination of the conditions and ideas that fascinate us most. For example, our Rod Laver Footbridge project is a new bridge spanning a railway line to a tennis centre. It combines the pattern of the traditional railway truss with the pattern of a well-known Australian tennis shoe. This approach to design combines the unexpected yet relevant cultures of railway engineering and tennis, in an outcome which is particularly Australian. These kinds of new connections inspire us and lead us to develop new forms, details, and experiences which belong solely to

The Rod Laver Footbridge with its iconic façade pattern inspired by the sole of the Dunlop Volley sneaker

each place. This is what we mean when we say we're interested in the extraordinary.

Which Australian buildings do you most admire and why?

We admire the State Library of Queensland. It is a bold, pragmatic building that seeks out ideas. Its outdoor public rooms capture what it is like to be a part of Brisbane. The original library building was adapted into a new work that addresses both the river and the landscape in interesting, new ways. It has a myriad of shaded places that create comfortable subtropical experiences for any combination of movement, rest, reading, research, small meetings, large public gatherings, and work.

What could the rest of the world learn from Australian architecture?

Australian architecture has a diversity of approaches that often bring ideas to the fore. The best work is pragmatic, intriguing, and culturally connected to place. We are conscious of this history and are connected to it. A good example is our project at the University of Queensland – the David Theile Olympic Swimming Pool. One of the aims for this project was to give the public realm an experience of water while maintaining the semi-private experience of bathing. The raised soffit, which floats over the change pavilions allows excellent ventilation, and is painted in a simple gloss and matt paint. This frugal technique using generic materials is enough to carry the experience of glinting light, the reflection of water, and the sounds of joy out to the street, whilst retaining privacy for the pool users. Delivering big ideas with minimal means – the world could do with more places like this.

State Library of Queensland

John Gollings © Penelope Seidler

« Riverside Centre

221 H

123 Eagle St, Brisbane
Harry Seidler
1986

Located on the waterfront of the Brisbane River, the Riverside Centre takes advantage of the site's picturesque views along the river. The 40-storey office tower does so through its triangular floor plan which allows for more than two-thirds of the offices to face the water. The lower buildings surrounding the tower define the large public space at ground level. A large curved beam further defines the open plaza at this waterfront edge. This open space comprises fountains, outdoor restaurants, seating, shops, a tavern, and trees. Inclining aluminium shades protect the full-height glass walls of the two sides of the tower which are more exposed to the sun. The elevations of the tower are pierced with recessed 'façade gardens'. *SZ*

Riparian Plaza

222 H

71 Eagle St, Brisbane
Harry Seidler
2005

Riparian Plaza is a multi-purpose building which accommodates both offices and residential units. It sits adjacent to Riverside Centre on the waterfront of the Brisbane River. Riparian Plaza is higher and larger in scale as its promenade continues along the river. The building offers facilities for the public, such as restaurants and plazas. Similar to the Riverside Centre, the tower's form takes advantage of the site, maximising views up and down the river. Column-free offices are located at the mid-section of the tower whilst luxurious penthouses make up the residential section at the top of the tower. Large curvilinear terraces project from each of these penthouses. Parking can be found at the bottom of the building. *SZ*

Fitzgibbon Community Centre 223 H
545 Roghan Rd, Fitzgibbon
Richard Kirk Architects
2012

In 2010, the Urban Land Development Authority commissioned the firm Richard Kirk Architect to design a community building for the new Fitzgibbon neighbourhood. This was to act as a mixed-use cultural centre, incorporating offices, meeting spaces, retail, and community halls, and serving as a centre point for the community. The Fitzgibbon Community Centre is a response to the common suburban landscape in which it is located. The regenerated bushland fringe had been previously used as a dumping ground for vehicles and refuse, degrading the landscape over time. The centre directly responds to this by redefining and redeeming its relationship to the environment and establishing the building as an artwork within the landscape. The building sits back from the street, with its façade line modified to incorporate the remaining trees on site. The 'heart' of the scheme is a large open covered space, which forms a gateway on the axis from the new commercial centre of Fitzgibbon to the bushland tracks and trails to the north. This gateway acts as a starting and finishing point for the trails, with essential amenities and a retail outlet. While formally abstract and demure the centre makes provocative use of materials, which highlight it as a landmark in the community. The building is fringed by sculptural blades of weathering steel, a material that responds to the corroded car bodies once found on site. These blades form a rippled screen to the street which reveals glimpses through the building when approached by vehicle. Behind this oxidised screen, the building is clad in stained plywood with ample operable glazing to allow natural ventilation, and large overhangs to provide natural lighting without overheating. This use of naturally weathering materials and passive climate controls allow the Fitzgibbon Community Centre to evolve and respond over time to its suburban landscape. *PA*

Peter Bennetts

Advanced Engineering Building 224 H
University of Queensland,
St Lucia, Brisbane
Richard Kirk Architects
2013

In 2009, Richard Kirk Architect was commissioned by the University of Queensland to carry out the Advanced Engineering Building (AEB) project, following a limited design competition. The AEB delivers on the university's vision to create a building to celebrate, collaborate, create, learn, innovate, and sustain, all within an integrated engineering landscape. The structure of the building is as open as possible, to allow a high level of visibility of processes and equipment to visitors and staff alike. A large foyer area can be used to showcase manufactured goods, stimulating interest in manufacturing processes. The layout is divided into three volumes that feed off a central and communal vertical street. Flexible learning spaces with laboratories allow for progressive teaching. The design concept prioritises passive design over the mechanical. An operable façade opens up the building, making it breathe and work with Brisbane's benign sub-tropical climate. The façade was also covered with a terracotta screen to ensure it remained open for longer. The AEB is a benchmark for sustainable architecture with a particular focus on the aesthetic, environmental, and structural strengths of using locally produced timber in a building – including structural façade glazing and long-span glulam roof trusses in one of Australia's largest timber-framed auditoriums. *PA*

Centre for Advanced Imaging 225 H

The University of Queensland,
St Lucia, Brisbane
John Wardle Architects, Wilson Architects
2013

The Centre for Advanced Imaging (CAI) captures highly experimental molecular imaging technology and the necessary support resources within a single facility. The CAI provides a rich collaborative environment for researchers in disciplines ranging from engineering, chemistry, physics, and computer science to biology, medicine, and psychology. This potent mix of researchers works on innovations in imaging technology, imaging biomarker development, and in biomedical research disciplines. The CAI facility accommodates NMR and EPR alongside the complementary use of MRI and PET imaging technologies in association with a cyclotron and supporting radiochemistry laboratories for research and commercial partnering. Traditionally, this type of facility is introverted in nature and protective of the complex machines within. This insularity is often exacerbated by the layers of structure necessary to provide a stable environment for experimentation free from vibration and magnetic interference. In contrast, the CAI is designed to include areas of interaction and collaboration across all levels, and these areas are concentrated at the ground and uppermost floors. A key theme is the connection of the interior to the landscape beyond – a remnant heritage grove of eucalypts, as well as sporting fields. Terracing, ramping, and garden beds step down from the interior to the natural ground line. A generous terrace at the uppermost floor provides great views out from the edge of the campus from this communal space. Sunshading blades create a vertical rhythm across the main façade, an allusion to the original landscape. Materially, the exterior envelope is either precast concrete in a sandstone hue that connects the building with its historic campus context, or a neutral charcoal metal panel that clothes the functions related to the technology within. The precast panels are carefully crafted, their profile attuned to keeping out the sun whilst their surface is inscribed with a pattern derived from imagery produced by the centre. The CAI is appropriately sited within the research precinct on the University of Queensland St Lucia Campus adjacent to the Gehrmann and Ritchie Buildings and with nearby access to the adjacent Queensland Brain Institute (QBI) and the Australian Institute for Bioengineering and Nanotechnology (AIBN). A strong central link has been forged between the two adjacent buildings to form an internal street between the campus interior and its outer edge. *PA*

Lady Cilento Children's Hospital 226 H

501 Stanley St, South Brisbane
Conrad Gargett, Lyons
2014

Melbourne architectural practice Lyons in joint venture with Brisbane architects Conrad Gargett completed the new Lady Cilento Children's Hospital in Brisbane. The twelve-storey 95,000-square-metre hospital is a significant new urban addition to Brisbane's Southbank precinct. Its brightly coloured exterior, incorporating the green and purple coloration of the native Bougainvillea plants in the adjacent parklands, speaks of a building designed for children. In its form and massing, it challenges the conventional model of podium and tower and delivers a medium-rise, sculpted building with landscaped roofscapes. The building is also highly functional and incorporates some of the world's most advanced diagnostic, interventional and treatment facilities. The colours used on the outside and inside of the building are derived from the colours of the Queensland landscape. These include muted neutral colour tones found in the Queensland outback landscape together with the more vibrant colours of the state's exotic birds, rainforest butterflies, and flora. Rooftop gardens, green walls, enclosed courtyard gardens, and views to surrounding parklands all form part of the hospital's healing environment. The green roofs on the upper levels are used by patients, families, and staff for passive and active recreation. *PA*

480 Queen Street

227 H

480 Queen Street, Brisbane
BVN Architects
2016

The development of 480 Queen Street establishes a new office building typology, the 'Campus Tower', for Brisbane's CBD and is designed to incorporate a carefully considered commercial and public realm. The 4,144-square-metre site provides a large parcel superbly located in the city to warrant a large-scale development. Its unique property shape and sloping terrain between Adelaide and Queen Streets are features that influence the building's cross section and distribution of building volume. The proposal offers significant public benefit through the provision of the publicly accessible pedestrian street and an elevated park that aligns with the cathedral ground plane across Adelaide Street. This large-scale green space adds to the identity of the sub-tropical region in a genuine and contemporary manner: an elevated, verdant landscape that references the historic terrain that was the foreground to the cathedral. Lower forms utilise the metaphor of stacked art and polished stone, producing a building character that suits the demands of contemporary office accommodation. Elevations to the cathedral and river sides are emphasised by 'revealing' coloured, jewel-like surfaces behind the 'cut' glass surface. These cut façade's portions form a contextually appropriate backdrop to St John's Cathedral and a unique, contemporary, and iconic building within the city's skyline. *PA*

Christopher Frederick Jones

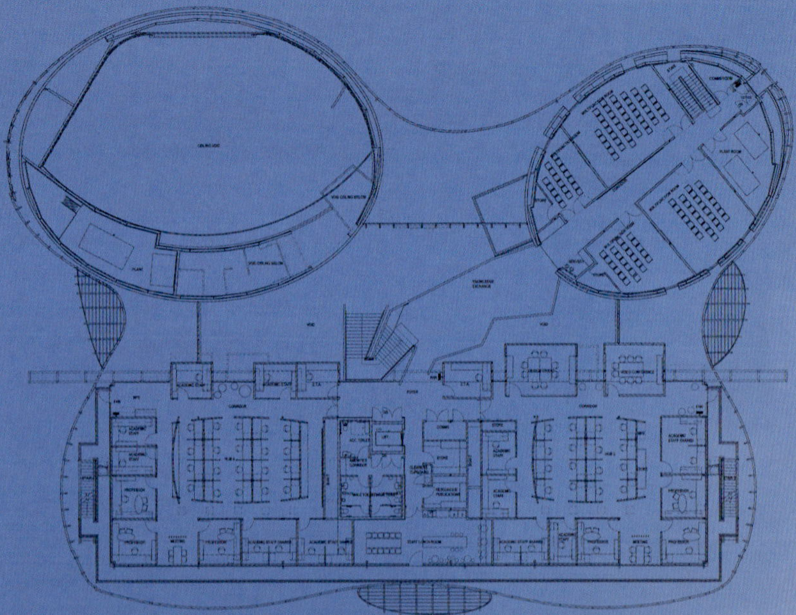

Floor Plan

The Cairns Institute

228 H

105 McGregor Rd, Smithfield
Woods Bagot and RPA Architects
2013

The Cairns Institute is a tropical research centre which lies within the James Cook University (JCU) campus. Designed by Woods Bagot and RPA Architects, the design reflects the beautiful, tropical landscape of far-north Queensland while also providing a contemporary research and collaboration environment with the highest technological standards. Cradled on three sides by rain forested slopes, the site draws the tropical landscape into the heart of the campus, creating a stimulating environment for students and staff. Intrinsic to the design proposition is the celebration and enrichment of the institute's rainforest backdrop. The façade is layered and evolutionary, the building form is informed by the surrounding landscape. The design goal of this project was to create a building that blurred into the landscape itself. An evolving landscape skin, a 'trellis', defines the building and encapsulates aesthetics and sun control, as well as a variety of micro climate ecologies around the building that are suited to their function and orientation. The design also assists in minimising running costs for JCU whilst contributing to the quality of environment, and is in line with the university's aspiration to achieve a sustainable outcome for the building. The design team, led by Woods Bagot Brisbane Director Mark Damant, created a building that represents its place and its context while employing innovative architectural elements. 'A truly imaginative and integrated design solution that was distinctive and uniquely desirable to JCU's community was paramount,' said Damant. *PA*

Index of Buildings

The digits indicate the building number.

Sydney

Canberra

Hobart and Surroundings

Melbourne

Adelaide

Index of Buildings

The digits indicate the building number.

Perth

Darwin and Surroundings

Brisbane and Surroundings

The Icon in St Kilda, Melbourne, a highly criticised apartment block by Jackson Clements Burrow and nicknamed Lego Building, 2016 (right)

sellmycastle.com.au
Punt

Index of Architects

The digits indicate the building number.

Index of Architects

The digits indicate the building number.

Author and Contributors

Sarah Zahradnik is a German born, Australian Architect. She graduated from the University of South Australia with a masters in Architecture. Since then she has worked in offices in Australia, Brazil, Mexico and Germany. She is currently working in an architectural office in Melbourne.

David Bridgman, Australian architect, architectural historian, and author. He has lived in Darwin for most of his career and has written major works on tropical architecture. He holds a doctorate and a degree in architecture from RMIT. He has also lectured at Charles Darwin University.

John Gollings, born in Melbourne, is a photographer specialising in the built environment. He studied the arts and architecture at Melbourne University and RMIT. He operates from a collaborative design, photography, and 3D-rendering studio in Melbourne and works extensively in Asia.

Harry Seidler, Austrian-born Australian architect (1923 – 2006). He first studied building and construction in England, then architecture in Canada and in the US. He is one of Australia's most admired architects of the modernist movement consistently following Bauhaus principles.

Attributions

SZ *Sarah Zahradnik*
VB *Vladimir Belegolovsky*
NM *Natascha Meuser*
PA *Project Architects*
DP *DOM publishers' Editors*

Sarah and John at his exhibition, 'John Gollings: The History of the Built World', the first major survey of his work, December 2017

Bibliography

The bibliography includes two works – an encyclopaedia and a historical survey – that offer a comprehensive overview of Australian architecture. Other books delve into more specialist topics, such as European-style housing in Australia, the use of steel, the Modern Movement, and the challenges of building in the country's tropical regions. Books that focus on particular regions – South Australia, East Australia, Canberra, Melbourne, and Sydney – were also consulted. The list also includes a volume on the works of Harry Seidler, and Robin Boyd's seminal work of architectural criticism, *The Australian Ugliness*. Two special issues of magazines – *Architectural Review* and *Domus* – offer a glimpse into the architectural discourse that was taking place in the early post-war years and in the 1980s.

The Australian Ugliness
Robin Boyd
Melbourne, 1960

A seminal text in which the architect and author Robin Boyd attributes the 'ugliness' of Australian architecture to a phenomenon he calls 'Featurism' – a prioritisation of decorative and kitchy 'features' at the expense of coherence, and the cloaking of an environment's material reality with distracting veneers.

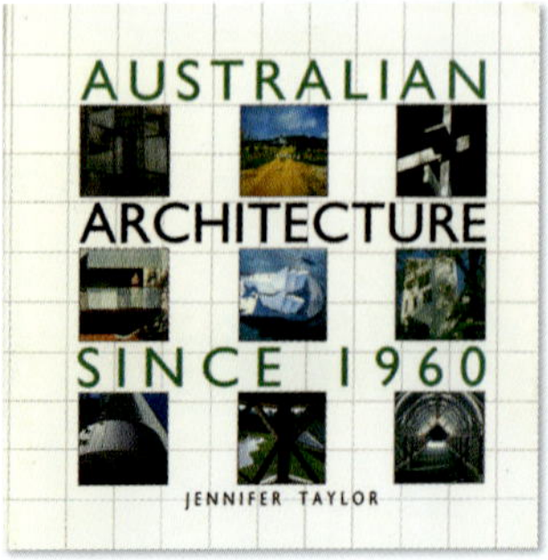

Australian Architecture Since 1960
Jennifer Taylor
Sydney, 1986

The mid-twentieth century saw the acceptance, propagation, and critical questioning of the Modern Movement. The author explores how changing attitudes to buildings and the built environment in Australia informed and influenced the urban forms in Australia up to the mid-1980s.

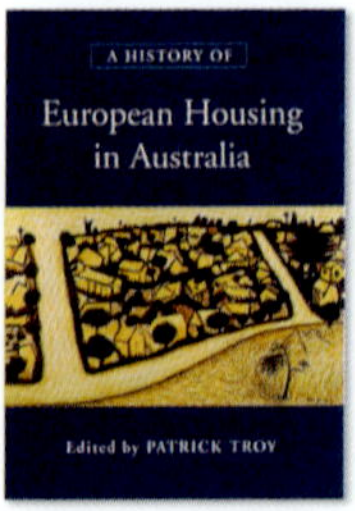

European Housing in Australia
Edited by Patrick Troy
Cambridge (UK), 2012

A collection of essays by scholars from a wide range of disciplines. It attempts to explain the social, cultural, administrative, and technical history of 'European' housing in Australia, starting from its origins in the first colonial settlements, and explores what makes Australian housing distinctive in social terms.

***The Encyclopedia of Australian Architecture*, edited by Philip Goad and Julie Willis**
New York, 2012

A major, comprehensive reference work on Australian architecture, offering over 1,000 entries from 225 contributors. It documents and analyses works of architecture in Australia from the country's indigenous beginnings to its colonial, modern, and contemporary eras.

Architecture in Australia
J. M. Freeland
Melbourne, 1968

An account of the history of Australian architecture. The book begins with an overview of the first European settlements and the methods colonial architects adopted to overcome early challenges. The author then presents a survey of the major architectural phases of Australia up to the mid-twentieth century.

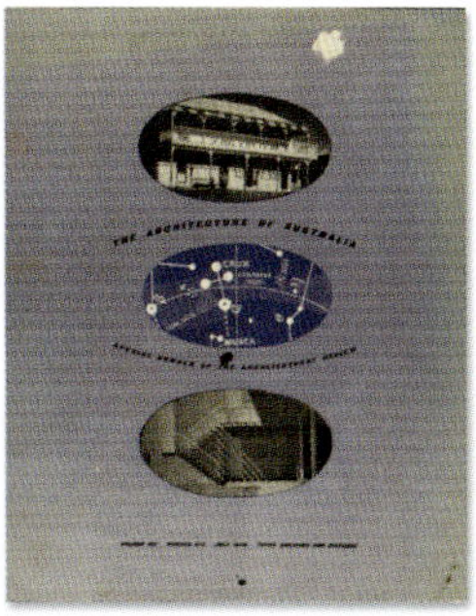

'The Architecture of Australia'
Special issue of the *Architectural Review*, vol. CIV, number 619, July 1948

This special issue of the monthly London-based magazine gives a fascinating insight into the architectural discourse on Australia that was taking place during the early post-war years in Europe. Central preoccupations include zoning, regional planning, green belts around towns and cities, and the merits of garden cities.

'Ciao Australia'
Special issue of *Domus*
Milan, August 1985/663

A special issue of the bilingual Milan-based monthly architecture and design magazine. It opens with an interview with Harry Seidler and presents various works of architecture, furniture, fashion, design, and art in Australia. Featured architects include Glen Murcutt, Edmond & Corrigan, and Ken Woolley.

Bibliography

Canberra: Myths and Models
K. F. Fischer
Hamburg, 1984

Canberra was founded as a planned city in 1913. From the very beginning, the concept of the 'ideal city' shaped the city's planning. Karl Friedhelm Fischer charts and analyses the history of Canberra by examining how the concept of the 'ideal city' changed throughout the Australian capital's young history.

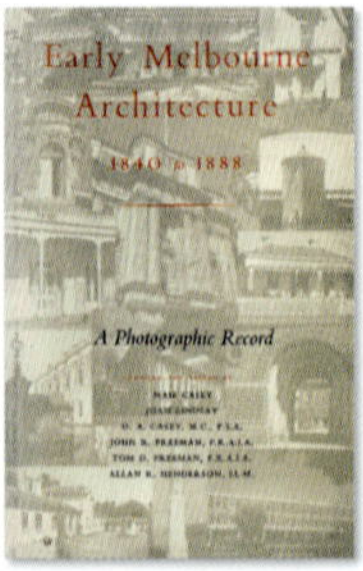

Early Melbourne Architecture
Edited by Maie Casey et al.
London, 1953

A collection of photographs, annotated by the editors, illustrate the works of architecture of early Melbourne from 1840 to 1888. The book offers an insight into the city's early public buildings, some now already demolished, which were still heavily influenced at the time by the styles that were prevalent in Britain.

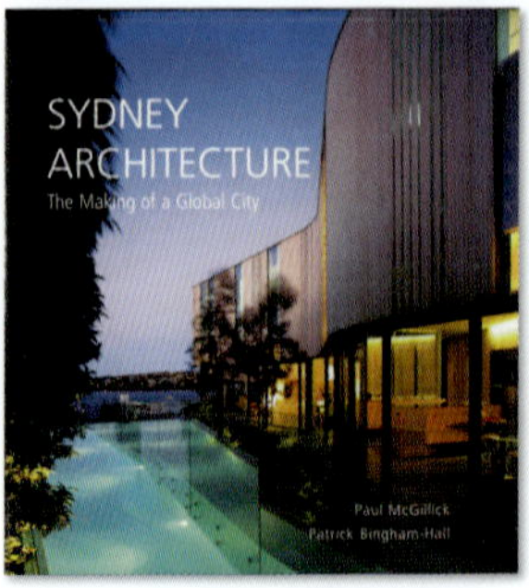

Sydney Architecture
Paul McGillick and Patrick Bingham-Hall
Signapore, 2005

A catalogue of the most representative works of architecture in Sydney. The projects are annotated by the authors, who comment on the historical context and architectural qualities of each building. The introduction presents an overview of how historical events shaped the evolution of the city's architecture.

Architecture in Tropical Australia
Balwant Singh Saini
London, 1970

A study of how the climate in Tropical Australia determines the needs of the inhabitants, whether these relate to physiological comfort or general living conditions. The author offers an in-depth account of how design, planning, and choice of building typology can help meet these needs.

Architecture in South Australia
South Australian Institute of Architects
1960

A collection of photographs compiled by the South Australian Institute of Architects as a contribution to the Adelaide Festival of Arts, 1960. It illustrates buildings from the earliest years of the state's history, but primarily focuses on projects built between 1930 and 1960.

Architecture in Steel
Alan Ogg
Red Hill, 1987

A detailed study of the use of steel in architecture, exploring both the technological and ideological aspects of the material. The author offers an account of the material's history and presents exemplary case studies drawn from both international and Australian architecture.

The Architecture of East Australia
Edited by Bill MacMahon
Stuttgart/London, 2001

A guide to the architecture of East Australia, divided into chapters that are each dedicated to a specific location. The editor's introduction offers a historical overview of the evolution of architecture in Eastern Australia. The project descriptions focus on prominent buildings and are listed chronologically.

Harry Seidler: Lifework
Vladimir Belogolovsky
New York, 2014

Harry Seidler, one of Australia's most prominent architects, designed innovative and sculptural buildings throughout his career, which spanned six decades. His work was characterised by a sensitivity to site, space, and structure. This book gives a complete view of the modern master's body of work.

The *Deutsche Nationalbibliothek* lists this publication in the *Deutsche Nationalbibliografie*; detailed bibliographic data are available on the Internet at http://dnb.d-nb.de.

ISBN 978-3-86922-523-4

www.dom-publishers.com

Copy-editing
Kathleen Owens

Design
Sarah Zahradnik

Final Artwork
Atelier Kraut

Illustrations
Natascha Meuser

Maps
Katrin Soschinski

Printing
Tiger Printing (Hong Kong) Co. Ltd.
www.tigerprinting.hk

DOM
publishers